The Basics of American Politics

TWELFTH EDITION

Gary Wasserman
John Hopkins University, Nanjing Center

PEARSON

Longman

New York San Francisco Boston
London Toronto Sydney Tokyo Singapore Madrid
Mexico City Munich Paris Cape Town Hong Kong Montreal

To My Students, Chinese and American

Executive Editor: Eric Stano
Senior Marketing Manager: Elizabeth Fogarty
Media and Supplements Editor: Kristi Olson
Production Manager: Denise Phillip
Project Coordination, Text Design, and Electronic Page Makeup: WestWords, Inc.
Cover Designer/Manager: Wendy Ann Fredericks
Interior Illustrations: David Omar White
Cover Photo: Todd Gipstein/National Geographic/Getty Images
Manufacturing Buyer: Lucy Hebard
Printer and Binder: Courier Corporation
Cover Printer: The Lehigh Press, Inc.

Library of Congress Cataloging-in-Publication Data
Wasserman, Gary, 1944–
    The basics of American politics / Gary Wasserman.—12th ed.
      p. cm.
    Includes index.
    ISBN 0-321-31795-5 (pbk.)
      1. United States—Politics and government. I. Title.
  JK276.W36 2005
  320.473—dc22

                                                          2004026281

Please visit our website at http://www.ablongman.com

ISBN 0-321-31795-5

1 2 3 4 5 6 7 8 9 10—CRS—08 07 06 05

CONTENTS

PREFACE

The first version of *The Basics* came from my frustration in teaching the introductory American government course. Students in my classes were not buying the assigned text because it was too expensive. They were not reading the chapters because they were too long. And they were not answering test questions because they were too complicated. They also found the texts pretty boring. So I wrote a book that was shorter, simpler, and cheaper than any other text. While over the editions it has grown longer, more complicated, and certainly more expensive, I hope it holds to that initial motivation.

The new edition of *The Basics* reflects the recent—and intense—changes in American politics.

- National security issues, in their many forms, understandably dominate this edition. Aspects of war range from discussions of Iraq's conflicting media images and a Marine's view of embedded reporters, to the White House spin on damaging 9/11 revelations and Congress's dependence on the executive. The tension between prosecuting terrorism and protecting civil liberties merits a case study as well as a review of the Patriot Act.
- Elections bring changes and demand attention. A new case study covers a presidential campaign's innovative use of the Internet; an update of the application, and avoidance, of the new campaign reform law, which leads to discussing the continuing role of money in elections; and the 2004 election results—their impact on Congress, the presidency, and the political parties.
- New discussions cover a range of topics: President Bush's unconservative approach to federalism; White House spin on 9/11; the presidential leadership style on Iraq; the revival of affirmative action in the University of Michigan case; free speech bake sales on campus; and redistricting: the incumbent protection racket.

INSTRUCTOR SUPPLEMENTS FOR QUALIFIED COLLEGE ADOPTERS

LongmanParticipate.com 3.0 Faculty Teaching Guide (ISBN: 0-321-31708-4). This easy-to-use guide to Longman's market-leading American government Website (www.longmanparticipate .com) walks instructors through registration and gives step-by-step advice for integrating the site's activities into the course.

Instructor's Manual/Test Bank (ISBN: 0-321-35513-X). This combined supplement written by Melanie Brumberg of California University of Pennsylvania, includes chapter overviews, chapter outlines, learning objectives, key terms, and valuable teaching suggestions. In addition, the test bank contains hundreds of challenging and thoroughly revised multiple-choice, true-false, and essay questions along with an answer key.

TestGen-EQ CD-ROM (ISBN: 0-321-35511-3). The printed test bank is also available through our computerized testing system, TestGen-EQ. This fully networkable, user-friendly program enables instructors to view and edit questions, add their own questions, and print tests in a variety of formats.

American Government Digital Media Archive (ISBN: 0-321-27068-1). Use this new CD-ROM to add video clips, images, and charts and graphs to your lectures or Power-Point presentations. The CD-ROM contains dozens of video clips and images from America's political past and present, as well as charts and graphs from Longman texts.

American Government Video Program
Qualified adopters can peruse our list of videos for the American government classroom.

STUDENT SUPPLEMENTS
AVAILABLE TO QUALIFIED COLLEGE ADOPTERS

NEW! LongmanParticipate.com 3.0.
Longman's bestselling interactive, online tool. Students will find a wealth of simulations, interactive timelines, comparative exercises, and case studies—all updated with the most current examples and data. The new 3.0 version includes 12 new simulations—over 30 simulations in all!

Visit us on the Web at www.longmanparticipate.com and see a sample chapter now!

This site will get students to experience what they only read about in their text. *LongmanParticipate.com* is the most interactive and comprehensive Website available for American government. Developed and revised by American government faculty from around the country, *LongmanParticipate.com 3.0,* and the over 100 activities it contains, will engage students in the course in a way nothing else can.

To order Wasserman's text packaged with a free subscription to *LongmanParticipate.com 3.0*, please contact your local Allyn & Bacon/Longman representative.

You Decide! 2005 Edition Current Debates in American Politics (ISBN: 0-321-33343-8). Edited by John T. Rourke of University of Connecticut, this exciting debate-style reader examines provocative issues in American Politics today. Questions include: *Does antiterrorism legislation threaten your civil liberties?* And *Is it un-American to criticize U.S. foreign policy in the post 9-11 world?* The topics have been selected for their currency, importance, and student interest, and the pieces that argue various sides of a given issue come from recent journals, congressional hearings, think tanks, and periodicals. (FREE when packaged with any Longman American Government text!)

Culture War? The Myth of a Polarized America (ISBN: 0-321-27640-X). By Morris P. Fiorina (Stanford University), Samuel J. Abrams (Harvard University), and Jeremy C. Pope (Stanford University), this is the first book in the "Great Questions in Politics" series. This reader combines polling data with a compelling narrative to debunk commonly-believed myths about American politics—particularly the claim that Americans are deeply divided in their fundamental political view. (Discounted when purchased with any Longman American Government text!)

Getting Involved: A Student Guide to Citizenship (ISBN: 0-205-30933-X). A unique and practical handbook that guides students through political participation with concrete advice and extensive sample material—letters, telephone scripts, student interviews, and real-life anecdotes—for getting involved and making a difference in their lives and communities. (FREE when ordered packaged with the text.)

Ten Things Every American Government Student Should Read (ISBN: 0-205-28969-X). We asked American government instructors across the country to vote for the ten things beyond the text that they believed every student should read. The top vote-getter in each category was put into this unique reader and edited by Karen O'Connor of The American University. (FREE when ordered packaged with the text.)

New! Discount Subscription to the *New York Times*. A 10-week subscription for only $20!

Discount Subscription to *Newsweek* magazine. Students receive 12 issues of *Newsweek* at more than 80 percent off the regular price. An excellent way to keep students up on current events.

Choices: An American Government Reader. This reader allows instructors to choose from a database of over 300 readings to create a customized reader that exactly matches their course needs.

Discounted Penguin-Putnam Paperback Titles. Longman offers 25 Penguin-Putnam titles at more than a 60% discount when packaged with Wasserman's text. Titles include De Tocqueville's *Democracy in America* and Lewis's *The Jungle*. Go to www.ablongman.com/penguin for a complete list.

ResearchNavigator.com. This complete online research resource features the *New York Times* Search-by-Subject database of articles; ContentSelect, a customized, searchable collection of 25,000+ discipline-specific articles; the *New York Times* "Themes of the Times" collections; Link Library; and more. Access codes come in the Research Navigator Guide, which is FREE when packaged with any text.

***Writing in Political Science*, 3/e, by Diane Schmidt**
Taking students step-by-step through all aspects of writing in political science, this guide features samples from actual students and expanded information about using the Internet. (Available at a significant discount when ordered packaged.)

***Texas Politics Supplement*, 3/e, by Debra St. John**
(ISBN: 0-321-18841-1). Ninety-page primer on state and local government and issues in Texas. (FREE when packaged.)

***California Politics Supplement*, 3/e, by Paul Schmidt**
(ISBN: 0-321-21735-7). Seventy-page primer on state and local government and issues in California. (FREE when packaged.)

***Florida Politics Supplement*, by John Bertalan**
(ISBN: 0-321-14632-8). A fifty-page primer on state and local government and issues in Florida. (FREE when packaged.)

ACKNOWLEDGMENTS

Thanks to Mark K. McBeth at Idaho State University, Donald V. Gawronski at Mesa Community College, and Eric S. King at Virginia Union University for providing insights to assist in this edition.

Thanks to David Omar White for his cartoons, to Nadia Khawaja for her research, and to Erich Wasserman of FIRE, and to Jim Smith and Greg Andrews of Smith, Dawson, and Andrews for their insights and support. Eric Stano and Denise Phillip at Longman Publishers, and Jami Darby at WestWords, Inc., have brought needed patience and welcomed intelligence to the editorial and production process.

This edition was completed at the pioneering Hopkins-Nanjing Center in Nanjing, China where I taught American government to Chinese graduate students. I appreciate the support of Co-Directors Robert Daly and Huang Chengfeng.

Gary Wasserman
Nanjing, China

CHAPTER 1

What Is Politics?

THE FIRST DAY OF CLASS

The first day of my American government class, the professor comes in and asks us to sit in alphabetical order. Do you believe this? Of course all the freshman sheep shuffle along. But since I am sitting next to the rear door—for a quiet exit during the lecture—I don't want to move. So I ask him whether he might want us to wear Mentally Ill from Amityville t-shirts to his next class. A bit too cute, perhaps, because he asks me if I think politics goes on in the classroom.

I reply, "No, we study politics, but very few of us actually participate."

"Incorrect," he responds, and would I mind leaving his class?

"Yes, I would mind," I say, "considering the costs of my first seven years at college."

"Will you *please* leave?" he says.

OK, so I start to go. He then stops me and asks why I am departing. I remind him that while he may have missed it, he has just asked me to depart. But he persists and asks why I'm doing what he asked. Maybe I have missed something. I respond that he is *the kahuna* here. I am just a barely paying student.

"In other words," he says, "my position as the teacher influenced you to do something you didn't want to do. In fact, it influenced everyone to sit in alphabetical order. So we just saw a process of influence in this classroom that affected a group of people. That's politics. . . ."

"Oh, by the way, do you have a cigarette?"

"Hey, you can't smoke in here."

"You mean my power as a teacher is limited. In this case by your right to have a nonsmoking classroom. And of course all of you have other rights that limit any teacher's power. If this gentleman here didn't have such a good sense of humor he might bring me before some university committee for harassment. This too is politics."

This story reveals a process of influence between the teacher and the students. This relationship is not only an educational one but a political one as well. It is political in the sense of political scientist Harold Lasswell's famous definition of *politics as the process of who gets what, when, and how.* The teacher (who) gets the student to leave the class (what) immediately (when) by using his authority to persuade and threaten him (how). This indeed is politics.

Our definition of politics centers on actions among a number of people involving influence. How do people get others to do what they wish? How does our society or any group (like that classroom) distribute its valued things, such as wealth, prestige, and security? Who gets these *values,* and how? The dialogue hints at an answer in the concepts of *power* and *authority.*

POLITICS AND POWER

Notice that the teacher influenced the student to do something he didn't want to do (leave the class). The teacher demonstrated his power over the student, though limited by the student's rights. *Power* is simply the *ability to influence another's behavior.* Power is getting people to do something they wouldn't otherwise do. Power may involve force (often called *coercion*), or persuasion, or rewards. But its essence is the ability to change another's actions. The more power one has over another, the greater the change, or the easier the change is to accomplish. Having more power also could mean influencing more people to change.

Power involves a relationship between people and groups. When someone says that a person has a lot of power, one should ask: Power to influence whom to do what? What is the power relationship being discussed? Take the statement "The United States is the most powerful nation in the world today." If this means that because of its huge wealth, large army, and educated population, the United States can influence any other country however it wishes, the statement is wrong. These resources (wealth, army, and population) can give only a *capacity* for power. Whether this capacity is converted into effective influence will depend on the relationship in which it is applied. Certainly the United States has greater wealth, population, and troops than Iraq. Yet in 2004 the American attempt to stabilize the country and bring about a representative government sympathetic with American goals in the region seemed beyond America's power. While the use of U.S. military forces demonstrated American strength it also showed the limits (uncertain future outcomes) and costs (allies support, casualties, and money) of using that capacity to influence Iraqi behavior.

People generally do not seek power for its own sake. They usually want it for other values it can get them—for the fame or wealth or even affection they think it will bring. Power, like money, is a means to other ends. Most people seek money for what it can buy—whether possessions, prestige, or security. Just as some people go after money more intently than others, so too do some people seek power more than others. Of course, power, like money, does not come to everyone who seeks it.

Elites

Those who do gain power often are called a political elite. *Elites* are those who get more than others of the values society has available (such as wealth and respect). We could answer the "who" part of the question "who gets what, when, and how?" by saying the elite are those who get the most.

There may be different elites depending on what value is being considered. In a small town, the owner of the largest business may be getting most of the wealth in the community, whereas the poor but honest mayor may have most of the respect. In most cases, however, the values overlap. The wealthy businessman will get plenty of respect, and the mayor will use people's respect for her to make income-producing contacts and investments.

To see the difference between an elite and the rest of us, we can look at one value (wealth) in one society (the United States). Clearly, wealth is not distributed equally among the population; some (the elite) get more than others. The top fifth of the American population gets almost 50 percent of the national income while the bottom fifth receives 3.6 percent. The top 1 percent of the nation owns 33 percent of the wealth. More than 32 million Americans live below the official poverty line. Further, inequality seems to be growing. Between 1970 and 1999 the average annual compensation of the top 100 chief executive officers (CEOs) of American corporations went from $1.3 million—39 times the pay of an average worker—to $37.5 million, more than 1,000 times the pay of the average worker. (See "Guess Who's Coming to Dinner.")

Authority: Legitimate Power

Often, members of an elite reinforce their position by gaining authority. *Authority* is legitimate power. By *legitimate* we mean even more than "legal": The word implies something *accepted as right*. This correctness or *legitimacy* is connected in people's minds to both the position and the wishes of the authority. People also may think something is legitimate if it was chosen using an agreed-upon procedure, such as an election. People recognize certain others as having the right to influence them in certain ways, and not in other ways as we saw in the cigarette incident in class. Most people feel that a vice president *should* follow the wishes of the president; students *should* listen to their teacher; children *should* obey their parents. People have many reasons for obeying authorities including habit, the authority figure's personal appeal, desire to be accepted by the group, and self-interest. But although they may not always follow it, people widely recognize authority as deserving obedience and that is what gives it legitimacy.

Guess Who's Coming to Dinner

Imagine one hundred people at the banquet seated at six tables. At the far right is a table set with English china and real silver, where five people sit comfortably. Next to them is another table, nicely set but nowhere near as fancy, where 15 people sit. At each of the four remaining tables 20 people sit—the one on the far left has a stained paper tablecloth and plastic knives and forks. This arrangement is analogous to the spread of income groups—from the richest 5 percent at the right to the poorest 20 percent at the left.

Twenty waiters and waitresses come in, carrying 100 delicious looking dinners, just enough, one would suppose, for each of the one hundred guests. But, amazingly, four of the waiters bring 20 dinners to the five people at the fancy table on the right. There's hardly room for all the food. (If you go over and look a little closer, you will notice that two of the waiters are obsequiously fussing and trying to arrange ten dinners in front of just one of those five.) At the next-fanciest table, with the 15 people, five waiters bring another 25 dinners. The 20 people at the third table get 25 dinners, 15 go to the fourth table, and ten to the fifth. To the 20 people at the last table (the one with the paper tablecloth), a rude and clumsy waiter brings only five dinners. At the top table there are four dinners for each person; at the bottom table, four persons for each dinner. That's approximately the way income is distributed in America—fewer than half the people get even one dinner apiece.

Source: From *Equality* by William Ryan. Copyright © 1981 by William Ryan. Reprinted by permission of Pantheon Books, a division of Random House, Inc.

Thus authority is an efficient form of power. If people feel they *should* follow the wishes of an authority, then there is no need to force or even to persuade them to do so. The cost of influence is lowered for the authority. If, however, people do not respect the author-

ity's legitimacy, its power can disappear quickly. For example, in April 2001, rioting took place in Cincinnati, Ohio, by black youths

enraged at the shooting death of an unarmed black teenager by a policeman. Several days of rioting resulted in widespread damage and bitterness toward the largely white police force. Because the police had lost their legitimacy in the eyes of many in the black community, the cost to the police of influencing their behavior went up. The police could still force people off the street; an element of force lies behind most authority. But anyone can clear a street with a gun. Only an accepted authority can do it with just a word.

Power and authority, then, are central to politics. They are also central to many other aspects of life—almost all human interactions involve people trying to influence others. In a political science course, we could study the politics of a school or a hospital or a family—who influences, who is influenced, and what is the process and limits of that influence. But most students of politics are interested in a bigger question: How does our whole society decide who gets what, when, and how? To find out, we need to study the most important organization that decides who is to get the values of our society—government.

THE NEED FOR GOVERNMENT

Government is one of humanity's oldest and most universal institutions. History records very few societies that have existed with no government. *Anarchy* (a society without government) may be an interesting theory, but it seldom has been applied for long. Instead, people have lived under forms of government that vary from the tribal council of a Native American village to the complex party dictatorship of Communist China. Why is government so common?

One answer is that government is as common in society as is *political conflict*—the dispute over distribution of a society's valued things. These values (such as wealth) are limited, but people's demands for them are pretty unlimited. This imbalance means conflict. Whenever people have lived together, they have needed a way to regulate the conflicts among them. The question is not *whether* there will be conflict, but *how* the conflict will be handled. Who will decide on the rules that determine who wins and who loses? And how does one get the loser to accept the decision? The usual way to channel political conflict and thus preserve society, is to have some form of government.

Most governments in the world today claim to be democratic. A *democracy* is a form of government in which most people can effectively participate. Because it is generally impractical for all the people to take part in their government directly, their participation is usually through representatives whom they choose in free elections. (What many countries call "free elections," without competing political parties, freedom of speech and an independent press, would not impress many Americans. Admittedly many foreigners were equally unimpressed by our 2004 choice of two wealthy Yale graduates for president.) Hence, the people rule themselves indirectly through their representatives, in a form of government often called a *representative democracy.*

An essential part of democracy is a tolerance of different opinions and interests. Unlike ideologies like militant Islam or communism, democratic politics doesn't assume that some groups, like Christians or capitalists, are wrong and shouldn't participate in politics. Politics in a democracy acts like a marketplace, continually reacting to demands by different groups and reaching compromises among them. As British political scientist Bernard Crick wrote, "democratic politics . . . chooses conciliation rather than violence . . . as a way to maintain order and adapt to change." Reaching decisions this way means that democratic politics is likely to be messy, with few clear-cut victories by anyone. It also accepts that groups must be free to speak for their own interests and that none has a monopoly on the truth.

Yet establishing governments, even democratic ones, does allow some people great power over many others. This power includes the ability to coerce others more effectively than if government didn't exist. As illustrated by the mass murders of Jews by Nazi Germany and the more recent genocide of Tutsis in Rwanda, control of government may even mean the power to kill millions of your own citizens.

The politicians who wrote the Constitution understood the problem of power as we will see in the next chapter. The journalist Robert D. Kaplan described our Founders as "constructive pessimists" who "worried constantly about what might go wrong in human relations." James Madison's famous quote in *The Federalist Papers* No. 51—"If men were angels, no government would be necessary"—justified the elaborate handiwork of checks and balances, and divisions of power and civil liberties designed to limit the future leaders of the United States. Yet as the 2000 conflicted presidential election and a contested war in Iraq remind us, the control of powerful judicial and political offices remains a clear and present challenge to democracy.

What Is Government?

Government is a political association that does two things:

1. It makes rules determining who will get the valued things of a society.
2. It alone regulates the use of legitimate force in society.

The first part of the definition deals with how society distributes the values it has available—wealth, respect, safety, and so on. The second part deals with how these decisions are enforced. Government, then, has the final word over who gets what and has the ultimate say over how it will be done.

The government does not always *directly* determine who will get the valued things in a society. The United States is a capitalist system, based on the private ownership of the economy. This means that the government doesn't directly decide on what jobs people will do, what products they will make, or who will get the income from the sale of the products. Instead, in theory, the United States government only protects and legitimates the private distribution of most of society's values. Our government is set up to minimize government interference.

But this noninterference also can be viewed as a decision supporting the status quo or existing distribution of values in American society. The government not only refuses to interfere but also prevents others from interfering in the status quo. For example, it enforces laws such as those supporting repayment of debt and punishment of robbery. In practice, these and other government functions, such as providing a sound currency, protecting from domestic unrest, and safeguarding private property, do mean government intervention. Most groups, whatever their political leanings, favor intervention if it favors them.

At the same time, the government sets limits on the private distribution of values. While allowing people to accumulate wealth, the government puts higher taxes on those with higher incomes. It also supports welfare programs to help the people who are getting the least of society's wealth. Both taxes and welfare illustrate the government's use of its legitimate power (authority) to place limits on the private distribution of this value of wealth.

Making and Supporting Decisions

The government also may intervene more directly in disputes among its citizens. Citizens of a town near a river may not be able to swim there because a paper mill dumps sewage into it. The citizens of the town or the owners of the mill may ask the government to settle the dispute. The appropriate part of the government may respond by passing a law, or by a ruling of an administrative agency such as the Environmental Protection Agency, or by a court decision on whether the town or the paper mill will get the use of the river (the "valued thing").

How the government supports its decision brings us to the second aspect of government—its exclusive regulation of legitimate force. In enforcing its decisions, the government may employ, allow, or prevent the use of force. Either the paper mill or the town's swimmers may be ordered not to use the river and may be fined or arrested if they do so. Only the government is allowed to regulate what kind of force is used, and how.

The government is not the only group in society that can legitimately use force. Parents may discipline their children to keep them from swimming, or the paper mill may employ guards to keep people off their property. But only the government can set limits on this force. Most governments permit parents to spank their kids yet forbid physical abuse of children. The paper mill's guards may be forbidden to use guns to keep swimmers out. Government does not *monopolize* the use of legitimate force, but it alone *regulates* its use.

THE STUDY OF POLITICS

What is the study of politics? One thing you will notice about political science is that it's a lot like other *social sciences* such as history, economics, sociology, and psychology. Each studies aspects of the relations among people. In any large group of people, many social interactions are going on. Each of these disciplines may look at the same group and ask different questions about the relationships that are occurring. This division of labor is partly traditional and partly a way of separating complicated human relations into more easily understood parts. Political science fits in by studying one type of interaction between people—that involving power and authority. The following example will make the approaches of the other disciplines clearer and distinguish them from political science.

Political Science and Microsoft

What questions would an economist, a psychologist, and a historian ask about the operations of a "society" like the giant computer software company Microsoft? An *economist* might ask questions about the production and distribution of the various Microsoft operating systems and other programs. In designing its Microsoft Network, how did the company attract subscribers and content providers? How were buyers of the Windows program discouraged from using a rival web browser from Netscape? A *psychologist* might concentrate on the motives and goals of Bill Gates, the founder of Microsoft and probably the richest man in America. What is the psychological makeup of this successful entrepreneur? How does he deal with subordinates and competitors? A *historian* might look at the origins and development of Microsoft. What factors within the industry explain why in a few years its operating systems ran more than four-fifths of the world's computers? Why did it become a multi-billion dollar corporation while competitors fell by the wayside?

Of course, these different fields of study overlap. Members of one discipline often are interested in the findings of another. Economists may find answers to their questions about how focused and innovative the company is in a psychological study of Bill Gates. The historian might ask the economist about Microsoft's mergers with potential competitors to determine the logic behind its expansion. Certainly the economist and the psychologist would want to know about the history of the corporation before studying their particular parts of it.

A political scientist, although interested in the other disciplines' findings, would most likely focus on this central question: *Who is getting what, when, and how?* If Bill Gates runs Microsoft, how does he and his executives reach decisions and implement them? How has the government influenced their decisions, and why did the Justice Department bring and then settle its antitrust suit against Microsoft? How did Microsoft gain preeminence in its industry, and how do its leaders keep it, and themselves, on top? Political science focuses on the study of power and authority—on the powerful, the ways in which they exercise their authority, and the effects they produce.

As Lasswell wrote, "The study of politics is the study of influence and the influential."[1] That is the core of what a political scientist would want to find out about Microsoft.

Why Give a Damn About Politics?

After looking at what politics is and what government and political scientists do, you could still be asking one basic question: Who cares? Why give a damn about politics? Often students say: "Politics is just ego. I don't want to get involved in it." The problem is that you are already involved. Apathy is as much a political position as is activism. Either position will influence who gets what in our society. Safe streets, good schools, and clean food are political decisions influenced by who participates in making them, who is prevented from participating, and who chooses not to participate.

Our lives are webs of politics. Think of what you have done today and how politics has influenced you. What you had (or didn't have) for breakfast was probably influenced by the price and availability of the food. The quality of the food you ate was regulated by a government agency that made sure those Grade A eggs were Grade A and that the milk was indeed pasteurized. The cost of that milk or those eggs was affected by the decisions of government to aid farmers, as well as the

---

[1] Harold Lasswell. *Politics: Who Gets What, When, How.* New York: World, 1958, p. 13.

ability of farmers' groups to influence the government (through campaign contributions, for instance). The news you heard on the radio of what the government was doing for the economy was conditioned by what officials felt they should tell the public and what media editors felt was newsworthy. The college you attend, the tuition increases you pay, the student loans or other aid you may or may not receive, are all the results of someone's choices in the political game. (See "Who Needs Government?")

Sometimes the influence of politics is subtle. Many of the ways we expect to be treated in our daily lives reflect recent changes in the laws. A few examples would include the rights of women and homosexuals not to be harassed, or that elderly workers can't be fired because of their age, or the right to learn in a smoke-free class. These evolving rights can be supported by our participation in joining demonstrations, wearing buttons, and going to court. We are rights-bearing citizens often without thinking that these too are the result of political choices.

Of course people don't usually participate in the government decisions that affect their lives. Let's take a personal example. Studies of American government have often pointed out that federal regulatory commissions have not effectively regulated the businesses they oversee. These commissions have tended to be closely tied to the powerful

Who Needs Government?

Former Senator Ernest Hollings of South Carolina tells this story:

A veteran returning from Korea went to college on the GI Bill; bought his house with an FHA loan; saw his kids born in a VA hospital; started a business with an SBA loan; got electricity from TVA; and then, water from a project funded by the EPA. His kids participated in the school lunch program and made it through college courtesy of government-guaranteed student loans. His parents retired to a farm on their social security, getting electricity from the REA and the soil tested by the USDA. When the father became ill, his life was saved with a drug developed through NIH; the family was saved from financial ruin by Medicare. Our veteran drove to work on the interstate; moored his boat in a channel dredged by Army engineers; and, when floods hit, took Amtrak to Washington to apply for disaster relief. He also spent some of his time there enjoying the exhibits in the Smithsonian museums.

Then one day he wrote his congressman an angry letter complaining about paying taxes for all those programs created for ungrateful people. In effect, he said, the government should get off his back.

Source: Jonathan Yates, "Reality on Capitol Hill," *Newsweek,* November 28, 1988, p. 12.

economic interests they supervise. The lesson was brought home to me in graduate school.

Some years ago the cargo door blew off an American Airlines DC-10 flying over Windsor, Canada, causing violent decompression. The pilot managed to land the empty jumbo jet safely. The government's independent National Transportation Safety Board investigated the near disaster. Their recommendations went to the Federal Aviation Administration (FAA), the government regulatory commission in charge of airline safety. The safety board recommended that the FAA order that all cargo doors have modified locking devices and that McDonnell Douglas, the plane's builder, be required to strengthen the cabin floor.

The FAA, headed by a political appointee, was operating under a policy of "gentlemen's agreements" with the industries it was regulating. After discussions with the plane's manufacturers (who were large contributors to President Nixon's reelection campaign), they allowed McDonnell Douglas to modify the door on its own instead of under FAA supervision and simply to issue advisory service bulletins for the 130 or so DC-10s already in operation. McDonnell Douglas was allowed to reject as "impractical" the idea of strengthening the floor.

Somehow the changes were not made on the door of a DC-10 flown by Turkish Airlines. The plane, flying from Paris to London in March 1974, crashed, killing all 346 people aboard. It was at the time the world's worst air disaster. The cargo door had blown off. This loss produced explosive decompression, collapse of the cabin floor, and loss of control. Passengers still strapped in their seats were sucked from the plane. A subcommittee of the House of Representatives, in a report on the crash, attacked the FAA for its "indifference to public safety" and for attempting to "balance dollars against lives."

A teacher and friend of mine, Professor Wayne Wilcox of Columbia University, was on the plane. With him were his wife and two children.

We have no choice over *whether* to be involved in the political game. But we can choose *how* to be involved. We can choose whether to be a *subject* in the political game or an *object* of that game. The question is not whether politics affects us—it does and will. The question is whether we will affect politics. The first step in this decision is choosing how aware we wish to be of the game. This book may, with luck, be a start of your awareness.

WHAT IS THIS BOOK ABOUT?

This book is, in a way, a scorecard covering the major players in the game of national politics. This first chapter introduces some of the terms and substance of politics—the means (power and authority) and goals (values) of the game. Chapters 2 and 6 cover the formal constitutional rules and the civil liberties and rights under which the competition proceeds. Chapters 3, 4, and 5 deal with the governmental players—the president and bureaucracy, Congress, and the federal courts—their history and structure, their strengths and weaknesses. Chapters 7 and 8 are about four important nongovernmental players—voters, political parties, interest groups, and media. Though they are not official parts of the government, they have great influence over the outcome of political conflicts. Finally, the last chapter goes into different theories of who wins and loses, who plays and doesn't play the game.

Overview of book

Let's be clear about this "game"; it is not "Monday Night Football." It is important, complex, ever changing, and never ending, and may involve questions of life and death. Actually, many games are going on at the same time with overlapping players and objectives. They are games in which the participants often disagree, even on the goals. For the goals (unlike the touchdown in football) vary with the objectives of the players. A business group may seek higher profits from its involvement in a political issue, a consumer organization may want a lower-priced product, and a labor union may demand higher wages for its workers. They may all compete for their differing objectives over the same issue. They all seek to use power to obtain the values they consider important. We can analyze objectively how they play the game, but which side we root for depends on our own interests and ideals.

Another problem is that the players we've grouped together may not see themselves as being on the same team. Each participant, whether the bureaucracy, Congress, or the media, is hardly one player seeking a single goal. They are not only players but also *arenas* in which competition goes on. We may read of Congress opposing the president on an issue, but a closer look will find the president's congressional supporters and opponents fighting it out in the committees of Congress. Some of the media may oppose a certain interest group, while allowing or limiting the use of television news and radio talk shows as arenas for the group's views.

Finally, in this brief introductory text all the political players are not discussed. State and local governments are certainly important in national politics. Ethnic groups and foreign governments may have a role in the outcome of the competition. Someone even more basic is missing. As one student asked, Where are the people? What ever happened to the American people in this game? Are they players or observers?

Politics today is a spectator sport. The audience is on the sidelines. To be sure, people do influence the players. The president and Congress are selected by election, interest groups depend on their members' support, and political parties need popular backing. But though it is played for the crowd—who certainly pay for the game—the competition itself generally doesn't include them. Whether it will change so that they participate will depend on the players, the rules of the game, and the people watching.

Thought Questions

1. In the opening dialogue of this chapter, we discovered politics in a place that may seem unlikely—a classroom. Describe some other common situations in which politics goes on.
2. How do authorities gain legitimacy? How do they lose it? Can you think of recent examples of both?
3. People sometimes justify their apathy by the way politicians behave. Do you think this attitude is justified?
4. Have any decisions in your life been affected by government action? Did you have anything to say about those actions? If you didn't, do you know who did?

Suggested Readings

Crick, Bernard. *Democracy: A Very Short Introduction.* New York: Oxford University Press, 2002. Pb.
A historical disscussion of the definitions, conditions, and development of modern democracy.

Golding, William G. *Lord of the Flies.* New York: Capricorn Books, 1959. Pb.
A pessimistic novel (even before the TV series *Survivor*) on what happens to a group of British children on a deserted island without adults or government, but with a lot of politics.

Klein, Joe. *Primary Colors: A Novel of Politics.* New York: Random House, 1996.
A *Newsweek* columnist's fictional account of the nitty gritty of President Clinton's campaign.

Mathews, Christopher. "American: Beyond Our Grandest Notions." New York: The Free Press, 2002.
A pleasant if cheerleading read by a TV host about what makes the United States different and better.

Ophuls, William. *Requiem For Modern Politics.* Boulder, Colorado: Westview Press, 1997.
A harsh, difficult, and brilliant critique of modern American politics from the viewpoint of our environment.

Warren, Robert Penn. *All the King's Men.* New York: Harcourt Brace Jovanovich, 1946.
A terrific novel about a terrifically manipulative politician modeled on Louisiana's Huey Long.

CHAPTER 2

The Constitution: Rules of the Game

THE SECOND DAY OF CLASS

On the second day the professor comes in and says we're going to be a focus group. We'll do public opinion interviews to see what a small bunch of people think. He says to us, what words come to mind when you hear "politician"?

Well, this question I happen to know the answer to.

"How about 'Slime balls'?"

High fives all around.

Then the teach says, "What about 'politics'?"

Not too hard—"Corrupt," "Games," "Boring."

So then he says, "Well what about when I say 'Founding Fathers'?"

"Patriots," "Freedom," "George Washington."

"How about 'The Constitution'?" he says.

"Liberty," "Equality," "Bill of Rights". . . .

Some of us are catching on.

Then he lets us have it. "Didn't the framers of the Constitution run for election and make promises to win peoples' votes? And not all of them were perfect in their personal lives. Didn't they cut secret deals and wheel and deal to write the Constitution and get it adopted? Most people at the time were unhappy with the results. And with their leaders."

Sounds to me like our Founding Fathers were a bunch of politicians.

The Constitution did not fall from the sky. It was created by political leaders trying to form a government while dealing with immediate problems and conflicts, all within the understandings of their time. It has lasted because the politicians into whose care it was given proved flexible enough to adapt it to different times, and because it commanded loyalty as a symbol of a nation's traditions and ideals. But the Constitution has never been "above politics." Its words cannot be understood apart from the politics in which they were written then, and applied now.

So far we have discussed what the game of politics is about, what winning means, and why one plays. This chapter deals with the principles and procedures of the competition. It first discusses the politicians who wrote the Constitution, their debates, the interests they represented, and the compromises they reached. The Constitution contains the official rules of the American political game; it also establishes three major players and their powers—the president, Congress, and the Supreme Court. Further, it places limits on the game, providing protection for players and people. And by creating a central government that shares power with state governments, the Constitution establishes the playing field of federalism. What led to the adoption of the Constitution, its meaning, how it has changed, and its influence today are the subjects of this chapter.

BACKGROUND TO THE CONSTITUTION

On July 4, 1776, the Declaration of Independence proclaimed the American colonies "Free and Independent States." This symbolized the beginning not only of a bitter fight for independence from Great Britain, but also of a struggle to unify the separate and often conflicting interests, regions, and states of America. Only after a decade of trial and error was the Constitution written and accepted as the legal foundation for the new United States of America.

The politicians who gathered in Philadelphia in May 1787 to write the Constitution were not starting from scratch. They were able to draw on (1) an English political heritage, (2) American models of colonial and state governments, and (3) their experience with the Articles of Confederation.

The framers were inheritors of an English legal heritage that included the *Magna Carta,* which, in 1215, had declared that the power of the king was not absolute. It also included the idea of natural rights, expressed by English philosophers, most notably John Locke, who wrote that people were "born free" and formed society to protect their rights. Many colonists felt that they were fighting a revolution to secure their traditional rights as Englishmen, which they had been denied by an abusive colonial government.

Their 150 years as colonies had taught the states much about self-government that they used in the Constitution. Even the earliest settlers had been determined to live under written rules of law resting on the consent of the community: The *Mayflower Compact* was signed by the Pilgrims shortly before they landed at Plymouth in 1620. Similar documents had been written in other colonies, most of which had their own constitutions. Other aspects of colonial (and English) governments, such as two-house legislatures, also were later to appear in the Constitution. After the Revolution, in reaction to the authority of the royal governor, the colonists established the legislature as the most important branch in their state governments.

Most of the colonies had a governor, a legislature, and a judiciary— a pattern that would evolve into the constitutional separation of powers. Most had regular elections, though generally only property-owning white males could vote. There was even an uneasy basis for the federal system of local and national governments in the sharing of powers between the American colonies and a central government in England. Perhaps most important was the idea of limited government and individual rights written into the state constitutions after the Revolution.

But unity among the colonies was slow in coming. Attempts to tighten their ties during the Revolution were a limited success. Most political theorists of the time thought democracy could only exist in small states. The First Continental Congress in September 1774 had established regular lines of communication among the colonies and gave a focus to anti-British sentiment. The Second Continental Congress, beginning in Philadelphia in May 1775, created the Declaration of Independence. At the same time a plan for confederation—a loose union among the states—was proposed. The Articles of Confederation were ratified by the states by March 1781 and went into effect even before the formal end of the American Revolution in February 1783.

The Articles of Confederation (1781–1789)

The shortcomings of the Articles of Confederation are not difficult to list. No real national government was set up in the articles. Rather, they established a "league of friendship" among the states, which didn't have much more authority than the United Nations does today. The center of the federation was a *unicameral* (one-house) legislature, called the *Confederation Congress*. Each state had one vote, regardless of its size. Most serious actions required approval by nine states. Amendments to the articles needed approval by all 13.

The confederation had no executive branch and no national system of courts. Perhaps most important, the Congress had no ability to impose taxes; it could only *request* funds from the states. Each state retained its "sovereignty, freedom, and independence." Nor did the Congress have any direct authority over citizens who were subject only to the government of their states. In short, the Congress had no ability to enforce its will on either states or citizens.

The confederation did have some strengths, however. Unlike the United Nations, it had the power to declare war, conduct foreign policy, coin money, manage a postal system, and oversee an army made up of the state militias. The articles were also anti-elite in requiring compulsory rotation in office, what we would today call a type of *term limits*—no member of the Congress could serve more than three years in any six. Finally, real accomplishments were made under the articles, such as the start of a national bureaucracy and the passing of the *Northwest Ordinance,* which established the procedure for admitting new states into the union.

But by 1787, the inadequacies of the articles were more apparent than its strengths. Too little power had been granted to the central authority. Many people worried that Britain, France, or Spain would attack America because of its weak central government. The confederation was in deep financial difficulty: Not enough funds were coming from the states, the currency was being devalued, and the states were locked in trade wars, putting up tariff barriers against each other. In late 1786 Shays's Rebellion, an angry protest by Massachusetts farmers unable to pay their mortgages and taxes, reinforced the fears of many among the property-owning elite that strong government was needed to avoid "mob rule" and economic disruption.

The Constitutional Convention

Against this background, the convention met in Philadelphia from May 25 to September 17, 1787. The weather was hot and muggy, making tempers short. All the meetings were held in secrecy—the press was excluded. One reason was that the Congress had reluctantly called the convention together "for the sole purpose of revising the Articles of Confederation." Yet within five days of organizing, the convention had adopted a Virginia delegate's resolution "that a national government ought to be established consisting of a *supreme* legislative, executive, and judiciary." In other words, the convention violated the authority under which it had been established and proceeded to write a completely new United States constitution in a single summer.

The Constitution was a product of a series of compromises. The most important compromise, because it was the most divisive issue, was the question of how the states would be represented in the national legislature. The large states proposed a legislature with representation based either on the taxes paid by each state to the national government or on the number of people in each state. The small states wanted one vote for each state no matter what its size. After a long deadlock, an agreement called the *Great Compromise* established the present structure of Congress—representation based on population in the lower house (House of Representatives) and equal representation for all states in the upper one (Senate).

Other compromises came a bit more easily. Southern delegates feared the national government would impose an export tax on their agricultural goods and interfere with slavery. A compromise was reached that gave Congress the power to regulate commerce but not to put a tax on exports. In addition, the slave trade could not be banned before 1808. The slave issue also was central in the strangest agreement—the Three-Fifths Compromise. Here the debate was over whether slaves should be counted as people for purposes of representation and taxation. The South, which did not want to treat slaves as people, did however want to count them that way. It was finally agreed that a slave should be counted as three-fifths of a person for both. (This provision was later removed by the Thirteenth and Fourteenth Amendments.) Another key issue, the right of a state to withdraw or *secede* from the union, was simply avoided. The questions of secession and slavery had to wait for a later generation to answer in a bloody civil war.

The Framers

It is a bit surprising how quickly and relatively painlessly the Constitution was drafted. No doubt the writing went so smoothly partly because of the qualities of the leaders in Philadelphia. The universally respected General Washington chaired the meetings, bringing with him the pragmatism of a successful landowner and the commitment of a nationalist. Alexander Hamilton, the self-assured financial genius, often dominated debates, while the shy but equally brilliant James Madison often secured a consensus at discussion's end. Benjamin Franklin, at 82, added the moderation and insights of age.

The delegates possessed a blend of experience and learning. (See "Colonial Drinking and Voting.") Of the 55 delegates, 42 had served in the Continental Congress. More than half were college educated and had studied political philosophy. As a relatively young group, the average age being 40, they may have reflected a generation gap of their own time. Having politically matured during the revolutionary period, they were less tied to state loyalties than were

Colonial Drinking and Voting

[James] Madison . . . believed deeply in a government based on the consent of the people, *as long as the direct involvement of the people was strictly limited.* Early in his political career he had seen the ways of popular politics, and the experience made him uncomfortable. In Madison's Virginia, men got elected to office by plying the freeholders with bumbo—in the vernacular of the day. Rum punch was preferred, accompanied by cookies and ginger cake and occasionally a barbecued bullock or a hog. For one election, in 1758, George Washington supplied 160 gallons of liquor to 391 voters—a stiff one and a half quarts per voter.

That was the way it was done. Though good enough for the likes of Washington, Jefferson, Henry, Mason, and the rest, to young Madison it was a "corrupting influence," inconsistent with the "purity of moral and republic principles." During his second run for the Virginia House of Delegates, in 1777, he decided to set an example. He refused to supply the bumbo.

Madison lost that election—to a tavernkeeper.

Source: Fred Barbash, *The Founding.* New York: Simon & Schuster, 1987, p. 131.

older men whose outlook was formed before the war. They were nationalists building a nation, not merely defending the interests of their states.

But there was more to the consensus than this. The framers were not exactly a representative sample of the population of America at the time. They were wealthy planters, merchants, and lawyers. Fifteen of them were slaveholders, 14 were land speculators. The small farmers and workers of the country, many of whom were suffering from an economic downturn, were not represented at Philadelphia. Nor did leaders who might speak for this poorer majority, such as Thomas Jefferson (who was in Paris as ambassador and disliked the face-to-face disputes in political meetings) or Patrick Henry (who stayed away because he "smelt a rat"), attend the convention. Only six of the 56 men who signed the Declaration of Independence were at the convention. The delegates were a conservative, propertied elite, worried that continuing the weak confederation would only encourage more and larger Shays's Rebellions. Thus the debates at the convention were not between the "haves" and the "have-nots," but between the "haves" and the "haves" over their regional interests.

Motives Behind the Constitution

Much scholarly debate has gone on about the motives of the framers since Charles Beard published his book *An Economic Interpretation of the Constitution of the United States* in 1913. Beard argued that the convention was a counterrevolution engineered by the delegates to protect and improve their own property holdings by transferring power from the states to an unrepresentative central government. Certainly the 40 delegates who held nearly worthless confederation securities stood to profit from a new government committed to honoring these debts. Certainly their interests as creditors and property holders would be better protected by a strong central government. Nor did the delegates particularly favor democracy. Most thought that liberty had to be protected *from* democracy (which they thought of as "mob rule") and agreed with Madison's statement in *The Federalist Papers* No. 10 that "those who hold and those who are without property have ever formed distinct interests in society."

Critics of Beard's theory argue that the framers' motives were more varied. They reason that the delegates wanted to build a new nation, to reduce the country's numerous political disputes, and to promote economic development that would benefit all. They point out that having a central government able to raise an army to protect the states from foreign attack appeared to be the most important reason that George Washington, among others, backed the Constitution.

Is the Constitution Antidemocratic?

There is an argument that the Constitution was an antidemocratic attempt to limit popular participation in government. Many of the framers saw liberty and democracy as very separate, with peoples' liberties often needing constitutional protections from democratic pressures. Certainly the selection of the president, the senate, and the Supreme Court, as well as many constitutional procedures, like the veto, were seen as restraints on democracy. Critics often quote an antidemocratic framer like Roger Sherman of Connecticut who wrote that the people "should have as little to do as may be about the government. They . . . are constantly liable to be misled."

The late Thurgood Marshall, the Supreme Court's first black justice, pointed out that the Constitution's preamble that begins "we the people," did not include the majority of America's citizens—women and minorities. He called the Constitution "defective from the start" because it required tremendous social upheaval "to attain the system of constitutional government, and its respect for the individual freedoms and human rights, we hold as fundamental today." He warned against a complacent belief in the original vision of the founders. Instead, Marshall praised those who through the Civil War created virtually a new constitution using the Fourteenth Amendment to ensure the rights of all Americans.

But the arguments of the two sides don't necessarily cancel out each other. The framers' *public* interest of building a strong nation and their *private* interest of protecting their property could work together. Like most people, they believed that what was good for themselves was good for society. It was not surprising by standards of the day that most of the population (workers, the poor, blacks, women) was not represented at Philadelphia. Nor should it be surprising that the delegates' ideas for a government did not work against their own economic interests and, in many cases, aided them. (See "Is the Constitution Antidemocratic?")

Federalists Versus Anti-Federalists

There were divisions within the elite. Many of the debates during the writing and ratification of the Constitution divided people into two camps: the Federalists and the Anti-Federalists.

The *Federalists* generally favored a strong federal (national) government, with protection of private property rights and limits on popular participation in government. (Alexander Hamilton, a leader of the Federalists, described the people as "a great beast.") In the debates

over the Constitution, the Federalists
pushed for high property qualifications
for voting, an indirectly elected Senate
modeled after the English aristocratic House of Lords, a lofty indirectly
elected president, and a strong nonelected judiciary. The Federalists, being
more pessimistic about human nature
(including the nature of the rulers),
wanted these "cooling-off" devices in the government to filter down the
popular will and create guardians of the people's real interests.

    The *Anti-Federalists* were more optimistic about human nature
though just as suspicious about the nature of those in power. Led by
men like Patrick Henry and George Mason, they favored strong state
governments because they felt the states would be closer to the popular will than a strong central government. They wanted fewer limits
on popular participation and pushed for the legislative branch to have
more power than the executive and judicial branches. Believing that
the majority was responsible, though agreeing that it needed cooling
off, they wanted government to be accountable to elected officials.

    The Constitution is a compromise between these two positions. It
was designed to prevent tyranny from the bottom—the people (whom
the Federalists feared), and from the top—the rulers (whom the Anti-
Federalists feared). Both sides generally believed that the government that governed best governed least.

Ratification and the Bill of Rights

The struggle for ratification of the Constitution focused the debate
between the Federalists and Anti-Federalists. Conventions in nine
states had to approve the Constitution before it could go into effect.
Because a majority of the people were against the Constitution, the
fight for ratification wasn't easy. The Anti-Federalists wanted a more
rigid system of separation of power and more effective checks and
balances. Fearing that the president and Senate would act together as
an aristocratic clique, they proposed compulsory rotation in office (as
under the Articles of Confederation).

    The Federalists' difficulty came from supporting a strong central
government that could tax and endanger peoples' liberties—the very
arguments that they had *argued against* during the Revolution. They
criticized the Anti-Federalists for their lack of faith in popular elections
and for ignoring the advantages of a national union. Their propaganda
campaign in the newspapers pointed out the failures of the confederation, reassured people that the proposed president would be more like a

governor than a king, and dismissed charges that the judiciary would be a threat to individual liberties. A series of these essays in a New York newspaper written by Madison, Hamilton, and John Jay was later republished as *The Federalist Papers*. The book stands today as the most famous commentary on the framers' thinking regarding their Constitution.

The debate over whether to include the *Bill of Rights*, the first ten amendments in the Constitution, became a key issue in the struggle over ratification. The Philadelphia convention, dominated by Federalists, had failed to include a bill of rights in the original document, not so much because of opposition to the goals of the bill, but from a feeling that such a statement was irrelevant. (A proposed bill of rights was voted down unanimously near the end of the convention partly because everyone was worn out and wanted to go home.) The Federalists, from their conservative viewpoint, believed that liberty was best protected by the *procedures*, such as federalism, and checks and balances, established by their constitutional government. No matter what ideals were written down, such as freedoms of speech, press, and religion, the Federalists argued that support for them would depend on the "tolerance of the age" and the balance of forces established by the Constitution.

For the Anti-Federalists, the Bill of Rights was a proclamation of fundamental truths—natural rights due to all people. No matter that another generation might ignore them, these rights were sacred. Any government resting on the consent of its people must honor them in its constitution. Although the Anti-Federalists had lost the battle in Philadelphia, they eventually won the war over the Bill of Rights. Massachusetts and Virginia agreed to accept the Constitution with the recommendation that such a proclamation be the first order of business of the new Congress. It was, and the Bill of Rights became the first ten amendments to the Constitution on December 15, 1791.

FOUR MAJOR CONSTITUTIONAL PRINCIPLES

The United States Constitution did three things in establishing a government. First, it *established the structure* of government. In setting up three branches of government within a federal system, it gave the country a political framework that has existed down to the present. Second, the Constitution *distributed certain powers* to this government. Article I gave legislative powers, such as the power to raise and spend money, to Congress. Article II gave executive powers to the president, including command over the armed forces and wide authority over foreign policy. Article III gave judicial power, the right to judge disputes arising under the Constitution, to the U. S. Supreme Court. Third, the Constitution *restrained the government* in exercising these powers. Government was limited, by the

Bill of Rights for example, so that certain individual rights would be preserved.

The Constitution, then, both *grants* and *limits* governmental power. This can be most clearly illustrated by looking closely at four major constitutional principles: separation of powers, and checks and balances, federalism, limited government, and judicial review.

Separation of Powers and Checks and Balances

The first major constitutional principle is actually two: separation of powers, and checks and balances. But the two principles cannot be understood apart from each other, and they work together.

Separation of powers is the principle that the powers of government should be separated and put in the care of different parts of the government. Although never exactly stated in the Constitution, this principle was in practice in the governments of the colonies. The idea that power was needed to balance power was a key concept of the French political theorist Baron de Montesquieu who was often quoted at Philadelphia. (See "Madison on Separation of Powers and Government.") The writers of the Constitution divided the federal government into three branches to carry out what they saw as the three major functions of government. The *legislative function*—passing the laws—was given to Congress; the *executive function*—carrying out or executing the laws—was given to the president; and the *judicial function*—interpreting the laws—was given to the Supreme Court.

Madison on Separation of Powers and Government

But the great security against a gradual concentration of the several powers in the same department consists in giving to those who administer each department the necessary constitutional means and personal motives to resist encroachments of the others. . . . Ambition must be made to counteract ambition. The interest of the man must be connected with the constitutional rights of the place. . . . If men were angels, no government would be necessary. If angels were to govern men, neither external or internal controls on government would be necessary. In framing a government, which is to be administered by men over men, the great difficulty lies in this: You must first enable the government to control the governed; and in the next place, oblige it to control itself.

Source: James Madison, *The Federalist Papers* No. 51.

Though nice and neat, the principle is probably unworkable. The purpose of separation of powers was to allow ambition to counter ambition, to prevent any one authority from monopolizing power. Yet simply dividing the powers of government into these three branches would probably make the legislature supreme—as it had been in the colonies. As the starter of the governmental process, the legislature could determine how, or even if, the other branches played their roles. Although Congress was accepted as the most important branch, something was needed to curb legislative power. That something was checks and balances.

Checks and balances create a mixture of powers that permits the three branches of government to limit one another. A *check* is a control one branch has over another's functions creating a *balance* of power. The principle gives the branches constitutional means for guarding their functions from interference by another branch. Checks and balances blend together the legislative, executive, and judicial powers, giving some legislative powers to the executive, some executive powers to the legislative branch, and so on, to keep any branch from dominating another.

There are a number of examples of checks and balances in the Constitution. The president is given legislative power to recommend measures to Congress and to call Congress into special session, and some judicial power like the right to pardon (which President Clinton used extensively on his last day in office). The presidential veto gives the chief executive a primarily legislative power to prevent bills he dislikes from being passed into law. Congress can check this power by its right to override the veto by a two-thirds vote. The Senate is given an executive power in its role of confirming presidential nominations for major executive and judicial posts (which is also the power *not* to confirm, as President Bush found out when Democratic senators held up his appointments of federal judges). Further, Congress can refuse to appropriate funds for any executive agency, thereby preventing the agency from carrying out the laws.

But the system of separation of powers and checks and balances is even more elaborate. The way each branch of government is set up and chosen also checks and balances its power. For example, Congress is divided into two houses, and both must approve legislation before it becomes law. Limited terms of office and varied methods of selection help keep any one person or branch from becoming too strong. The House of Representatives was to be popularly elected for two-year terms; senators were elected for six years, originally by their state legislatures (changed by the Seventeenth Amendment to popular election); the president was elected for four years by an electoral college not a popular vote; and federal judges were to be appointed by the president, confirmed by the Senate, and to serve for life during good behavior. All these procedures were designed to give government officials different interests to defend varied bases of support, and protection from too much interference by other officials.

The institutions that result from this dividing and mixing of powers are separate bodies that in practice *share* the overall power of government. Each needs the others to make the government work, yet each has an interest in checking and balancing the powers of the others. This elaborate scheme of separation of powers and checks and balances was certainly not designed to be the most efficient form of government—as we can see today with the repeated complaints about political "gridlock." Rather, it was established "to control the abuses of government"—to oblige the government to control itself. It set up a structure that historian Richard Hofstadter has called "a harmonious system of mutual frustration."

Federalism

Federalism calls for political authority to be divided between a central government and the governments of the states. Both the federal and state governments may act directly on the people and each has some *exclusive powers*. Federalism, like separation of powers, distributes political authority to prevent power from being concentrated in any one group. It is a constitutional principle around which major political arguments continue down to the present day.

Actually, the men who wrote the Constitution had little choice. The loose confederation of states hadn't operated well, in their eyes, and centralizing all government powers would have been unacceptable to the major governments of the day—those of the individual states. Federalism, then, was more than just a reasonable principle for governing a large country separated by regional differences and slow communications. It also was the only realistic way to get the states to ratify the Constitution.

American federalism has always involved two somewhat contradictory ideas. The first, expressed in Article VI, is that the Constitution and the laws of the central government are supreme. This condition was necessary to establish an effective government that would be able to pass laws and rule directly over all the people. The second principle ensures the independence of the state governments: The Tenth Amendment *reserved powers* to the states or the people not delegated to the central government. These substantial reserved powers include control of local and city governments, regulation of business within a state, supervision of education, and exercise of the general "police power" over the safety of the people.

The conflict between the two principles—national supremacy and states' rights—came to a head in the Civil War, which established the predominance of the national government. That is not to say that the question was settled once and for all. Even today in issues such as gun control and immigration, state governments often clash with the federal government. Such conflicts can be expected from a constitution that not only divided the powers of government into a federal system but also clearly set up the basis for national union.

As political issues—whether regulating the economy or protecting the environment—became national, so too did solutions center in the national government. In practice there are few domestic programs today that are solely run by the federal government. Almost all require cooperation by the states and often the cities. In the best cases, this arrangement helps adjust the programs to local conditions; in the worst, it may delay needed changes. Either way, federalism now exists far less as separate boxes of powers than as a mix of overlapping relations between the states and the federal government, sometimes called a *marblecake.*

This mix of relations can be seen in looking more closely at public education. Public schools in this country are governed by local school boards. The boards set teachers' salaries and make the basic decisions concerning day-to-day operations of a public school system. Local taxes on property in the school district are usually the basic source of public school funds.

No Child Left Behind and Federalism

The education reform called 'No Child Left Behind' was the first legislation sent to Congress by President Bush. It passed both houses of Congress and was signed by the president in January 2002. It showed his willingness to strengthen the federal government's role in education, even if it undermined the conservative position of strengthening federalism.

Although its impact on education is not yet clear, the law has antagonized state and local officials, including conservatives, who felt that Washington was stepping over traditional lines of federalism. In states like Vermont and Utah, legislators have demanded that their states turn down the federal money rather than conform to what they saw as burdensome federal rules.

The approach in "No Child Left Behind" was to hold states, districts and schools accountable for student performance. The federal government would reward improved student achievement, as measured by annual state reading and math tests. There were also penalties to states for failure. If after a few years these schools did not meet performance goals, federal funds would be provided to parents to help them relocate their children in other schools.

Public education in the United States is not, however, solely a local government responsibility. State governments provide a large part of the funds for local education. These funds from state taxes are partly supplied to school districts according to financial need. This equalizes local revenues from property taxes, which vary widely from poorer to wealthier school districts. In addition, state governments usually control teacher qualifications, set educational standards in public schools, and approve the textbooks to be used.

The federal government also is involved in public education. Federal aid programs help equalize state funding just as state funds are used to reduce the differences among local school districts. Some "strings" are attached to these federal funds. In President Bush's recent education plan, "No Child Left Behind," the federal government set standards for student achievement, backed by tests, and left it to the states how to implement them. Federal monies would both help states achieve these standards and penalize them if they didn't. This same kind of funding and regulation of public education is found in government activities ranging from pollution control to public highways. (See "No Child Left Behind and Federalism.")

TABLE 2.1 87,504 GOVERNMENTS IN THE UNITED STATES	
TYPE OF GOVERNMENT	NUMBER
National	1
State	50
County	3,043
Municipal	19,372
Towns	16,629
School districts	13,726
Special Districts	34,683
TOTAL	87,504

Source: U.S. Census Bureau, Statistical Abstract of the United States: 2001, (Washington D.C.: Government Printing Office, 2001), Table No. 413.

The Debate over Modern Federalism

At first glance *modern federalism* appears far different from the original creation. While the Constitution remains an important limit on centralized power, the federal government has grown much stronger. Yet most of the nonmilitary services provided by government are supplied by state and local governments in complex, overlapping relationships with Washington. In some ways federalism makes it easier for citizens to participate in decisions because they occur closer to home. In other ways it's more difficult because people need to keep track of separate decisions being made in a variety of places. (See Table 2.1.)

Before being elected, George W. Bush accused his opponent of favoring "top-down Washington directives" and declared himself in favor of local and state policy making. As president he has gone in the other direction, resisting state and local initiatives, and centralizing policy making in the federal government. Besides expanding the federal role in his education reforms the Bush administration has blocked state efforts to buy prescription drugs in Canada, challenged Oregon's assisted suicide law, and resisted states' attempts to issue tougher air pollution standards. Opponents of the proposed amendment to ban gay marriages pointed out that it would limit a traditional state responsibility to regulate marriage. In short, where federalism clashed with administration objectives, federalism lost.

Are local and state governments closer to the people and therefore produce better policies than the national government? Historically, the answer to this question has depended on how satisfied people have been with what government does. The growth of the federal government has been fueled by big problems and popular demands for their solution. As the economy became national, issues like regulating corporations, protecting workers, providing housing, and guarding the environment seemed beyond the states' capacities to solve. By responding to these challenges the national government appeared both efficient and representative, certainly more so than state and local governments.

These liberal activist programs produced opponents. Business opposed protection for labor unions, environmental restrictions, and consumer guidance that curtailed the marketplace. Wealthy and middle-class families disliked paying taxes for programs that benefited poor people. Elected officials worried about expanding government spending that led to more bureaucracies. Public opinion shifted. More people trusted state and local governments than trusted Washington and wanted them to take the lead in solving national problems.

In the 1980s, President Reagan pioneered a "New Federalism" that gave large block grants to states and localities to use with few controls from Washington. President Clinton continued this conservative trend—curiously to a greater extent than President Bush. Clinton's welfare reform legislation reflected the principle of reducing federal programs and shifting more responsibility to the local level. It ended the federal government guarantee of support for needy children and transferred control over welfare to the states by giving them block grants to use at their discretion.

This devolution of power to the states and local governments had a number of motivations behind it. One was money. For the first time in the modern era, state and local governments by the mid-1990s had more money to spend than Washington. With this money came an expansion in manpower in their bureaucracies to some 16 million, while the federal payroll continued to fall to under 2 million employees. With public confidence behind devolution, even Democrats saw political advantage in allowing the states to do more, as the federal government did less. The Supreme Court joined in with decisions favorable to shifting power away from the central government. And ambitious state governors grabbed headlines by suing tobacco companies and helping senior citizens pay for prescription drugs. Even the rise of deficits in the national government and the cutbacks in state and local programs because of budget shortfalls in the first years of the new century did not immediately reverse this trend. Federalism was alive and well.

Almost 100 years before, Woodrow Wilson, the only political scientist to become president, wrote that the relations of the states and federal government cannot be settled "by one generation, because it is a question of growth, and every new successive stage of our political and economic development, gives it a new aspect, makes it a new question." To see federalism as a flexible system for representing the varied interests of a large, diverse country is not far from what we have today. Actually it's not far from what the framers of the Constitution had in mind. (See "Case Study: Federalism at 55 MPH," p. 38.)

Limited Government

The principle of *limited government* means that the powers of government are limited by the rights and liberties of the governed. This principle is basic to the very idea of constitutional government: The people give the government listed powers and duties through a constitution, while reserving the rest to themselves. This *political compact* means that government actions must rest on the *rule of law,* approved, however indirectly, by the consent of the governed. Furthermore, the Constitution sets up procedures, such as separation of powers and federalism, to ensure that the government remains limited to its proper duties and powers. For example, the president may not exercise powers given by the Constitution exclusively to Congress.

Limited government guarantees citizens their *rights against* the government as well as *access to* the government. Civil liberties and rights guarantee the openness and competitiveness of the political process, which means not only the right to vote but also the freedom to dissent, demonstrate, and organize to produce alternatives, in order to make the right to vote meaningful. Civil liberties are supposed to protect the citizen from arbitrary governmental power. Under civil liberties would fall a citizen's right to a fair and speedy trial, to have legal defense, and to be judged by an impartial jury of his or her peers. Further, government cannot take life, liberty, or property without due process of law, nor interfere with a citizen's right to practice religion, nor invade her or his privacy. In short, the people who make the laws are subject to them. (See Chapter 6 on civil liberties and rights.)

Judicial Review

An important means of keeping government limited and of maintaining civil rights and liberties is the power of judicial review vested in the Supreme Court. *Judicial review,* the last constitutional principle, is the judicial branch's authority to decide on the constitutionality of the acts of the various parts of the government (local, state, and federal). The political importance of judicial review could be seen in the 2000 presidential election where the Supreme Court ruled that Florida's method of recounting votes was unconstitutional and thus decided the election.

Although judicial review has become an accepted constitutional practice, it is not actually mentioned in the document. There was some debate in the first years of the Constitution over whether the Court had the power merely to give nonbinding opinions or whether it had supremacy over acts of the government. Most people at that time agreed that the Court did have the power to nullify unconstitutional acts of the state governments, but opinion was divided over whether this power extended to the acts of the federal government. In 1803, the case of *Marbury* v. *Madison* clarified this power that the Court probably already had. The Supreme Court first struck down an act of Congress which gave a duty not mentioned in the Constitution to the Court. This power has since become a firmly entrenched principle of the Constitution, though limited by the Court's own practices and by the practices of the other branches of government.

Judicial review has put the Court in the position of watchdog over the limits of the central government's actions and made it the guardian of federalism. The latter function, reviewing the acts of state and local governments, has historically been the Court's most important use of judicial review. Though relatively few federal laws have been struck down by the Court, hundreds of state and local laws have been held to violate the Constitution. As Justice Oliver Wendell Holmes said over 80 years ago, "The United States would not come to an end if we lost our power to declare an act of Congress void. I do think the Union would be imperiled if we could not make that declaration as to the laws of the several states." (See Chapter 5 on the judicial branch.)

HOW IS THE CONSTITUTION CHANGED?

To say that the Constitution has lasted over 200 years is not to say it is the same document that was adopted in 1789. The Constitution has changed vastly; in practical ways, it bears little resemblance to the original. Most of the framers would scarcely recognize the political process that operates today under their constitution. Changes in the Constitution have been made by four major methods: formal amendment, judicial interpretation, legislation, and custom.

Amendments

Although the amendment process is the first way we usually think of for changing the Constitution, it is actually the least common method. Only 27 amendments (including the first ten amendments, which can practically be considered part of the original document) have been adopted. (The Equal Rights Amendment and the Washington, D.C., Voting Rights Amendment were proposed by Congress but not ratified by the needed three-fourths of the state legislatures.) As those recently proposing to change the electoral college have discovered, adopting amendments is meant to be difficult. Though the Constitution's framers recognized the need for change in their document, no matter how farsighted, they wanted to protect it from temporary popular pressure. Hence, they required unusually large majorities for adopting amendments.

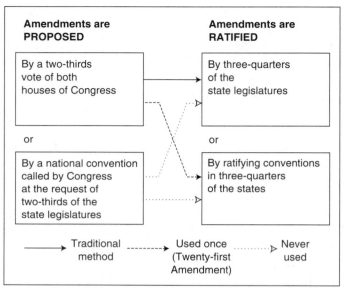

FIGURE 2.1
Amending the Constitution.

Article V of the Constitution provides a number of methods for adopting amendments. (See Figure 2.1.) Amendments may be *proposed* by a two-thirds vote of each house of Congress or (if requested by two-thirds of the state legislatures) by a national convention called by Congress. They must be *ratified* by conventions in three-fourths of the states, or by three-fourths of the state legislatures (the choice is up to Congress).

The national convention has never been used; all amendments have been proposed by Congress. The most recent attempt occurred in the late 1980s, when 32 states of the needed 34 passed resolutions calling for a constitutional convention to draft a new amendment requiring a balanced budget. Only the Twenty-first Amendment, repealing Prohibition, was ratified by state conventions. The idea behind this one use of state conventions was that the state legislatures were still full of the same representatives who had passed Prohibition in the first place and conventions seemed likely to be the fastest way to change it. A major reason that the national convention method has never been used to propose amendments is Congress's jealousy toward another body trespassing on its powers. Another is worry over how many other amendments might be proposed by such a convention. After all, the Constitution was written by an earlier runaway convention set up only to amend the Articles of Confederation. (See "The Long and Winding Road of the Twenty-seventh Amendment.")

The Long and Winding Road of the Twenty-seventh Amendment

"No law varying the compensation for the services of the Senators and Representatives, shall take effect, until an election of Representatives shall have intervened."

————The Twenty-seventh Amendment

The Twenty-seventh and last amendment to the Constitution took 200 years to ratify. Referred to as the Madison Pay Raise Amendment, it began its journey as one of the original 12 amendments to the Constitution, the first ten of which became the Bill of Rights. Initially, only six states ratified the Madison Amendment. No further action was taken from 1789 to the late 1970s, with the exception of Ohio's ratification in 1873. Since 1978, 33 states ratified the amendment with the vote by Michigan on May 7, 1992, pushing it over the three-fourths of the states needed to ratify.

Most recent amendments to the Constitution have had deadlines of seven years for passage, but the Madison Amendment was not given any time limits. Some in Congress cited a Supreme Court decision that ratification must reflect "a contemporaneous consensus," arguing that the states that approved the amendment prior to 1978 would have to vote again. However, Congress did not have the political stomach to formally confront the issue due to members' defensiveness about their own recent pay raises. Thus the Amendment became part of the Constitution on May 18, 1992.

Judicial Interpretation

If the amendment process is the least-used method of changing the Constitution, interpretations by the Supreme Court are probably the most common. Practically every part of the Constitution has been before the Supreme Court at some time or another. The justices have shaped and reshaped the document. Modern Court decisions have allowed Congress great scope in regulating the economy, prohibited legal segregation of races, allowed local communities to determine the limits of obscenity, and established "one man, one vote" as a constitutional principle governing election to the House of Representatives. The Supreme Court has also given practical meaning to general constitutional phrases such as "necessary and proper" (Article I, Section 8), "due process of law" (Amendments 5 and 14), and "unreasonable searches and seizures" (Amendment 4). No wonder the Supreme Court is sometimes called "a permanent constitutional convention."

Legislation

Although legislation is passed under the Constitution and does not change the basic document, Congress has been responsible for filling in most of the framework of government outlined by the Constitution. Congress has established all the federal courts below the Supreme Court. It has determined the size of both the House of Representatives and the Supreme Court. The cabinet and most of the boards and commissions in the executive branch have been created by congressional legislation. And most of the regulations and services we now take for granted, such as social security, have come from measures passed by Congress.

Custom

Custom is the most imprecise way in which the Constitution has changed, yet one of the most widespread. Many practices that have been accepted as constitutional are not actually mentioned in the document. The growth of political parties and their role in Congress, the presidential nominating conventions, the breakdown of an independent electoral college, and the committee system in Congress are just a few customary practices not foreseen by the Constitution.

Custom also has changed some practices that, at least on the surface, seem to have been clearly intended by the framers. The Eighth Amendment, forbidding "excessive bail," has not prevented courts from setting bail for serious offenses that is too high for the accused to raise. Although Congress has the right to declare war (Article II, Section 8), presidents have entered conflicts that looked very much like wars (Korea, Vietnam, Afghanistan) without such a declaration. Customs also have been broken and reestablished by law. The custom that a president serves only two terms was started by Washington and cemented by Jefferson. Broken with much debate by Franklin D. Roosevelt in 1940, the custom was made law in the Twenty-second Amendment, adopted in 1951, to keep FDR's example from being followed in the future.

WHY HAS THE CONSTITUTION SURVIVED?

How the Constitution has been changed does not entirely explain why it has survived. Indeed, many of the framers saw the Constitution as an experiment not likely to last more than a generation. Various explanations have been offered for why the Constitution has endured to become the oldest written constitution of any country.

The major reason it has lasted probably lies not in the Constitution itself, but in the stability of American society. Upheavals like the

A British View on the Constitution's Survival

The late nineteenth-century British scholar and diplomat, James Bryce, believed the Constitution deserved "the veneration" bestowed on it. He thought much of its value came from the "political genius" of the Anglo-American race.

> The American Constitution is no exception to the rule that everything which has the power to win the obedience and respect of men must have its roots deep in the past and that the more slowly every institution has grown, so much the more enduring it is likely to prove. There is little in the Constitution that is absolutely new. There is much that is as old as Magna Carta.

Source: James Bryce, *The American Commonwealth.* New York: Macmillan, 1910, vol.1, p. 28.

Civil War, the Indian campaigns and massacres, and foreign wars all have been handled within the same constitutional structure. The Constitution has been made more democratic to include "out" groups, such as immigrants, former slaves, women, and the poor, that were originally excluded from political participation. The Constitution's emphasis on procedures has served it well through the wars and depressions as well as the peace and prosperity of various ages.

Other explanations for the Constitution's durability focus on the document. One maintains that it is a work of genius. William Gladstone, the nineteenth-century British prime minister, described it as "the most wonderful work ever struck off at a given time by the brain and purpose of man." Incorporating centuries of English political traditions as well as the framers' own experience, the Constitution set out the principles and framework of government in concise, well-written phrases. (See "A British View on the Constitution's Survival.")

The shortness of the document (only some 7,000 words with all its amendments) is another major reason for its durability. Although it sets out the basic principles and structures of a government, the Constitution leaves much only generally stated or not mentioned at all. In a word, the Constitution is *vague.* Many of the most enduring constitutional phrases ("freedom of speech," "due process of law," "all laws which shall be necessary and proper," "privileges or immunities of citizens") have been applied differently at different times in our history. Other principles, such as majority rule and individual liberties, sometimes seem contradictory. It is left to the political players of each age to resolve the conflicts between groups claiming constitutional support. This flexibility has been one of the Constitution's major strengths in adapting to new political pressures and allowing people to reach compromises under competing principles.

CASE STUDY

FEDERALISM AT 55 MPH

When the Senate voted to repeal the 55-mile-an-hour (MPH) speed limit it was hailed as a victory for states' rights and federalism. But a closer look shows the issue to be a bit fuzzier; it illustrates both the inconsistencies and the politics that surround the practice of modern federalism.

Highways, Safety, and the Federal Government

In June 1995, the Senate began debate on spending $13 billion to upgrade highways across the country and establish a National Highway System. Attention quickly centered on proposals dealing with various federal laws that had been enacted to conserve fuel and to protect the public safety, especially the 55 MPH speed limit. The new Republican majority focused on federal government involvement with issues that they felt should be left to the states.

Twenty-one years earlier the public concerns had been much different. In 1974 following the Arab oil embargo and in the middle of the "energy crisis," Congress passed a national speed limit of 55 MPH. (While, under federalism, Congress couldn't directly legislate a speed limit, it accomplished the same thing by threatening to withhold highway money from states that did not comply with the federally set speed limits.) Conservation of gasoline was the major motivation, although safety also was mentioned. It quickly became one of the nation's most ignored laws; anyone traveling 55 MPH on an interstate risked getting run over by one of the numerous drivers rocketing past. It was especially unpopular in western states where people drove long distances with few cars on the road.

In 1987 Congress allowed states to raise the federal limit to 65 MPH in rural areas. The federal speed limits were kept largely because they were seen as a safety measure that saved an estimated 4,750 lives a year and prevented countless injuries. In addition many environmental laws to reduce air pollution, particularly ozone, required lower automobile speeds.

Driving for Federalism

The 1995 Senate debate focused on Washington's role in enforcing highway safety. One freshman senator denounced speed limits, as well as seat belt and helmet laws, charging they represented a "paternalistic . . . Washington knows best" attitude that had been rejected by voters who elected a Republican majority the previous November. Another Republican called the laws "fiscal blackmail" because the legislation allowed the federal government to withhold highway money from states that did not obey the speed limits.

Defenders of federal involvement argued that it was needed to force reluctant states to impose safety rules that saved lives and billions of dollars in medical costs. "People will die," said freshman Senator Mike DeWine (R-Oh.), whose 22-year-old daughter had been killed in an auto accident the year before.

But by 65 to 35 the Senate voted to repeal the speed limits. Oklahoma Senator Don Nickles's question on safety seemed convincing: "Are we taking a position that we need to have the national government mandate speed limits because states do not care about safety, states do not care about fatalities?" The regional pressure from western states, and from Republicans claiming a mandate to return power to the states on issues from the environment to welfare reform, helped to carry the day.

Muddying the Federal Role

This strong endorsement of federalism was not the whole story of the Senate's actions on the Highway bill. Indeed, its other actions muddied up the seemingly clear sense of direction on speed limits and illustrated that positions on federalism must exist in a political setting.

On the same day that the speed limit for cars was repealed, the Senate voted to *keep* the federal government limits for big trucks and buses, which were viewed as more dangerous. The next day, the Senate voted to repeal federal penalties forcing states to require motorcyclists to wear helmets. Senator Ben Nighthorse Campbell (R-Co.)—who regularly roared around Washington on a Harley-Davidson—argued that the federal government should not tell people "how to dress for recreational pursuit."

But later in the session the Senate rejected an effort to repeal more popular federal requirements that people use seat belts. And when Senator Robert Byrd of West Virginia proposed requiring tough new state laws against drinking and driving by minors, it passed 64 to 36. The proposal would withhold 10 percent of a state's federal highway funds if it did not adopt "zero tolerance" policies banning any drinking by drivers under age 21. Public support for seat belt use and concern over deaths from drunk driving were cited by newspapers as overwhelming the drive to roll back the federal government's role in highway safety. Federalism took a backseat to safety.

By November the "Bill Ending Speed Limits" (as the newspapers called it) overwhelmingly passed both houses of Congress in substantially the same form that the Senate had approved in June. President Clinton, while objecting to changes in the speed limit and helmet laws, signed it into law.

Conclusion

After the Senate action, the conservative columnist George Will wrote, "The speed limit issue, having been an energy issue and then a safety issue, now is a federalism—10th Amendment—states rights issue, with anti-paternalism in the bargain." He was partly right. Federalism, the proper division of power between the states and central government, was an important concern in the debate over repealing federal highway speed limits. But the other issues of safety and protecting the environment had not disappeared. They were still in the political arena because they were still public concerns. And they influenced the federal role on the 55 MPH speed limit.

Federalism in real life is not just an abstract constitutional principle. In whatever issue packaging it appears, federalism must compete with other policy choices. This will make the modern practice of federalism at times appear hesitant and uncertain. But as the Senate actions on highway safety illustrate, the application of federalism can only be as consistent as the politics swirling around it.

Sources: The *Washington Post,* June 21, 22, 25, 1995; The *Dallas Morning News,* June 26, 1995; and *Congressional Quarterly,* June 24, 1995.

WRAP-UP

We have covered quite a bit in this chapter. In looking at the writing of the Constitution, we saw how the colonists drew from English political thought, the models of colonial government, and their own experiences with the Articles of Confederation in shaping the Constitution. The framers also were influenced by who they were. As a wealthy elite, they sought to establish a government that would further the interests of the nation and their own economic concerns. They divided into Federalists and Anti-Federalists over how strong the government should be and how personal rights would be best protected. Ratification and the addition of the Bill of Rights forged an uneasy agreement between the two groups.

The Constitution that has developed centers on four major principles: separation of powers, and checks and balances; federalism; limited government; and judicial review. Although these principles remain fundamental, the Constitution has been changed vastly by four main methods: formal amendment, judicial interpretation, legislation, and custom. The changes it has undergone have enabled the Constitution to endure. Perhaps more important to its survival, however, have been the stability of American society and the ambiguity of the document itself. The flexibility of the document can be seen in the modern example of the principle of federalism being applied in the case of the 55 mph speed limit.

But does the flexibility and ambiguity of the document mean that the Constitution, as a body of rules governing the American political game, is meaningless? That essentially it serves the interests of those in power, and its interpretations change only as those interests change? Perhaps. Certainly any document that has legitimized a political system that imported and enslaved most of its black residents, placed its citizens of Japanese descent in detention camps, allowed sweatshops and child labor, and ignored great wealth alongside extreme poverty, has much to answer for. Is the Constitution a grab bag of obsolete principles used to rationalize domination by the few?

As I said in Chapter 1, politics is not primarily about words—it is about power and ideals. Can we blame a body of principles and procedures for the power or lack of power or for the ideals or lack of ideals of the players in the game? All great historical documents, from the Bible to the Constitution, have been differently applied by different leaders at different times.

More than the rules of the game, then, the Constitution stands as a symbol of the ideals of a people. But it is a symbol with power. That a president is accused of violating the law does mean that he has to answer to impeachment procedures in Congress. That people have a constitutional right to elect representatives can immediately change what laws are passed and the direction the government takes. That the press has the right to report and publish government mistakes— from a Watergate break-in of opposition party headquarters to pictures of Iraqi prisoners being tortured—does affect whether voters keep officials in office. Even the hypocrisy of politicians in bowing to principles they may wish to ignore shows the strength of the symbol.

Yet the substance of the principles in the Constitution must ultimately rest on the political relationships of the players. The *right* to vote is meaningless without the *will* to vote. Freedom of speech means nothing if no one has any informed criticism to make. Judicial safeguards, such as the right to a lawyer, could be lost (and indeed was ignored in the government's recent treatment of some accused terrorists) without anyone necessarily changing a word of the Constitution. Power without principle may be blind, but principle without power is paralyzed.

The rules of this game, then, are not fixed or unchanging. Though written in the traditions of the past, they exist in the politics of the present. They are not only historical guidelines but future goals as well. Therefore they remain unfinished as must any constitution setting out to "secure the Blessings of Liberty to ourselves and our Posterity."

Thought Questions

1. How did the Constitution as written by the framers reflect the politics of the time and their need to resolve sectional differences? Give examples of the impact of these politics in each branch of government.
2. How important was the principle of federalism to the senators voting on the speed limit? Were the senators voting against the principle "unprincipled"?
3. How efficient are the political structures set up by the Constitution in dealing with contemporary problems? Do the goals of efficiency and democracy in the Constitution work against each other?
4. "Americans can afford optimism partly because their institutions, including the Constitution, were conceived by men who thought tragically." Comment.

Suggested Readings

Beard, Charles A. *An Economic Interpretation of the Constitution of the United States.* New York: Macmillan, 1935. Pb.
    The famous criticism of the framers' economic motivations in writing the Constitution.

Berkin, Carol. *A Brilliant Solution: Inventing the American Constitution.* New York: Harcourt, Inc. 2002.
    An historian gives a lively account of the human stories behind the writing of the Constitution.

Cross, Christopher. *Political Education.* New York: Teachers College Press, 2004, Pb.
    A balanced analysis of the federal role in education and how federalism has often stood in the way of what was best for our schools.

Ellis, Joseph J. *Founding Brothers: The Revolutionary Generation.* New York: Vintage Books, 2000. Pb.
    Well written Pulitzer Prize-winning stories of the flawed but fascinating fraternity of men who unexpectedly made the new American republic work.

Hamilton, Alexander, James Madison, and John Jay. *The Federalist Papers.* New York: New American Library, 1961.
    The classic work on what the framers thought about their Constitution.

Sunstein, Cass R. *Designing Democracy: What Constitutions Do.* New York: Oxford. 2001. Pb.
    A challenging comparative study by a leading scholar of how constitutions help democracies work.

CHAPTER 3

The Executive Branch: The Presidency and Bureaucracy

Whatever the flaws of the men who have held the office, the president remains the superstar of the American political game. Although the head of just one of the three branches of the U.S. government, the president is the only official—along with the vice president—elected by the entire country. He stands as the representative of the federal government and, in times of crisis, a symbol for the nation to rally around. Yet the presidency remains an intensely political office filled by the leader of a political party and the target of partisan attacks.

Historically Americans have idolized their president. Often, he represents the country's belief in its religious mission as "the last best hope of mankind," and he is expected to act on his own for the good of the nation. But he also is selected by the voters, and is expected to personally remain one of the people. These roles create conflicts, especially when they clash with the reality of limited executive power. The result: presidents who disappoint.

Not surprisingly Americans have swung back and forth in how powerful they want their presidents. In times of crisis like now, people demand strong leaders. Yet this often leads to popular concerns about the consequences of that strength. In more peaceful periods the call is heard for less activity from the executive branch. Yet this inactivity is soon dismissed as weakness from the chief executive. Today President Bush has vigorously used the military and diplomatic tools available to the chief executive. With this considerable power over national security has come responsibility for the results, both good and bad.

Modern presidents have faced the tension between too much and too little power with varying success. They have often tried to contrast themselves with their predecessors. Underlying Richard Nixon's resignation in 1974 was the public's fear of the president's growing—and illegal—use of his authority, underlined by the Watergate scandal. Distancing himself from Nixon, a more open Jimmy Carter fell victim to the popular view that the president was too weak to solve the country's major problems including lines at gas stations and inflation. Ronald Reagan brought a smiling conservatism to the office. His efforts to extend the powers of the office in order to limit the growth of the federal government seemed to achieve more, at least in raising the popularity of his Republican party. Inheriting the optimism of the Reagan years, George Bush Sr.'s low-key concentration on governing proved popular at first, and less so later on.

President Bill Clinton, with his populist charm, shaped an administration that emphasized youth and change. While often bogged down in scandals, investigations, and worse, Clinton was propelled by a buoyant economy, the excesses of his opponents, and his own political skills. George W. Bush's aw-shucks leadership style and businesslike administration didn't quite remove the doubts about his disputed election and his intellect. Then September 11 silenced dissenters in a flurry of patriotism. His political smarts helped put his party in control of the federal government and he in command of his party. Yet in facing the voters in 2004 he led a country bitterly divided over his direction of the war in Iraq and the economy at home. In winning reelection in 2004, he cemented his conservative leadership over a united government and a divided country. (See "W: The Misunderestimated President.")

This chapter is about the president and the executive branch he heads. We will trace the history of the growth of the presidency from the limited powers granted to the office in the Constitution. Next we

W: The Misunderestimated President

In February 2001 Secret Service agents wounded a man with a gun near the White House. Reporters asked where the president was at the time. The answer: George W. Bush was in the gym working out— in the middle of the morning, in the middle of the work week.

While most politicians brag about how smart they are and how hard they work, President Bush promotes the opposite image. He talks about his afternoon naps and projects a laid-back style that have led some to label his a "no-sweat" presidency. This may be calculated to lull opponents who have derided Bush's work habits and intellectual talents. But after his convincing reelection where opponents couldn't blame Florida miscounts, a 5–4 Supreme Court decision, the Electoral College or Ralph Nader, some began to agree with the President's complaint that he had been "misunderestimated."

Bush clearly has talents, including the ability to not anguish over his decisions, to appear in public as a regular guy and to delegate authority to his staff and cabinet. On this last point Bush explained picking a high-powered Cabinet this way, "It says I'm not afraid to surround myself with strong and competent people."

Nor is it clear that intellectuals make the best presidents. While brilliant men like Jefferson and Wilson have made good presidents, so have decidedly last-in-their-class types like Harry Truman and Ronald Reagan. Americans seem to prefer sunny, optimistic presidents, rather than tormented, complex intellectuals. These apparently simplistic leaders are not necessarily naïve. At first there seemed to be nothing smart about President Bush going into several dozen extremely close races in the 2002 election to campaign for potential losers. Many said he would be blamed for bad outcomes. So George W. Bush made a dumb move. But the GOP won most of those seats. Dumb like a fox.

discuss the different approaches to being president and the various roles of the office he fills. Then there are the departments of the federal bureaucracy under the president, and the problems of controlling the bureaucracy. Finally, a case study looks at the president under the worst of circumstances, the days following September 11, 2001.

THE PRESIDENT AND THE CONSTITUTION

The Constitution in Article II grants a president far less power and far fewer duties than it gives Congress in Article I. Yet the opening sentence of the article ("The executive Power shall be vested in a President of the United States of America") and other broad phrases ("he shall take Care that the Laws be faithfully executed") have been used by presidents to justify enlarging their powers. As we will see, presidential practice has vastly expanded the Constitution's ideas of executive powers.

In setting requirements for the office, the Constitution states that the president must be at least 35 years old, a resident of the United States for 14 years, and a native-born citizen. The president can be removed by impeachment or, because of the Twenty-fifth Amendment, if he is disabled. His term of office is fixed at four years. Under the Twenty-second Amendment, passed in 1951, presidents are limited to two terms.

During the last months of his final term the president often is called a *lame duck:* Because he cannot be reelected, his influence—and his accountability—are lessened. For political reasons, the term often is expanded to label presidents in their last term as being powerless. More appropriately, after the election in November 2000 and his successor's inauguration in January 2001, President Clinton was a lame duck.

The Electoral College

As we were reminded in 2000, presidents are not chosen by direct popular elections. All the votes across the United States are not added up on election day with the candidate receiving the most declared the winner. Rather, presidents are chosen through the *electoral college.* Each state is granted as many *electors,* members of the electoral college, as it has senators and representatives combined (the District of Columbia gets three votes). On election day the votes *within each state* are added up, and the candidate with the most votes receives *all* that state's votes in the electoral college, except for Maine and Nebraska, which don't use this "winner-take-all" system. When the counting has been done in each state, the number of electoral college votes for each candidate is added up. If any candidate has a majority (270 votes, which is 50 percent plus 1), he or she becomes president. If no candidate wins a majority (probably because several candidates have split the votes), the Constitution provides that the election will be decided by a majority vote in the House of Representatives with each state delegation casting one vote.

Sometimes the presidential electoral system doesn't seem to work. Back in 1800 and 1824 the House of Representatives had to decide on a president when no candidate received a majority of the vote. In 1876 Democrat Samuel Tilden lost to Rutherford Hayes when a Republican-dominated Electoral Commission awarded the Republican the election even though Tilden had won the popular vote. Then in 2000 Al Gore won the popular vote by over 500,000 votes yet lost the electoral college, and the presidency, to George W. Bush by 271 to 267. It was an election that came down to a difference of a few hundred votes in Florida and a contested recount halted by the U.S. Supreme Court.

In a uniquely close race like 2000 the messiness of an election is exposed to public view. This mess includes the states determining their own election laws as well as designing and supervising the ballots. It also includes the electoral college. A product of compromises at the Constitutional Convention, the electoral college reinforces federalism by strengthening the smaller states. It was designed to keep partisans— whether state officials, legislators, or supreme court justices—from deciding who will be president. As Alexander Hamilton wrote in *The Federalist Papers* No. 68, "They have not made the appointment of the President to depend on any preexisting bodies of men who might be tampered with beforehand to prostitute their votes."

The electoral college was created by the authors of the Constitution as another way of filtering the passions and prejudices of the mass of voters. The development of political parties (see Chapter 7) has undercut the purpose of the college, for electors are now pledged to one party's candidate at the time of the elections. After the mess of the 2000 election there were calls for replacing the "outmoded" electoral college with a direct popular vote—which would require a constitutional amendment. Since many states and political interests benefited from the present system these voices for change quickly faded.

Vice President

The major constitutional duties of the vice president are to preside over the Senate and to succeed the president if the office should become vacant. (The speaker of the House of Representatives and the president *pro tem* of the Senate are next in line.) Traditionally the vice presidency has been seen as a limited, frustrating office. John Nance Garner, Franklin Roosevelt's vice president, commented that his position was "not worth a pitcher of warm spit." But this view is out of date. Just the fact that 13 vice presidents have become president, and that half of our last eight presidents were vice presidents at some time, has increased the political importance of the office.

Today scholars speak of a "new vice presidency." Vice presidents such as Al Gore and Dick Cheney have played key roles in their administrations. They have represented the chief executive in visits overseas, lobbied for him in Congress, campaigned in midterm elections, and served as a top presidential adviser. Al Gore was treated as a partner of President Clinton and became the president's chosen successor and "deputy president."

George W. Bush went a step further. He elevated his vice president to become the most powerful in the nation's history. Dick Cheney came to the office with experience as a Washington insider—former White House chief of staff, secretary of defense during the 1991 Persian Gulf War, and a congressman from Wyoming. At the age of 60 with a history of heart problems, Cheney was the first vice president in memory not to have his own presidential ambitions. He headed the transition out of which emerged several old friends as cabinet heads and political appointees. The Iraq war saw Cheney's star rise even further. His strong advocacy for the war, his knowledge of national security, and his closeness to key bureaucratic players, made him the administration's day-to-day policy coordinator. Serving a president who avoided nuts-and-bolts administration, Cheney was sometimes called the "prime minister" in the White House, a somewhat inflated promotion.

HISTORY OF THE PRESIDENCY

Forty-three men have been president of the United States, from George Washington, who took office in 1789, to George W. Bush. (See Table 3.1 and Table 3.2 on pp. 49–50.) Between the two Georges, the influence and powers of the office of the presidency have expanded considerably, if not always in a pattern of constant growth.

Most members of the Constitutional Convention in 1787 did not see a *political* role for the president. They pictured the president as a gentleman-aristocrat—probably because they had George Washington in mind—who would stand above politics as a symbol of national unity. He would be selected by an electoral college to ensure that he wasn't dependent on popular support. Congress, not the president,

TABLE 3.1   PRESIDENTS OF THE UNITED STATES

Year	President	Party	Year	President	Party
1789	George Washington		1900	William McKinley	Republican
1792	George Washington		1901	Theodore Roosevelt[a]	Republican
1796	John Adams	Federalist	1904	Theodore Roosevelt	Republican
1800	Thomas Jefferson	Democratic-Republican	1908	William H. Taft	Republican
1804	Thomas Jefferson	Democratic-Republican	1912	Woodrow Wilson	Democratic
1808	James Madison	Democratic-Republican	1916	Woodrow Wilson	Democratic
1812	James Madison	Democratic-Republican	1920	Warren G. Harding	Republican
1816	James Monroe	Democratic-Republican	1923	Calvin Coolidge[a]	Republican
1820	James Monroe	Democratic-Republican	1924	Calvin Coolidge	Republican
1824	John Quincy Adams	Democratic-Republican	1928	Herbert C. Hoover	Republican
1828	Andrew Jackson	Democratic	1932	Franklin D. Roosevelt	Democratic
1832	Andrew Jackson	Democratic	1936	Franklin D. Roosevelt	Democratic
1836	Martin Van Buren	Democratic	1940	Franklin D. Roosevelt	Democratic
1840	William H. Harrison	Whig	1944	Franklin D. Roosevelt	Democratic
1841	John Tyler[a]	Whig	1945	Harry S Truman[a]	Democratic
1844	James K. Polk	Democratic	1948	Harry S Truman	Democratic
1848	Zachary Taylor	Whig	1952	Dwight D. Eisenhower	Republican
1850	Millard Fillmore[a]	Whig	1956	Dwight D. Eisenhower	Republican
1852	Franklin Pierce	Democratic	1960	John F. Kennedy	Democratic
1856	James Buchanan	Democratic	1963	Lyndon B. Johnson[a]	Democratic
1860	Abraham Lincoln	Republican	1964	Lyndon B. Johnson	Democratic
1864	Abraham Lincoln	Republican	1968	Richard M. Nixon	Republican
1865	Andrew Johnson[a]	Democratic (Union)	1972	Richard M. Nixon	Republican
1868	Ulysses S. Grant	Republican	1974	Gerald R. Ford[a]	Republican
1872	Ulysses S. Grant	Republican	1976	James E. Carter	Democratic
1876	Rutherford B. Hayes	Republican	1980	Ronald W. Reagan	Republican
1880	James A. Garfield	Republican	1984	Ronald W. Reagan	Republican
1881	Chester A. Arthur[a]	Republican	1988	George H. Bush	Republican
1884	Grover Cleveland	Democratic	1992	William J. Clinton	Democratic
1888	Benjamin Harrison	Republican	1996	William J. Clinton	Democratic
1892	Grover Cleveland	Democratic	2000	George W. Bush	Republican
1896	William McKinley	Republican	2004	George W. Bush	Republican

[a]Nonelected vice presidents nominated by the president and confirmed by Congress.

TABLE 3.2   VICE PRESIDENTS OF THE UNITED STATES

Year	Vice President	Party	Year	Vice President	Party
1789	John Adams		1900	Theodore Roosevelt	Republican
1792	John Adams	Federalist	1904	Charles W. Fairbanks	Republican
1796	Thomas Jefferson	Democratic-Republican	1908	James S. Sherman	Republican
1800	Aaron Burr	Democratic-Republican	1912	Thomas R. Marshall	Democratic
1804	George Clinton	Democratic-Republican	1916	Thomas R. Marshall	Democratic
1808	George Clinton	Democratic-Republican	1920	Calvin Coolidge	Republican
1812	Elbridge Gerry	Democratic-Republican	1924	Charles G. Dawes	Republican
1816	Daniel D. Tompkins	Democratic-Republican	1928	Charles Curtis	Republican
1820	Daniel D. Tompkins	Democratic-Republican	1932	John N. Garner	Democratic
1824	John C. Calhoun	Democratic-Republican	1936	John N. Garner	Democratic
1828	John C. Calhoun	Democratic	1940	Henry A. Wallace	Democratic
1832	Martin Van Buren	Democratic	1944	Harry S Truman	Democratic
1836	Richard M. Johnson	Democratic	1948	Alben W. Barkley	Democratic
1840	John Tyler	Whig	1952	Richard M. Nixon	Republican
1844	George M. Dallas	Democratic	1956	Richard M. Nixon	Republican
1848	Millard Fillmore	Whig	1960	Lyndon B. Johnson	Democratic
1852	William R. King	Democratic	1964	Hubert H. Humphrey	Democratic
1856	John C. Breckinridge	Democratic	1968	Spiro T. Agnew	Republican
1860	Hannibal Hamlin	Republican	1972	Spiro T. Agnew	Republican
1864	Andrew Johnson	Democratic (Union)	1973	Gerald R. Ford[a]	Republican
1868	Schuyler Colfax	Republican	1974	Nelson A. Rockefeller[a]	Republican
1872	Henry Wilson	Republican	1976	Walter F. Mondale	Democratic
1876	William A. Wheeler	Republican	1980	George H. Bush	Republican
1880	Chester A. Arthur	Republican	1984	George H. Bush	Republican
1884	Thomas A. Hendricks	Democratic	1988	Dan Quayle	Republican
1888	Levi P. Morton	Republican	1992	Albert Gore, Jr.	Democratic
1892	Adlai E. Stevenson	Democratic	1996	Albert Gore, Jr.	Democratic
1896	Garrett A. Hobart	Republican	2000	Richard Cheney	Republican
			2004	Richard Cheney	Republican

[a]Nonelected vice presidents nominated by the president and confirmed by Congress.

was to be the superior branch. Yet strong presidents confronting national problems soon increased these powers, although at times weak presidents and popular sentiment have reduced executive power. In the twentieth century, presidential power has irregularly expanded as a result of wars and domestic crises, such as economic depression.

George Washington sent troops to put down a rebellion among farmers in western Pennsylvania who were angered by a tax placed on whiskey. Washington's action in the Whiskey Rebellion was later claimed as the precedent for a president's *residual power* (also called *inherent power*)—powers not spelled out in the Constitution but that are necessary for the president to be able to carry out other responsibilities. The third president, Thomas Jefferson, as leader of the liberals, had fought against establishing a strong executive in the Constitution. Yet as president, he expanded the powers of the office. By negotiating and signing the Louisiana Purchase, gaining the approval of Congress only after the fact (perhaps inevitable in an age of slow communication), Jefferson weakened the principle of checks and balances. Congress not only played a minor role in doubling the size of the country but couldn't easily reverse the president's action once it had been taken.

Abraham Lincoln, the sixteenth president, disregarded a number of constitutional provisions when he led the North into the Civil War. Lincoln raised armies, spent money that Congress had not appropriated, freed slaves in the South, suspended certain civil rights, and generally did what he felt was necessary to help preserve the Union. He even sent money and troops to promote a rebellion in Virginia that created West Virginia, all without participation by Congress. Congress later approved these actions, but the initiative was clearly with the president.

This pattern of *crisis leadership* continued into the twentieth century. Most visible were aggressive presidents like Theodore Roosevelt, who pushed his pro-environment and antimonopoly policies, and Woodrow Wilson, who led the country into World War I. They were followed, however, by a series of weak presidents in the 1920s (Harding, Coolidge, Hoover), reflecting a national mood in the country that favored less government activity presided over by passive chief executives.

Franklin D. Roosevelt's coming into office in 1933 was shadowed by the Great Depression of the 1930s. FDR's tenure led to the president taking virtually full responsibility for the continual shaping of both domestic and foreign policy. His programs in response to the Depression (called the *New Deal*), and his leadership of the United States into the international role it would play during and after World War II, firmly established the strong leadership patterns we find today in the presidency. Roosevelt thus is called the first modern president.

FDR influenced the shape of the presidency more than anyone else in the last century.

TYPES OF PRESIDENTS

This growth of the presidency should not be seen as a straight line expansion of presidential powers between Washington and Bush II. There have been cycles in which the power of the office has waxed and waned reflecting factors of personality and politics. To simplify matters we will talk about three general approaches that various presidents have adopted toward the office and see which chief executives fit into each category.

Buchanan Presidents

The first category has been called *Buchanan presidents,* after James Buchanan, who is known mainly for his refusal to end southern secession by force in 1860. Presidents in this group view their office as purely administrative: The president should be aloof from politics and depend on leadership from Congress. Buchanan presidents adopt a *custodial* view of presidential powers: The president is limited to those powers expressly granted to him in the Constitution. Otherwise, they argue, there would be no limits on presidential power. Presidents who have followed this approach generally have been less active chief executives. They include William Howard Taft, Warren Harding, Calvin Coolidge, and Herbert Hoover—all Republican presidents in the early twentieth century.

Lincoln Presidents

Second, there are the *Lincoln presidents.* In this approach, the president is an active politician, often rallying the country in a crisis. Abraham Lincoln did so in the Civil War; Theodore Roosevelt did it later when he moved against the large business monopolies called trusts. In this century, the Lincoln president also originates much of the legislation Congress considers, he leads public opinion, and he is the major source of the country's political goals.

Lincoln presidents do not interpret the Constitution as narrowly as do Buchanan presidents. In their view the presidency is a *stewardship;* its only limits are those explicitly mentioned in the Constitution. The president's powers, then, are as large as his political talents. Following this approach have been activist presidents such as Andrew Jackson, Theodore Roosevelt, Franklin Roosevelt, Harry Truman, Lyndon Johnson, and Ronald Reagan.

Eisenhower Presidents

The two previous approaches to the presidency were outlined by Theodore Roosevelt, who as the energetic twenty-fifth president did much to expand the influence of the office. Another style of presidential leadership is a combination of the first two called the *Eisenhower president*. While General Eisenhower was a skilled politician, he concealed his own involvement in political business. He delegated responsibility widely, which allowed others to take the blame for policy failures while he preserved his own reputation of being "above" politics. This *hidden-hand leadership* hurt Eisenhower's ability to transfer his personal popularity to his party or his chosen successor in 1960, Richard Nixon. Some observers saw parallels to Eisenhower in George W. Bush's style of leadership.

Modern Presidents

While presidents never fall into exact categories, modern presidents have leaned toward the activist end of the scale. Lyndon Johnson sought not only to represent a national consensus but also to create and guide this coalition as well. President Johnson, a master politician, was well known for his midnight phone calls and political arm-twisting to gain support for his proposals. Richard Nixon tried to create an image of the presidency being above politics while using his powers as president for partisan and sometimes illegal activities climaxing in the Watergate scandal. After Nixon's resignation, Gerald Ford's calm, brief presidency began as the nation's first nonpopularly elected vice president—he had been selected by Nixon  and confirmed by Congress under the Twenty-fifth Amendment.

Jimmy Carter, though gaining high marks as a diligent honest manager, was criticized for his lack of political leadership. Trained as an engineer, Carter thoroughly (and often privately) surrounded himself with the details of policy decisions. By the end of his term a widespread feeling that the country's problems—inflation at home, Soviet advances in Afghanistan, hostages in Iran—were not being competently handled led to the Democrat's defeat for reelection in 1980.

Ronald Reagan came to the presidency with a career as an actor and two terms as a conservative Republican governor of California behind him. He excelled in the ability to communicate through the media, while delegating broad powers to his subordinates. His relaxed, sunny attitude toward the office and his advanced age (76 when he left office) led critics to accuse him of being a "nine-to-five" president. Yet his media and political skills helped to gain decreases in social programs, increases in defense spending, large tax cuts, and his vice president elected as his successor. His hard line toward communism may have contributed to the fall of communism in Eastern Europe and Russia. His state funeral in June 2004 revealed Reagan's widespread popular following almost 20 years after he had left office. (See "Hollywood and Presidents.")

Reagan's popularity also helped elect his successor, George Bush Sr., in 1988. His presidency had two faces. The one looking out

Hollywood and Presidents

How much are presidents part of America's mass culture? Just go to the movies.

Which is what film fans did one summer to watch the fantasy fighter pilot/president in *Independence Day* (1996) successfully beat back an alien invasion. Strong leadership was a theme in Hollywood's favorable view of chief executives, from D. W. Griffith's classic *Birth of a Nation* (1915) showing Lincoln as a symbol of peace, through the adventure story of Jack Kennedy in World War II in *PT-109* (1963) to the fictional tale of Teddy Roosevelt rescuing an American girl in Africa in *The Wind and the Lion* (1975).

However, mostly fictional and mostly weak Presidents have also surfaced. Satires have bumbling presidents in Stanley Kubrick's *Dr. Strangelove* (1964), Jack Nicholson being Jack Nicholson in *Mars Attacks* (1996), and Chris Rock in *Head of State* (2003).

With Clinton generally came youth, good intentions, and sex appeal in Hollywood's view of the White House. In *The American President* (1995), an attractive widower becomes more liberal and wins the girl. *Primary Colors* (1997), tracked Clinton's campaign and flaws, with insights on the trade-offs of politics. TV had the hit series *West Wing*, featuring a liberal president and his dedicated, mostly idealistic staff struggling with Washington and each other. The Bush presidency was present in the disaster film *The Day After Tomorrow* (2004) with a nasty vice president and a detached president, not doing much about global warming until it was too late. Stay tuned.

to foreign affairs beamed with success; the domestic side paled in comparison. Foreign policy gave Bush notable victories, some of his own doing (saving Kuwait), and some through a mixture of his own and others' efforts (the end of the Cold War). His domestic claims of being the "education president" and the "environmental president" just added to critics' complaints that he neglected these national concerns. A stalled economy drastically lowered his popular support, and he lost his 1992 bid for reelection.

Bill Clinton brought a zeal for campaigning to the White House plus 12 years experience as governor of Arkansas. With Democrats in control of both houses of Congress in his first two years in office, he got many of his proposals passed, including drastic deficit reductions. The defeat of his health care reform in 1994 and the Republican takeover of Congress moved Clinton to more limited objectives. As a moderate "New Democrat" (positioned between liberal and conservative), Clinton compromised with Republicans in areas like welfare reform while denouncing GOP cuts in social programs.

In his second term, Clinton took to the "bully pulpit" to address national problems like race and focus on international issues like trade with China and the Middle East conflict. While handicapped by scandals—and his own character lapses—President Clinton's public approval remained high enough to defeat the Republican effort to impeach him. But neither his popularity nor prosperity was enough to elect his vice president, Al Gore, in 2000.

The man who was elected, George W. Bush, took office as the first president since 1888 to lose the popular vote. His contested win in Florida; his lack of experience in national politics; the appearance of undeserved advancement from being the son of a former president, George H. W. Bush; and his bouts of garbled speeches all cast early doubt on his performance as president.

These low expectations made Bush's achievements even more impressive. In domestic affairs his broad income tax reduction, his education reform, and his Medicare expansion were hailed as major legislative victories. His early rallying of the nation in the war against terrorism gained him popular and political support, and muted the questions about his detachment toward governing. Yet the economy, though recovering, never replaced the jobs lost during his first term. The costs and violence of invading Iraq raised questions about his 'gut' judgments. But by mobilizing his conservative voter base, casting doubts on Senator John Kerry's leadership and raising fears of another terrorist attack, President Bush in his successful 2004 campaign seemed to overcome opposition to what critics charged was an unnecessary war. (See 'Bush Invades Iraq')

Bush Invades Iraq

On the day before Thanksgiving, ten weeks after the 9/11 attacks, President Bush pulled Secretary of Defense Donald Rumsfeld aside after a meeting to ask him to do a war plan for Iraq. These private instructions, in the midst of the conflict in Afghanistan, were to culminate in the invasion of Iraq in the spring of 2003. Both the strengths and weakness in the president's style of leadership were on display.

For supporters, Iraq showed a decisive leader setting goals and resolutely fulfilling them. In the months leading to the war, the president pushed an often reluctant national security bureaucracy toward war. Yet the justifications for the war—weapons of mass destruction and ties to terrorists—were later to be proven wrong. Expectations that the United States would be greeted as a liberator and that careful planning for postwar Iraq was not needed were equally mistaken. Reflecting Bush's preference for his own "gut" decisions, there were few second thoughts, and there was never a high-level meeting to debate the decision and costs of going to war.

This certainty (or arrogance) was underlined in the president's treatment of the only man who had faced a similar presidential decision to invade Iraq, who the president respected, and who could be expected to give an honest opinion. George H. W. Bush, the 41st president, had confronted Saddam Hussein in the 1991 Gulf War over Kuwait, and had held back from invading Iraq because of his concern for the costs of occupation and the threat of guerrilla war. Yet the president never spoke to his father about his decision.

Source: Bob Woodward, *Plan of Attack.* New York: Simon & Schuster, 2004.

A Psychological Approach

A well-known attempt to categorize presidents has concentrated on their psychological makeup. Political scientist James D. Barber uses this personality approach to focus on the style and character of various chief executives.[1] A president's *style* refers to his ability to act and to the habits of work and personal relations by which he adapts to his surroundings. A style is either *active* or *passive. Character* refers to the way a president feels about himself (his self-esteem).

[1]James David Barber, *The Presidential Character,* 3rd ed. Englewood Cliffs, N.J.: Prentice-Hall, 1985.

Character is either *positive* or *negative*. Putting style and character together, Barber comes up with four categories of personalities in which he places some of our recent presidents (Active-Positive, Active-Negative, Passive-Positive, Passive-Negative).

And so, for example, because of their activism in office, as well as their ability to gain satisfaction from their accomplishments, John Kennedy, Harry Truman, and Jimmy Carter are labeled Active-Positive. Not so fortunate are Active-Negative types like presidents Johnson and Nixon who, though intensely active, suffered from a low opinion of themselves and gained little personal satisfaction from their efforts. Passive-Positive presidents (one of whom, Barber believes, was Ronald Reagan) are easily influenced men searching for affection as a reward for being agreeable rather than for being assertive. President Eisenhower fits into the final category, Passive-Negative, combining a tendency to withdraw from conflict with a sense of his own uselessness. Only his sense of duty leads the Passive-Negative type into the presidency.

This last category gives us a clue to some of the shortcomings of Barber's personality approach. Having been Supreme Allied Commander during World War II, Eisenhower may have seemed Passive-Negative compared with other presidents, but could hardly have achieved what he did if these characteristics had dominated his entire career. The strength of his party, the interests he represented, and the political mood of the country are just some of the factors needed to understand the Eisenhower presidency. Studying a president's personality will provide interesting insights into how and why he acts. It does not, as Barber would agree, give us the full picture of the history, institutions, and political and economic interests that shape the presidency. Perhaps that is why Barber has been reluctant to place recent presidents, including Clinton and Bush, in one of these categories. (See "Presidential Mama's Boys.")

Presidential Hats

The reasons the presidency has expanded lie not only in the history of the office and the personality of the occupant, but also in the increasing expectations focused on the president. When a national problem arises—declining student test scores, rising unemployment, or terrorist threats—the president is expected to respond. The president also is legally required to handle a number of important duties, such as drawing up and presenting the federal government's annual budget. In fulfilling these responsibilities, the president wears six different hats, often more than one at a time.

Presidential Mama's Boys

One overlooked part of many presidents' emotional makeup has been their extraordinarily close relationship with their mothers. Harry Truman had a portrait of his mom hung in the White House, and Calvin Coolidge died carrying a picture of his. In Richard Nixon's Watergate farewell address, he called his mother a "saint." Lyndon Johnson declared his mother "the strongest person I ever knew." Sara Roosevelt rented an apartment in Cambridge to be near Franklin at college. Years later when some New York political bosses asked him to run for office, he responded, "I'd like to talk with my mother about it first."

It's no accident that most of our presidents were their mother's first boy. These mothers were strong, religious women who dominated the raising of their favorite sons. They single-mindedly pushed their sons to overcome the image of failure frequently found in their husbands' careers. Alas, our presidents' fathers were not great role models: Truman's lost his farm in speculation; both Eisenhower's and Nixon's dads were unsuccessful storekeepers; Lyndon Johnson's failed at farming and politics; and Reagan's dad had a drinking problem, as did Bill Clinton's stepfather. (George W's father is the exception here but those who know the family describe "W" as most like his mother from whom he gets his decisive good-versus-evil instincts.)

The sons of these laid-back fathers and strong mothers were hardly sissies. Rather, they became self-confident men who took their mothers' belief in them and turned it into real success.

Chief of State

The president is the symbolic head of *state* as well as the head of *government*. (In England, the two positions are separate: The queen is head of state, a visible symbol of the nation, and the prime minister is head of government, exercising the real power.) As *chief of state*, the president has many ceremonial functions, ranging from declaring National Codfish Week to visiting foreign countries (often in an election year). Because of this role, many people see the president as a symbol of the nation, blessed with extraordinary abilities. This perception raises public expectations, often unrealistically, but also gives him a political advantage. The difficulty in separating his ceremonial from his political actions was evident after September 11. President Bush rallied the nation at nationalist and religious ceremonies. Clearly he was speaking as a nonpolitical chief of state. Yet after the invasion of Iraq he landed a Navy jet on an aircraft carrier under a sign reading

'Mission Accomplished.' Democrats charged he was using the military as a patriotic prop for a reelection commercial.

Chief Executive

The president's second hat places him in charge, at least in theory, of the huge federal bureaucracy in the executive branch. His authority as *chief executive* comes from Article II of the Constitution, which states: "The executive Power shall be vested in a President of the United States of America." Executive power in this instance means the ability to carry out or execute the laws. By 2003 this meant the president headed a bureaucracy spending $1.8 trillion a year and employing 1.9 million civilians (down from 2.2 million in 1990). The federal government, with revenues larger than those of the top 40 U.S. corporations combined, ranks as the largest administrative organization in the world. Criticism of the bureaucracy is widespread. Presidential candidates in every election will inevitably pledge to restrain and reform "Washington." They follow a long bipartisan tradition of promising to get government "off the backs of the American people." But most presidents (including the current one) have ended up increasing the budget and adding to the bureaucracy.

Chief Diplomat

The repeated attempts of recent American presidents and their secretaries of state to mediate the Middle East conflict illustrate the importance of the chief diplomat role. The president has the power to establish relations with foreign governments, to appoint U.S. ambassadors, and to sign treaties that take effect with the consent of two-thirds of the Senate. Over the years, the president has become the chief maker and executor of American foreign policy. Despite the Senate's power to approve treaties and Congress's power to appropriate money for foreign aid and to declare wars, the political checks on the president's power in foreign affairs are far fewer than those on his conduct in domestic matters.

After World War II, in an age of cold war when the United States and the Soviet Union seemed to be competing in every sphere, this authority over foreign policy elevated the president's standing to ever greater heights. Often presidents went so far as to argue that the health of the economy, the effectiveness of the educational system, and even racial discrimination affected our standing abroad, and thus involved the president in how they should be resolved.

The Senate's power to approve or reject treaties also has been changed by practice. Since its refusal in 1920 to approve U.S. membership in the League of Nations, the Senate has seldom not ratified a treaty.

However, most international agreements involving the United States never reach the Senate. Because *executive agreements* do not require the approval of the Senate, their use has increased to the point where a president may sign hundreds of them in a single year. Presidents argue that these agreements usually concern only minor matters, and that important issues, such as the START II Treaty reducing nuclear weapons, are still submitted to the Senate. Historically agreements that involved matters of far-reaching importance were kept secret from the public and Congress. Both Wilson and Franklin D. Roosevelt used executive agreements to aid the Allies in the two world wars, thus involving the country in those conflicts before war was declared. Attempts by Congress to limit the president's use of executive agreements have all failed, although Congress can refuse to appropriate funds to carry out the agreements.

Commander-in-Chief

When George W. Bush mobilized U.S. military forces to drive Saddam Hussein from power in Iraq in the Spring of 2003, he was clearly acting as commander-in-chief. He was less successful in gaining the support of the United Nations and most of our allies. The president often wears his military helmet with his chief diplomat hat. The principle behind this presidential role is *civilian supremacy* over the military: An elected civilian official, the president, is in charge of the armed forces. In practice, this authority is given to the secretary of defense, who normally delegates his command to members of the military. This role is not limited to actions abroad, as shown by President Bush Sr.'s use of federal troops in Florida in 1992 to help victims of Hurricane Andrew. Its political importance is further reflected by the fact that national defense costs some $300 billion a year, over 16 percent of the government budget.

Although the Constitution gives Congress the power to declare war, Congress has not done so since December 1941 when the United States entered World War II. Presidents, in their role as commander-in-chief, initiated the country's involvement in the Korean and Vietnam Wars. Congress supported both actions by appropriating money for the armed forces. Criticism of the president's role in Vietnam led to the *War Powers Act* of 1973 to restrict the president's war-making powers. The law, passed over President Nixon's veto, limited the president's committing of troops abroad to a period of 60 days, or 90, if needed for a successful withdrawal. If Congress does not authorize a longer period, the troops must be removed.

The effectiveness of the War Powers Act is questionable even though presidents generally feel the need to gain congressional approval for any major use of the military. In the first Gulf War (1991),

Congress frequently referred to the Act while former President Bush cited it as unconstitutional. But Bush Sr. implicitly honored it by seeking a congressional resolution of approval for sending troops to recapture Kuwait. In the 1999 Kosovo conflict, Congress refused to endorse the bombing, refused to declare war, and then, confusing everyone, proposed giving the president twice as much money for the war as he requested.

In gaining approval for using force against Iraq in October 2002, Congress passed a resolution authorizing the president to use armed forces "as he determines to be necessary and appropriate" to defend the nation against "the continuing threat posed by Iraq." He was encouraged to work with the UN and to report to Congress within 48 hours of any military action. The resolution described itself as "specific statutory authorization" under the War Powers Act. Mr. Bush argued that he already was permitted to act as commander in chief without a formal declaration of war, but that he wanted Congress to be involved to reflect national unity. Many Democrats, including Senator John Kerry, argued that this resolution was not the equivalent of a declaration of war. In short, Congress and presidents have agreed to disagree on the War Powers Act.

Chief Legislator

Although the Constitution gives the president the right to recommend measures to Congress, it was not until the twentieth century that presidents regularly and actively participated in the legislative process. The president delivers his *State of the Union address* to a joint session of Congress at the beginning of every year to present the administration's annual legislative program. He also gives an annual budget message, an economic message and report, and frequently sends special messages to Congress supporting specific legislation. Historically, most bills passed by Congress originate in the executive branch.

Presidents often try to lead Congress by controlling the *national agenda,* which consists of the important political issues that the public concentrates on at any one time. So in the first half of 2001 President Bush campaigned successfully for public support of the tax cut that became law that summer. The terrorists' attacks meant that guarding the country against that threat now drove the agenda. Budgets, legislation, and executive branch actions soon conformed to this priority. Despite President Bush's success in gaining much of what he wanted in tax cuts and counterterrorism measures, presidents are frequently not successful in gaining unity behind their national agenda. An indifferent public, a skeptical press, and entrenched interest groups can combine to derail this strategy.

In dealing with Congress a president has a number of advantages, many of which President Bush has displayed. His willingness in 2004 to risk his own political standing to elect Republicans included recruiting new candidates to run, taking polls for them, raising money, and giving them the publicity that comes from a popular president's visit to their states. President Bush is noted for "killing Congress with kindness"—inviting members to dine at his Camp David retreat, giving them nicknames, and phoning their sick relatives. Such courtesies build loyalties. More forceful leverage can influence legislators' votes on specific bills. (See "Presidential Arm-Twisting.")

The president's main constitutional power as chief legislator is the *veto*. If a president disapproves of a bill passed by Congress, he may refuse to sign it and return it to Congress with his objections. The president can also *pocket veto* a bill by refusing to sign it within ten

---

Presidential Arm-Twisting

West Virginia Senator Robert Byrd, who has had his arm twisted by presidents of both parties, offers an imaginary dialogue of what a White House phone call is like:

"Hello, Mr. President."

"Bob, I have been wanting to talk to you about something. . . . I know you have some moneys in the appropriations bill for the Gallipolis Locks and Dam."

"Yes, sir."

"The people of West Virginia, in my opinion, are to be complimented in having you as their Senator. I know you have worked hard for that funding. . . . By the way, Bob, we have this piece of legislation that is going to be coming up in the Senate in a few days to authorize moneys for the Contras in Central America. Gee, I wish you would support that, Bob. . . . It will be used only for food and medicines. . . . I respect you for your opposition to that funding, but I wish you would see your way to vote with us next time on that. Can you do it?"

"Well, I will certainly be glad to think about it, Mr. President. . . . "

"Well, Bob, I hope you will. And by the way, that money for the heart research center in Morgantown that you have worked for, I will bet your people love you for that."

"Yes, Mr. President. There is a lot of support for that in West Virginia."

"Bob, I have given a lot of thought to that. Be sure and take another look at that item we have, funds for the Contras."

Source: New York Times, July 26, 1985, p. A10. Copyright © 1985 by The New York Times Company. Reprinted by permission.

days of Congress adjourning. Congress may override the veto by a two-thirds vote of those present and voting in each house. Prior to 1969 approximately 1 of every 18 vetoes were overridden. Since 1969 Congress has been more successful, overriding one out of every five. The veto is most often used as a threat in negotiations to influence a bill while it is still being considered by Congress. Nearing the end of his four-year term of office, President Bush had not yet used his veto even once.

In 1996 as part of the Republican majority's "Contract with America," Congress passed a Line Item Veto allowing the president to veto sections of some money bills. Supporters hoped that the line item veto would reduce Congress's spending tendencies. During its 1997 term the Supreme Court ruled that the line item veto unconstitutionally expanded presidential powers (*Clinton* v. *City of New York*). Because the Supreme Court had the last word, presidents must still accept or reject the entire bill before them. They have no line item veto.

Party Leader

A president is head of his party. As party leader, the president is given a number of major duties: to choose a vice president after his own nomination; to distribute a few thousand offices and numerous favors to the party faithful; and to demonstrate that he is at least trying to fulfill the *party platform,* the party's program adopted at his nominating convention. The president also is the chief campaigner and fundraiser for his party. He names the national chairperson and usually exercises a great deal of influence over the national party machinery.

The president's grip on his party has traditionally been limited by the decentralized nature of American parties. Congressional members of the president's party can oppose his proposals, and he has no direct power to refuse members of Congress their party's nomination, or to keep them from reaching positions of power through seniority. Yet President Bush led a party in 2004 which dominated all three branches of the national government even while public opinion polls showed Americans evenly split between the two parties. Through pressures on lobbyists for financial support, redistricting manipulation in the House and a clear ideological agenda, the GOP came close to national political control.

President Bush's skillful use of his informal power over his party produced a great deal of loyalty in the GOP for him. This took place through fundraising, distributing partisan favors and jobs, and recruitment. On just this last point, Karl Rove, President Bush's chief political advisor, was reported to have telephoned leading Republicans in states with key congressional races. He pressured some to run in the

GOP primary and some to stand aside for stronger candidates. One Minnesota Republican who dropped out of running for the Senate put it this way; "Once the White House says, 'We've made a decision and we're going in a different direction,' there's not much you can say."

THE PRESIDENT AND THE PUBLIC

A major result of the president's many powers and roles is his influence over mass opinion. His visibility, his standing as a symbol of the nation, and his position as a single human being compared with a frequently impersonal government, give the chief executive a great deal of public support in the political game. The White House offers its occupant what Theodore Roosevelt called "a bully pulpit."

"Going public" has become an essential part of presidential power. A president with visible public support can increase his overall prestige within Washington as well as his influence on a specific issue. By rallying public opinion, pressure can be brought on official Washington—usually Congress—to support the chief executive.

Mobilizing public opinion behind the president results from careful planning. The White House staff sells the president's message through techniques used in election campaigns. Polling of public opinion will first be used to determine which issues and arguments have the greatest positive impact. Then the topic may be presented in a nationally televised speech, or the president may hit the road to push his plan through meetings or press interviews. Cabinet secretaries and allies in Congress may meet with groups to reinforce the message. All of this can be directed by a "war room" set up in the White House to coordinate the campaign. These tactics were used by President Bush in the spring of 2003 to gain public support for his budget proposals and tax cut. While 9/11 was a unique event, the president's reaction reflected his familiarity with campaigns to mobilize public opinion. Whether it works or not, "going public" is an essential presidential weapon in keeping popular backing. (See Case Study: "September 11: A President's Trial by Fire.")

This visibility may work against him. After all, a president is chosen by election and has to keep the voters happy to keep himself and his party in office. Usually this means accomplishing his administration's goals as well as maintaining his own personal popularity. But these two aims are not always compatible. Two presidents, Lyndon Johnson—despite domestic legislative successes—and Richard Nixon—despite foreign policy achievements—left office widely unpopular. Johnson was unpopular because of the Vietnam War and Nixon because of Watergate. In both cases the public attention focused on them by the mass media hastened their decline. George W. Bush faced a public in 2004 polarized by a costly war in Iraq, and administration policies which seemed to turn American troops into harsh jailers and allies into anti-Americans. (See "Presidential Privacy and the Press: FDR.")

Some presidents have been lucky. President Reagan was one of the most skillful chief executives at using the media to directly reach out and touch people with his sincerity. President Clinton's folksy manner and detailed command of issues did not quite overcome media suspicion of his honesty. He preferred going around national reporters by favoring out-of-Washington speaking and interviews with local reporters—a practice continued by President Bush. A 1998 sexual scandal in the White House remarkably improved President Clinton's standing with the public. People disconnected Mr. Clinton's moral lapses from positive judgments of his presidential performance, not least because of his White House public relations skills.

Early in his term, President Bush was dismissed by the press for his inability to speak English coherently. But what looked like dumb to some of the media elite seemed like folksiness to some of the

Presidential Privacy and the Press: FDR

Franklin Roosevelt, a polio victim, was wheelchair-bound. He was protected by the press in ways that seem amazing to modern presidents. Of 35,000 press photographs of FDR in the archives only two showed his wheelchair. When he occasionally fell in public, photographers would take no pictures and live radio broadcasts would not mention it.

The press's rule of thumb was that a president's private life should stay private unless it seriously interfered with his job performance. But this rule extended into 1944 (the year before his death) when FDR's failing health was a legitimate concern. His hearing had deteriorated to where he had to have questions at his press conference repeated for him. Publishers like Henry Luce of *Time Magazine*—a strong Republican—refused to print photos showing the president's poor health. World War II was going on and this was seen as giving comfort to the enemy.

public. He was not as familiar with policy details as Clinton, so he delegated public discussion on these issues to his vice president or the cabinet. He was shrewd enough to defend his policies by staying "on message" which meant following the single theme that his advisors had laid out for that appearance. Of course 9/11 and early victories in Afghanistan and Iraq helped, at least until Iraq bogged down. By the end of his first term though most people thought the country was heading in the wrong direction, they were willing to stick with a presi-

White House Spin: Iraqi Ties with Terrorists

"Spin" is slang for putting favorable interpretations on information. The Bush White House needed this skill in June 2004 to counter the 9/11 Commission's report that concluded there was no "collaborative relationship" between Saddam Hussein's Iraq and Al Qaeda in the terrorist group's attack on the United States. This lack of cooperation between Iraq and the 9/11 terrorists was bolstered by FBI and CIA officials, and by Republican commission members.

The problem facing the administration was that ties between Iraq and the 9/11 terrorists had been one of two justifications for the war against Iraq. (The other was Iraqi weapons of mass destruction which had not been found.) In his State of the Union address, Mr. Bush had charged that Saddam Hussein "aids and protects terrorists, including members of Al Qaeda." And just the Monday before the report, the vice president said in a speech that Iraq had "long-established ties with Al Qaeda." Senator John Kerry charged that Bush had "misled" the American people about the need for the war.

The White House "spin" on this damaging report was to deny any real differences with the commission. A White House spokesman said, "It is not inconsistent for Iraq to have ties with Al Qaeda and not to have been involved in 9/11 or other potential plots against America." President Bush denied ever saying that Al Qaeda and Iraq had "orchestrated" the 9/11 attacks. Attacking the messenger was another acceptable part of the spin strategy for dealing with bad news. Vice President Cheney charged on TV the next day that the press reports on the commission findings were "irresponsible" and done for "malicious" reasons.

The success of the spin was reflected in polls taken both before and after the commission report showing that around 40% of the public thought that Saddam was linked to 9/11.

Source: New York Times, June 17, 2004; and *Washington Post,* June 18, 2004.

dent they seemed to trust to fix it. (See "White House Spin: Iraqi Ties with Terrorists.")

While keeping up his standing with other branches of the government and the public at large, the president must still try to carry out the tasks of his office and the goals of his administration. In doing so, his most critical relationship is with the bureaucracy, the huge organization that manages programs ranging from launching shuttles into orbit to teaching adults to read. What makes up this bureaucracy and how the president tries to control it are the focus of the rest of this chapter.

THE FEDERAL BUREAUCRACY

The federal bureaucracy carries out much of the work of governing. Despite the negative sound of the word, a *bureaucrat* is simply an administrator, a member of the large administrative organization— the bureaucracy—that carries out government policies. The United States' bureaucracy is generally competent and uncorrupt, distinguishing it from many other bureaucracies around the world. It is what makes the country well governed. The great historical growth of the national government and the tasks it has confronted have produced an administrative system unequaled in size and complexity. Whether this bureaucracy is the servant or master of government varies from case to case.

Most of the bureaucracy is within, or close to, the executive branch. Its structure can be broken down into the executive office of the president, the cabinet departments, the executive agencies, and the regulatory commissions. (See Figure 3.1.)

Executive Office of the President

In 1939 the *executive office* was established to advise the president and to assist him in managing the bureaucracy. It has grown steadily in size and influence and today it includes over a dozen agencies and some 1,400 people. (See Figure 3.2.) Three of the most important agencies of the executive office are the White House office, the National Security Council, and the Office of Management and Budget. The *White House office* is a direct extension of the president. Its members are not subject to Senate approval. In recent years, centralization of executive power has increased the authority of the White House staff at the expense of the cabinet officers—and even the president. The White House chief of staff, at present Andrew Card, manages the staff, keeps

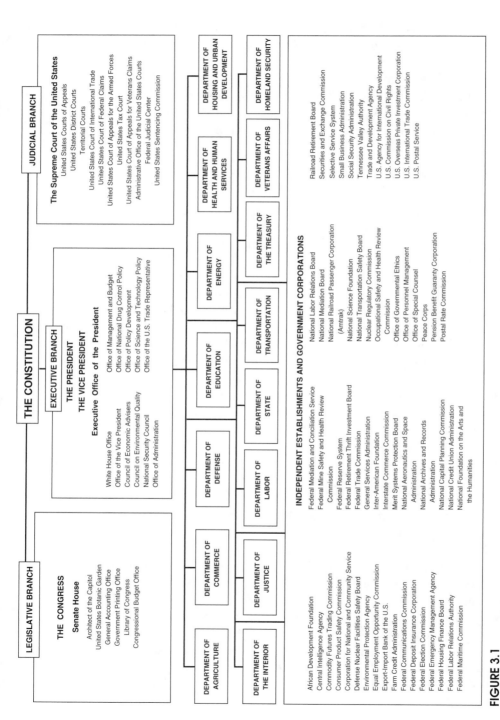

FIGURE 3.1
The Government of the United States.
Source: U.S. Government Manual.

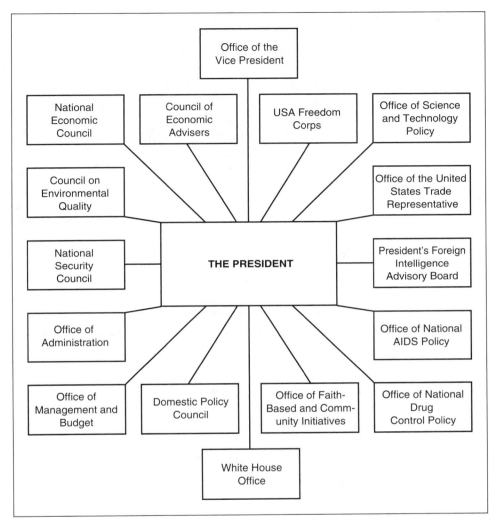

FIGURE 3.2
Some of the Offices in the Executive Office of the President.
Source: www.whitehouse.gov

the paperwork flowing, and serves as the gatekeeper determining who gets to see the president. The staff, often veterans of the election campaign, perform a variety of tasks from speech writing and negotiating with Congress, to steering attacks away from the president—calling themselves his "javelin catchers."

The White House staff is frequently part of the problem. Strong chiefs of staff have alienated Congress by their arrogance. In the Clinton White House led by a famously undisciplined president, the staff often got the blame for poor planning. Past White Houses have taken on the trappings of royalty with the staff acting like a palace guard isolating the president. A special assistant to Lyndon Johnson described the staff's relationship to the president as that of a doting mother to a spoiled child—"Whatever he wants is brought to him immediately." (See "First Advisor, First Lady.")

The present White House has appeared well organized under a president noted for promptness, decisiveness, and the occasional inattention to details. In the crisp businesslike atmosphere of the office (no loosened ties allowed) the president, our first with an MBA degree, runs his staff like the chief executive officer of a large company. In carrying out the business of government, George W. Bush is noted for denying that partisan politics figure into his decisions. He freely delegates authority saying, "It's important to be able to delegate to people whose instincts you trust." Of course one of these people is his political advisor, Karl Rove, whose staff reviews

First Advisor, First Lady

There is no position of first lady mentioned in the Constitution. Yet despite frequent criticism president's wives have often acted as trusted advisors to their husbands. Much attention has been given to powerful recent first ladies like Hillary Clinton. But wives acting as presidential advisors is a common practice.

The following is an exchange between President Lyndon Johnson and his wife, Lady Bird, following a press conference. She appears to be knowledgeable in this taped recording and ready to criticize her powerful husband.

> *Lady Bird: You want to listen for about one minute to my critique, or would you rather wait until tonight?*
>
> *LBJ: Yes, ma'am. I'm willing now.*
>
> *Lady Bird: I thought you looked strong, firm, and like a reliable guy. Your looks were splendid. The close-ups were much better than the distance ones.*
>
> *LBJ: You can't get them to do it.*
>
> *Lady Bird: During the statement you were a little breathless and there was too much looking down and I think it was a little too fast. Not enough change of pace. Dropping voice at the end of sentence. There was a considerable pickup in drama and interests when the questioning began. Your voice was noticeably better and your facial expressions noticeably better.*

Source: Michael R. Beschloss, ed. *Taking Charge: The Johnson White House Tapes, 1963–1964.* New York: Simon & Schuster, 1997, 272–73.

policies, speeches, and presidential travel to increase their partisan advantage.

The *National Security Council (NSC)* was established early in the Cold War (1947) to coordinate American military and foreign policies for the president. These policies mainly involve the departments of State and Defense, which are represented on the council. (The Central Intelligence Agency, though an executive agency, also is a member of the NSC.) Presidents have varied in how much they wished to use the NSC. In President Bush's first term, his National Security Adviser, Condoleeza Rice, became a key player, coordinating agency input to the White House and planning for the war on terrorism and the invasion and occupation of Iraq. Rice also became a public defender of the president when dissenting bureaucrats, like counterterrorism advisor Richard Clarke, resigned and wrote a book charging that the Bush White House had ignored warnings before the 9/11 attacks.

The *National Economic Council (NEC)* was established in 1993 because President Clinton decided that the United States needed an organization similar to the NSC to manage orderly economic policy making. In its formal structure the NEC includes cabinet members plus various top aides, and coordinates the executive branch's economic activities.

The *Office of Management and Budget (OMB)* was created by President Nixon in 1970 to replace the Bureau of the Budget. Departments of the executive branch submit competing claims for shares in the federal budget to OMB. Besides preparing the budget, OMB is an important general-management arm of the president. It helps control the executive branch by overseeing the agencies and their success in accomplishing their programs. Preparing and administering the annual budget (which is then submitted to Congress for approval) gives OMB tremendous power within the government.

The *Council of Economic Advisers* is another important unit of the executive office. It is a three-member council of economic experts, appointed with Senate approval, which helps the president form a national economic policy and predicts future economic developments.

The Cabinet Departments

The *cabinet departments,* created by Congress, are the major agencies of the federal government. At first there were only 3 (the Departments of State, War, and the Treasury); today there are 15, the most recent being the Department of Homeland Security. The expansion of the cabinet has been due largely to the growth of problems that political and popular interests wanted the federal government to deal with. Recently there have been competing efforts to both remove departments and create new ones. President Reagan entered office promising to abolish two cabinet departments—Education and Energy—and left office having created a new one—Veterans in 1988.

Homeland Security came out of the widespread frustration with the bureaucratic "turf wars" that hindered the nation's security both before and after 9/11. While originally pushed by congressional Democrats over the administration's objections, it was soon embraced by the Bush White House. The Homeland Agency combined 22 agencies and some 170,000 employees in a cabinet department that aimed to centralize oversight of domestic security. It was the biggest government reorganization since the creation of the Defense Department in the late 1940s. The complexity of blending various agencies with different workplace cultures, payroll systems, computers, and physical locations behind a common mission underlined the difficulty of reorganizing any bureaucracy of government.

Each cabinet department is headed by a secretary, who is appointed by the president with the consent of the Senate (which is usually given). Cabinet secretaries hold office as long as the president wishes. Pressures from their staff and constant involvement with the problems of their agencies may cause secretaries to act more like lobbyists for their departments than representatives of the president. Because of this detachment they often play a secondary role to the White House office. Cabinet secretaries in many administrations can be heard complaining that they are not included in important decisions and that young White House staffers with large egos block their access to the president.

How much the president uses the cabinet as a whole is strictly up to him. The cabinet has no power as a body. Although many presidents, including Clinton and Bush, entered office promising to give the cabinet more power, things haven't worked out that way. President Bush seldom uses the cabinet as a whole, except for ceremonial photo opportunities and when he wants to demonstrate broad support for his proposals such as the tax cut. Former Treasury Secretary Paul O'Neill charged that the president didn't read his memos and spent little time mastering the details of policy decisions. The traditional lack of a policy-making role by the cabinet is illustrated in a story about President Lincoln being opposed by his entire cabinet on an issue. He remarked, "Seven nays, one aye; the ayes have it."

The amount of control cabinet heads have over their departments varies greatly. President Bush has allowed his cabinet secretaries considerable scope over their own departments, and strong secretaries like Defense Secretary Donald Rumsfeld have emerged. Even a cabinet head appointed to control a department for the White House, as Secretary of State Condoleeza Rice was in 2005, ends up lobbying for her agency's programs. Often a department may be a loose structure containing strong, relatively independent groups. For example, the attorney general has authority over the FBI, which is in the Justice Department. Yet the reports on FBI missteps in tracking the Arab terrorists who hijacked American planes illustrated the independence of the Bureau from any outside political control. The FBI's ability to keep separate from the new Homeland Security Agency showed that this autonomy was likely to continue.

The Executive Agencies

Executive agencies are simply important agencies of the executive branch that are not in the cabinet. Their heads are appointed by the president with approval of the Senate, but they are not considered major enough to be part of the cabinet. Examples of these are the Office of Personnel Management (OPM), the National Aeronautics and Space Administration (NASA), and the Central Intelligence Agency (CIA).

Under executive agencies we might include *government corporations,* which began as semi-independent but have come increasingly under presidential control. Government corporations, like private corporations, perform business activities such as operating a transportation system or developing and selling electricity. They are usually governed by a board of directors, have limited legislative control over them, and allow for flexible administration. The Tennessee Valley Authority (TVA) is a government corporation, set up in the 1930s to develop electricity for the Tennessee Valley. The U.S. Postal Service is another, established in 1970 when Congress abolished the Post Office as a cabinet department and set it up as a semi-independent, government-owned corporation.

The Regulatory Commissions

Regulatory commissions are charged with regulating and making rules for certain parts of the economy. Examples are the Federal Trade Commission (FTC) which oversees unfair business practices, consumer protection and the National Do Not Call Registry, and the Federal Communications Commission (FCC) regulating telephones, radio and TV. (The important Federal Reserve Board, under its chairman, Alan Greenspan, is a special type of regulatory agency that determines general monetary policies, like interest rates, for Federal Reserve Banks.) Although the president appoints the members of the commissions and chooses who chairs them, the commissions are relatively independent of all branches of the government. They are bipartisan (members come from both parties); the president has only a limited right to remove commissioners, who generally serve longer terms than the president; and there is no presidential veto over their actions. These commissions also have all three capacities of government: They can make rules that have the force of law (legislative), administer and enforce these regulations (executive), and conduct hearings and issue orders (judicial). Their decisions can be reviewed by federal courts, while their authority and budget can be reduced by Congress.

The logic behind these commissions is that Congress and the president felt that parts of the economy required detailed oversight on complicated matters that Congress didn't have the technical ability to ensure. They were independent because their decisions were not supposed to be made on a partisan basis, but instead should rest on their expertise. The independence of these commissions from the rest of the government has meant, however, that the public has little control over their activities. The commissions often come under pressure from the groups they are regulating, and the lack of governmental controls has sometimes led them to negotiate with, rather than regulate, important economic interests. They have been charged with being captives of the wealthy economic groups they oversee (see pp. 00–00). During the corporate scandals of 2002 auditors were discovered to have "cooked the books" at Enron to conceal stealing by that energy business's executives. The Securities and Exchange Commission (SEC) was accused of not closely regulating the auditors and corporate chiefs. However a few years earlier the SEC head, appointed by President Clinton, had been accused of overregulating by the same business groups that now demanded more government supervision.

PROBLEMS OF BUREAUCRACY

When Americans hear the word *bureaucracy*, they think of incompetence and red tape; faceless administrators blindly following rules despite their impact on peoples' lives. Yet bureaucracies are set up to apply standardized rules, to treat people the same or at least according to some standard operating procedure (SOP). The problems with bureaucracies seem to be related to their size rather than the nature of the public or private organizations they serve. As reflected by negative comments heard in Eastern Europe after the political upheavals in those countries, socialist and capitalist bureaucracies may have more in common than the political regimes they serve. The size and complexity of any large bureaucracy make it hard to tell who is responsible for a particular action, inhibiting public oversight.

Public distaste for the bureaucracy in the United States has helped antigovernment politicians gain positions of power, where they then faced the dilemma of both directing and depending on bureaucrats to carry out their policies. Of course the bureaucracy may also be a useful scapegoat that politicians can blame for failed policies. Whether in 2003 the CIA on its own misjudged the presence of weapons of mass destruction in Iraq, or was pressured to support administration policies, still remains uncertain. (See "Who is to Blame for the Bureaucracy?")

The fact that bureaucrats are experts in their own areas is a major source of their influence in government, but the limits of their vision present problems. A member of Congress or a president wanting information and advice on tax policy, housing, or safer space shuttles would probably go to the bureaucrat in charge of the issue. The problem is how to get these experts in the bureaucracy to see beyond their narrow fields of expertise to the broader public interest. Investigators looking into the FBI and CIA antiterrorist activities discovered that

Who Is to Blame for the Bureaucracy?

For many critics of big government Franklin Delano Roosevelt, the creator of the modern bureaucracy, is to blame for the government we have. The only president to be elected to four terms, FDR brought the United States through the Great Depression of the 1930s and World War II. To fight the depression, Roosevelt started 30 new federal agencies, including well-known programs like the Social Security Administration. Later, to pay for the war, payroll deductions allowed the government to automatically collect income taxes, and therefore to double the number of federal employees. Taxes poured into Washington at six times the rate as before the war.

The growth in government has continued since FDR. Government employment has tripled. Federal taxes now take 20 percent of the nation's gross domestic product, four times more than in Roosevelt's first years. Social Security and other entitlement programs which were part of FDR's New Deal take half of the entire federal budget.

Nor have recent politicians stopped this growth. The federal budget stands at nearly $2 trillion a year, three times what it was when Jimmy Carter was president. Under George W. Bush, the cost of government increased and no major agency of government has yet been abolished. In fact, no president of either party has stopped the growth of the modern bureaucracy. Perhaps this means the blame lies less with FDR and his successors than with the demands placed on government—from caring for the elderly to arming the military—by all of us.

the frequently rival agencies were reluctant to share information with each other on foreign terrorists. The FBI limited itself to crimes in this country; the CIA was restricted to intelligence gathering abroad. Valuable information that had been collected on Arab terrorists prior to 9/11 was neglected because the two agencies never combined the clues that each had. It was a harsh lesson on the costs of protecting bureaucratic turf.

Rise of the Civil Service

In the first century of the federal government, the usual method of choosing government bureaucrats was known as the *spoils system.* Taken from the phrase "to the victor belong the spoils," the spoils system meant that victorious politicians filled government positions with their supporters. This system of widespread patronage got its start during the administration of Andrew Jackson (1828–1836) and may have peaked under Abraham Lincoln (1860–1865). Those bureaucrats did not even need to be knowledgeable in their fields. But as the tasks expected of bureaucrats became more complex and corruption grew, pressure for reform also increased.

In 1881, President James Garfield was assassinated by a disappointed (and crazy) office seeker. The new president, Chester Arthur, backed by public outrage over the murder, supported the Civil Service Reform Act (also known as the *Pendleton Act*), which was passed by Congress in 1883. The act set up a bipartisan Civil Service Commission under which government employees were chosen by merit through examinations. At first only about 10 percent of federal employees were covered by civil service, but the system has grown and now covers practically the entire bureaucracy. This has considerably diminished the spoils system and has added stability to government activity. The president today fills only about 5,000 patronage jobs, of which fewer than one-third are at a policy-making level. While weakening the spoils system, it also has weakened presidential control of the bureaucracy; the bureaucrats know they will have their jobs long after the current administration passes into history.

Bureaucrats as Policymakers

The traditional idea of *public administration,* was that *policy* and *administration* were two different functions of government. The president and Congress, elected by the people, should make policy. The unelected bureaucracy should carry it out. The goal of bureaucracy was "efficiency." According to this ideal model, bureaucrats administer policy and supply expert knowledge to elected policymakers. Today most political scientists consider this traditional view incomplete, if not a bit naïve.

The political conflicts that influence policies do not stop when Congress passes a law. They continue when these policies are administered. In order to pass a bill, Congress often reaches a compromise that results in a vaguely worded law. That leaves it to the administrators to referee the debate—on, say, how clean is clean water—in applying the law. Before the bill is passed, bureaucrats may have influenced the process by their advice and information, even to the point of lobbying the bill through Congress. Afterward they often face applying the law to changed political and economic situations not foreseen by those who drafted it. And, of course, bureaucracies have interests of their own, such as increasing their budget or protecting their "turf." The result is that the model of a bureaucrat as a politically neutral administrator looks like a single musical note in a symphony of sounds. Bureaucrats carry other tunes as well.

Bureaucracies are involved in policy making because they exercise legislative, judicial, and executive power. For example, the Internal Revenue Service (IRS) holds hearings on tax cases and makes judicial findings. These legislative and judicial powers have been delegated by Congress. In exercising executive power, federal bureaucracies draw up long-range plans, and then make decisions about day-to-day operations, from aid to Afghanistan to use of the national forests. Other decisions, such as how to divide money among competing programs, involve the most serious policy questions in the government. Federal bureaucracies share in this decision making.

The President and the Bureaucracy

Curiously, the bureaucracy is both an important support for the president and a major limit on his actions. The federal bureaucracy gives the president access to more information than his opponents are likely to have, and allows him to create policies to which others must react. But to carry out his policies, the president must rely on the information, advice, and actions of subordinates. Keeping control over the 2 million employees of the executive branch is a full-time job in itself. As political scientist Richard Neustadt commented, the president spends much of his time finding out what his bureaucratic subordinates are doing in his name.

Members of the bureaucracy acting as policymakers may work to protect their own interests or may respond to pressures from economic concerns threatened by presidential policies. In doing so, they may ignore the president's orders, and delay or even sabotage his programs, even on trivial matters. (See "The President and the Mouse.") Often these departments have long-standing rivalries with each other: Labor versus Agriculture on food prices, or the FBI versus CIA on intelligence. The State Department's knock-down drag-out

The President and the Mouse

The problems presidents have with their bureaucracies are not always limited to major policy matters. An example from the Carter presidency:

> When a couple of mice scampered across the president's study one evening last spring, an alarm went out to the General Services Administration, housekeeper of federal buildings. Some weeks later, another mouse climbed up inside a wall of the Oval Office and died. The president's office was bathed in the odor of dead mouse as Carter prepared to greet visiting Latin American dignitaries. An emergency call went out to GSA. But it refused to touch the matter. Officials insisted that they had exterminated all the "inside" mice in the White House and this errant mouse must have come from outside, and therefore was the responsibility of the Interior Department. Interior demurred, saying that the dead mouse was now inside the White House. President Carter summoned officials from both agencies to his desk and exploded: "I can't even get a damn mouse out of my office." Ultimately, it took an interagency task force to get rid of the mouse.

Source: Hedrick Smith, "Problems of a Problem Solver," *New York Times Magazine,* January 8, 1978. Copyright © 1978 by The New York Times Company. Reprinted by permission.

fights with Donald Rumsfeld's Defense Department over policies in Iraq are the most publicized recent example. The president must act as a judge over these conflicts, yet maintain close ties with both sides. Cabinet officials appointed by the president may represent their own departments' interests against those of the president. Does the secretary of defense represent the president to the Defense Department, or the department to the president? Clearly both, but conflict often results. Presidential power thus often boils down to the power to persuade. The president's ability to gain acceptance for his policies depends on his skill in gaining public support, and then "selling" these policies to other political and bureaucratic players.

CASE STUDY

SEPTEMBER 11: A PRESIDENT'S TRIAL BY FIRE

It was a horrible day, for the nation and the president. On Tuesday morning September 11, 2001, four teams of 19 Arab terrorists took control of four California-bound jets at three East Coast airports. Using the planes as "smart bombs" they had crashed into both towers of the World Trade Center and the Pentagon. (The fourth plane, apparently thwarted by passengers, had crashed into a field in Pennsylvania.) The huge 110-story towers had imploded to the ground, thousands were killed and a stunned nation watched the doomsday images repeated endlessly on television. The nation's airports were closed, Congress evacuated the capital, rumors of further attacks spread, and Americans struggled to regain equilibrium and a lost sense of security.

A Challenged Leader

President Bush had problems trying to appear in command. His day had begun in an elementary school in Sarasota, Florida, where he had been plugging his education program. He had waited seven minutes after the second attack before leaving the class, and then took 12 hours to get back to the White House. Relying on his staff's security fears his jet had taken a zigzag course first to an Air Force Base near Shreveport, Louisiana, and then to a command post in Omaha, Nebraska, where he had conducted a meeting of the National Security Council by video phone to Washington. While the secret service worried that the attacks hadn't ended, the president's political aides had to face another issue: How could Mr. Bush appear in control and reassure the nation from a bunker in Nebraska? Or as a *USA Today* reporter sarcastically noted, "Not since the British burned the White House in 1814 has a President been persuaded by security concerns to avoid the capital."

Arriving back at the White House that night, President Bush addressed the nation from the Oval Office at 8:30 p.m. In his brief talk a "somber" chief executive sitting alone at his desk assured his audience that "Our country is strong. . . . Terrorist acts can shake the foundation of our biggest buildings, but they cannot touch the foundation of America." He declared that the government would continue "without interruption," that the search was underway to find those behind these evil acts, and that both allies and members of Congress would stand together to win the war against terrorism. He ended asking for prayers for those who grieve and promised "America has stood down enemies before, and we will do so this time."

In the coming days the president expanded on these themes. He would be shown offering sympathy, demonstrating national unity, defining an unseen enemy, and executing a strong response. Underlying his activities was a nagging doubt: Was this commander in chief, barely eight months in office, elected by a minority of voters, with almost no foreign policy experience, up to the enormous task? With the nation traditionally rallying around the president in a time of crisis, many of his actions in this first week were designed to answer that unspoken question. (See "Congress on September 11.")

Congress on September 11

On 9/11 Congress was reminded of its physical dependency on the executive in a graphic way. Unlike the executive branch, Congress then had no evacuation plan. Members wandered around, prayed with the chaplain or went home. Rumors circulated of more planes heading to Washington. Vice President Cheney ordered that the leaders of Congress be taken to a secure location—rumored to be West Virginia. When, later in the day, one Republican senator demanded in a phone call to Cheney that the leadership be returned to Washington so that Congress could convene, the vice president refused. The senator pointed out that Congress was an independent branch of government, not under executive control. Cheney replied, "We control the helicopters."

Source: Jeremy D. Mayer, *9–11: The Giant Awakens.* Belmont, California: Wadsworth/ Thomson, 2003, p. 24.

The President Responds

On September 12, his first full day back in the White House, President Bush focused on defining the issue, rallying an international coalition and asserting his presence in the midst of the tragedy. He escalated his language, calling the attacks "more than acts of terror; they were acts of war," thus laying the foundation for military action. He was shown calling world leaders, meeting security advisors, and discussing with congressional leaders new defense spending. The House passed a resolution of support, and administration officials, led by Secretary of State Colin Powell, sent stern public messages to other countries—"You're either with us or against us."

As the week went on the president overcame his tentative first day. He did this in a way that only an individual chief of state could do: by personally connecting to the range of emotions most Americans felt, from sadness to anger. He comforted victims, thanked rescue workers at the Pentagon and at the World Trade Center site and reflected stunned feelings of outrage. On Thursday when he got off the phone after talking with New York Mayor Rudolph Giuliani, a *Boston Globe* reporter described him this way, "The president's eyes glistened and welled with emotion as he blinked to hold back tears. 'I'm a loving guy,' he said. 'And I'm also someone, however, who's got a job to do and I intend to do it. And this is a terrible moment.'"

A president's religious role as a "democratic priest-king" was also visible. The president declared Thursday a national "day of prayers and remembrance." His proclamation read, "In the face of all this evil, we remain strong and united, one nation under God." During a televised service at Washington Cathedral on September 14, Bush said, "The commitment of our fathers is now the calling of our time. We ask almighty God to watch over our nation and grant us patience and resolve in all that is to come."

He was also the commander in chief, rallying the country for what lay ahead. In that same cathedral service Bush talked tough, "This conflict was begun on the timing and terms of others; it will end in a way and at an hour of our choosing." Two days after the attack the president declared that "The nation must understand this is now the focus of my administration." He asked Congress to authorize the use of force against those responsible for September 11, while adding that he did not need prior approval to launch a military attack. Congress for its part easily passed $40 billion in emergency spending. By September 15 the president had approved an antiterrorist global strategy involving intelligence, finance, diplomacy and the military. The CIA became the lead agency in the planning to overthrow the Taliban government in Afghanistan for harboring the Al Qaeda terrorists.

In the coming days the president pointedly did not do certain things. He did not blame anyone in the government for allowing the attack.

Although the hijackings represented an enormous intelligence failure the president made clear his confidence in the CIA by meeting with its director. Bush also tried to separate the terrorists from the religion of Islam they claimed to represent. He publicly met with American Islamic leaders, declaring that the hijackers had nothing to do with the peaceful intentions of most Moslems. When professional baseball resumed, he went to the mound to throw out the first pitch. The president made clear that he didn't want the national agenda disrupted by terrorism. He emphasized that his education reform, "No Child Left Behind," remained a top domestic priority.

A Call to Arms

The climax of the country's initial response to the terrorist attack came in President Bush's speech to a joint session of Congress on September 20. Using the Capitol as the stage and Congress as his cheering chorus a president not known for rhetoric gave an inspiring speech. He issued an ultimatum to the Afghan leaders to turn over the Al Qaeda terrorists responsible for the attack, and called on the nation and world to unite to destroy terrorism. "Tonight we are a country awakened to danger and called to defend freedom. Our grief has turned to anger, and anger to resolution. Whether we bring our enemies to justice, or bring justice to our enemies, justice will be done."

He framed the challenge not as a mere policy difference but as a challenge to America's core values. "They hate our freedoms—our freedom of religion, our freedom of speech, our freedom to vote and assemble and disagree with each other. . . . We have seen their kind before. They are the heirs of all the murderous ideologies of the 20th century . . . they follow in the path of fascism, and Nazism and totalitarianism. And they will follow that path all the way, to where it ends: in history's unmarked grave of discarded lies."

And when Bush concluded "In our grief and anger, we have found our mission and our moment." He was speaking for more than a generation of Americans. He was speaking of his presidency.

WRAP-UP

This chapter has introduced the executive players in the political game—the president and the bureaucracy. We have seen how the presidency has irregularly but vastly grown in influence from a limited grant of constitutional powers, and we have looked at three different presidential styles as well as a psychological approach to a president's personality. The six major hats a president wears—chief of state, chief executive, chief diplomat, commander-in-chief, chief legislator, and party leader—show how broad and public his power has become. In the last century, government power has been centralized, in the federal government relative to the states, and in the presidency relative to the Congress.

The bureaucracy within the executive branch generally reinforces the president's power. Yet its size, its roles in policy making, its complexity and its rivalries—from the executive office to the cabinet departments, executive agencies, and regulatory commissions—limit the president's control over the bureaucracy. In the aftermath of the terrorist attacks we saw a president use the powers of his office to unify, defend, rally, emotionally identify with and set direction for a country stunned by a sudden and terrible blow.

The president as both an individual and an institution will continue to play a central role in the American political game. Often presidents have seemed ineffective in managing the bureaucracy and getting their programs acted on by Congress. Dissatisfaction with government has often focused on the personal flaws of individual presidents. Most of us still look for a presidential Moses to lead us out of a wilderness of domestic and foreign troubles. Which is part of the problem.

Presidents are political leaders. They hold a powerful office restrained by historical, political, and legal limits. They may mislead us by overpromising, and they may disappoint us when their policies fail. But we also play a part. If we expect them to be heroes or symbols, priests or kings, we are bound to be disappointed. We may have to cool our expectations of what presidents can do to protect our country and improve our lives. In that way we can, as citizens of a democracy, more realistically judge the leader of the executive branch of government.

Thought Questions

---

1. What are the major reasons for the growth in the power of the president? Do you think that candidates' anti-Washington speeches will limit this growth?
2. How can the president gain control over the rivalries and independence of the executive branch bureaucracy?
3. Do you think the president is too powerful or not powerful enough? Will a president's power expand in a crisis like a war? Should it?
4. Many people say that they prefer one party to control the presidency and another party to control Congress. How does this weaken or strengthen the president?

Suggested Readings

Cabbage, Michael, and William Harwood. *Comm Check . . . : The Final Flight of Shuttle Columbia,* New York: The Free Press, 2004.
An interesting case study of the Shuttle Columbia disaster and the bureaucratic problems that led to it.

Johnson, Haynes, and David S. Broder. *The System.* Boston: Little, Brown, 1997. Pb.
Two top political reporters expertly dissect what happened to Clinton's health reform proposals, with some striking conclusions about politics.

Klein, Joe. *The Natural: The Misunderstood Presidency of Bill Clinton.* New York: Doubleday, 2002. Pb.
A brief insightful analysis of our endlessly fascinating forty-second president by a leading political reporter.

Langston, Thomas S. *With Reverence and Contempt: How Americans Think About Their President.* Baltimore: Johns Hopkins University Press, 1995.
Spirited if pessimistic essays on the dilemmas facing a president, and the public who raise him to nearly religious heights.

Shambaugh, George E., and Paul J. Weinstein. *The Art of Policy Making,* New York: Longman, 2003. Pb.
A practical guide for students to how executive decision making works, based on the Clinton administration.

Suskind, Ron. *The Price of Loyalty.* New York: Simon & Schuster, 2004.
George Bush's former secretary of the Treasury Paul O'Neill uses this book to even some scores and express his worry about a chief executive indifferent to the details of administering the government.

Woodward, Bob. *Bush at War.* New York: Simon & Schuster, 2002. Pb.
An insider's view, with all the self-serving limits, of the president leading his team into Afghanistan and war.

————. *Plan of Attack,* New York: Simon & Schuster, 2004.
A balanced account of how President Bush planned and implemented the war in Iraq. Based on interviews with the leading administration figures.

The 9/11 Commission Report. New York: W. W. Norton & Company, 2004.
Overcoming administration resistance to its creation and completion, this independent bipartisan panel examines the facts surrounding the largest loss of life from an enemy attack on American soil, to produce a well-written account along with recommendations for reform.

CHAPTER 4

The Legislative Branch: Congress

The Constitution is clear: Congress is to be the center of the American political game. The framers' experience with King George III of England and his autocratic governors had left the framers suspicious of strong executive authority. As a result, the Constitution gives many detailed powers and responsibilities to the Congress but far fewer to the president.

Through its major function, lawmaking, Congress creates the rules that govern all the political players. Article I of the Constitution gives Congress the power to levy taxes, borrow money, raise armies, declare war, determine the nature of the federal judiciary, regulate commerce, coin money, and "make all Laws which shall be necessary and proper for carrying into Execution the foregoing powers, and all other Powers vested by this Constitution in the Government of the United States, or in any Department or Officer thereof."

The powers of Congress limit many of the powers given to the president. The president was named the commander-in-chief of the armed services, but he could not declare war or raise armies—only Congress could. The president was to be the chief administrative officer of the government, but there would be no government to administer if the Congress did not create it. He could appoint executive officials and negotiate foreign treaties only if the Senate agreed. Both the raising of money through taxes and the spending of it by the government required congressional legislation. Finally, as the country was recently reminded, Congress was given the power to impeach and even remove the president.

Through most of the nineteenth century, Congress was the major player in shaping the nation's policies. By the end of the nineteenth century, Woodrow Wilson could proclaim, "Congress is the dominant, nay, the irresistible power of the federal system." Wilson was later to change his mind, and, since the Great Depression and World War II, the executive branch generally increased in influence compared with Congress. (Of course, even during this long cycle of executive ascendancy there were weak presidents and assertive congresses.)

Now, with Republican majorities in the House and Senate (as well as the presidency and a majority in the Supreme Court appointed by Republican presidents), there is the opportunity/threat of centralized leadership of the federal government. By the very way they are organized, representative assemblies are dependent on executive leadership for tackling major issues from education to foreign policy. Yet the two parties remain evenly divided in public loyalties, and instead of civility and bipartisanship in Congress there is polarized politics. The legislature remains necessary to the political game, but not sufficient to shape the nation's politics on its own—exactly what the Constitution intended.

In this chapter we will examine the structure and activities of Congress, how it was designed to operate, and how it actually carries out its functions today.

MAKEUP OF THE SENATE AND HOUSE

The Congress of the United States is *bicameral,* made up of two houses: the Senate and the House of Representatives. The Senate consists of two senators from each state, regardless of the size of the state. House members are distributed according to population so that the larger the state's population, the more representatives it gets. The Constitution requires that each state, no matter how small it may be, have at least one representative. These provisions are the result of a political compromise between the small states and the large states during the writing of the Constitution.

As the country has grown, so too has the size of Congress. The first Congress consisted of 26 senators and 65 representatives. With each new state added to the Union, the Senate has grown by two, so that it now has 100 members. As the nation's population grew, the size of the House of Representatives grew also. In 1922 the Congress passed a law setting the maximum size of the House at 435 members, where it remains today. In the first House each member represented around 50,000 citizens. The average representative now serves over 647,000 constituents.

Role of the Legislator

There are many questions about the role of a legislator, questions as old as the idea of representative assemblies. Should representatives follow their own judgments about what is best or do only what their constituents wish ("re-present" them)? What should representatives do if the interests of their district conflict with the needs of the nation as a whole? Should legislators recognize a "greater good" beyond their district?

Members of Congress are both *national* and *local* representatives. They are national representatives who make up one branch of the national government, are paid by that federal government, and are required to support and defend the interests of the nation. However, they are chosen in local districts or states. In running for election, legislators must satisfy local constituents that they are looking out not only for the national interest but for local interests as well. In controversial areas, such as cutting the defense budget by closing military bases, the national interest may be very different from local popular opinion. In the impeachment vote of Bill Clinton in late 1998, many Republican congressmen said they were ignoring polls favoring acquittal to vote their consciences. Yet they can't forget a warning heard often in Congress: "You have to save your seat before you can save the world"—a reminder that usually gives their voters' opinions the upper hand.

Casework or helping constituents solve individual problems with the government is a vital part of what senators and congressmen do. Most of a member's staff spend their time not on legislation but on constituency service for local voters. Given the growing role of government in peoples' lives and the ease of contacting congressional offices, via e-mail and faxes, casework has increased. Casework can give people influence in an often impersonal bureaucracy. It certainly helps incumbents get reelected.

Casework includes assisting veterans in getting information about government programs for the disabled, or intervening with an agency so a surviving child can get an overdue Social Security benefit. These are not always the most earth-shaking concerns. One Georgia congressman tells a story about receiving a call from a constituent that her garbage hadn't been picked up. The congressman asked her why she hadn't called the director of the Department of Sanitation. "Well, Congressman," she replied, "quite frankly, I didn't want to go up that high." (See "The Image of Congress.")

Who Are the Legislators?

Members of the House of Representatives must be at least 25 years old, citizens of the United States for seven years, and residents of the state in which they are elected. Senators must be 30 years old, citizens for nine years, and residents of the state that elects them. State residency is a fairly loose requirement. Hillary Clinton won a senate seat from New York in 2000 despite never living in the state before. Other states, like Arizona, have a five-year residency requirement to run for office.

Senators serve six-year terms and are elected by the entire state's population. Every two years, during national elections, one-third of the Senate seeks reelection. The other senators do not run because they are only one-third or two-thirds of the way through their terms.

The Constitution originally provided that members of the Senate would be elected by their state legislatures. This was done to remove the choice from the masses of citizens and ensure that more conservative elements would pick the senators. The Seventeenth Amendment changed this in 1913, and senators now are elected by the voters of their state.

Members of the House of Representatives (called *representatives* or *congressmen/women*) serve two years. They are elected from

The Image of Congress

Congress's lousy image is not new. In the nineteenth century Mark Twain remarked that "there is no distinctly native American criminal class except Congress." At best the public today sees Congress as slow, chaotic, and unresponsive to national needs. At worse Congress is a place of plotting, partisan rivalry, and scandal. Part of this image is because Congress is doing what the framers intended—slowing down the policy process to debate the issues of the day. The media darkens this image by finding the misdeeds of a few members easier to report than complicated legislation. As the respected reporter, David Broder said, "Scandals in Congress even of a petty nature are easier to sell to most editors than the stories of larger consequences."

Curiously most congressmen may not care about the image of their institution, they may even worsen it. There's a long tradition of members running *for* Congress by running *against* Congress. By pandering to the public's negative views of Congress, members can present themselves as lonely fighters against a corrupt legislature. The result is that people dislike Congress but reelect their own congressmen, over and over.

congressional districts within the states. No congressional district ever crosses state borders.

Congress is composed overwhelmingly of white males, and it tends to reflect the values of upper-middle-class America. Almost half the members of Congress are lawyers. Other common professions are business, banking, education, farming, and journalism. Women and blacks are underrepresented in Congress for many reasons, including the selection of candidates by party organizations and voter apathy. The 1992 elections, however, brought more women and minority group members into Congress than any previous election in American history. The 1994 congressional elections, sometimes referred to as "the year of the angry white male," leveled off this trend. Recent elections have resulted in the largest number of women in Congress in American history. (See "The 109th Congress.")

Careerism—the tendency for legislators to see service in Congress as a lifetime career—still exists. Tradition holds that the leadership in both houses consist of the most senior members. Although recent Republican speakers of the House drew attention by occasionally breaking with the seniority tradition in the appointment of committee chairs, the present House chairmen average more than

The 109th Congress

The 2004 elections cemented Republican control over the new 109th Congress. In the House the GOP increased its majority from 227 to 232 (with 202 Democrats and one independent from Vermont, Bernie Sanders). Most of these came from the defeat of five veteran Democrats from Texas who were gerrymandered out of their seats—and forced to run in unfriendly districts—by Republican leaders in the state. Redistricting plans drawn up by Republican legislatures throughout the country have likely made their party's majority in the House safe for the rest of this decade. The Democrats had now failed to gain control of the House for six straight elections.

The Senate also moved in a more conservative direction. The Democrats' minority leader, Tom Daschle, was defeated and five moderate Southern Democrats who retired were all replaced by committed Republican conservatives, giving the GOP 55 senate seats. There were only four Democratic senators left in the South, a drastic turnaround from when Democrats dominated that region. The 'individualistic' Senate which historically could be counted on to restrain the impulses of the rest of the government now seemed eager to follow the White House agenda.

The new congress was also more diverse, with more women, Hispanics and blacks. The House of Representatives had 65 women—23 Republicans and 42 Democrats—up from 59. The Senate added two Hispanics and one black, up from zero of both. This was the third black American elected to the Senate in 125 years, the first Cuban-born senator, and the first Hispanic-American in the Senate in nearly 30 years. The Senate kept its record high of 13 women. And House Democrats kept Californian Nancy Pelosi as their minority leader, which continued her as the first woman in American history to lead a political party in either house.

18 years of service. House Republicans have placed limits on the number of consecutive terms members can serve as committee chair and in leadership positions. The current unpopularity of *incumbents* has led many of the new members of Congress—calling themselves "citizen legislators"—to vow to stay in office for only a few terms. Some have broken that promise.

It does seem ironic that although high-level executive branch administrators and members of the judiciary may be appointed from outside fields, it's a lifetime career to become a leader in a representative assembly. The problem with careerism is that, although it may guarantee loyalty to their institution, it also may separate members from a changing society.

As popular disgust for entrenched government grew, proposals for *term limits* on members of Congress gained support. Twenty-three states adopted measures to limit the number of times their congressmen and senators could run for reelection. Congress tried to join in by voting on several different constitutional amendments that would restrict members to 6 or 12 years in office. They all failed.

Even more damaging for supporters of term limits was a 1995 Supreme Court ruling (*U.S. Term Limits* v. *Thornton*) that threw out term limits imposed by the states. The Court held that states could not restrict who could run for federal offices without an amendment to the Constitution. Support has cooled toward the idea, even among Republicans. As one supporter, former Senator Dan Coats of Indiana, said about the chances of Congress voting for such an amendment, "I don't think there's any way to get two-thirds of the people in this place who are willing to say good-bye to their jobs."

Malapportionment and Reapportionment

The drawing of House districts is up to the state governors and legislatures, who often use these powers to boost their own party and penalize the party that is out of power. In the past, *malapportionment* (large differences in the populations of congressional districts) was common in many areas of the country. Districts would be drawn up so that minority-party districts included more voters than majority-party districts. In this way, each minority-party voter would count for less. In 1960, Michigan's 16th district had 802,994 people, whereas the 12th had only 177,431. Both elected just one representative.

In addition, the art of *gerrymandering* was practiced. The name comes from Massachusetts Governor Elbridge Gerry, who in 1812 helped to draw a long, misshapen district composed of a string of towns north of Boston. When painter Gilbert Stuart saw a drawing of the oddly shaped district, he penciled in claws, wings, and a head and said, "That will do for a salamander!" His editor replied, "Better say a gerrymander." The two most common forms of gerrymandering are "packing" and "cracking." *Packing* involves drawing up a district so that it has a large majority of supporters, to ensure a "safe" seat. *Cracking* means splitting up opponents' supporters into minorities in a number of districts to weaken their influence.

Such practices have long been attacked by reformers. In 1962 a Supreme Court decision (*Baker* v. *Carr*) held that legislative districts must be as close to equal in population as possible. Many of the worst abuses of malapportionment were ended by this and later Court decisions. But politics remains vital to the drawing of districts, as can be seen in the conflicts caused by the latest census.

At the beginning of each decade the Census Bureau counts the nation's population, and the House of Representatives is reapportioned to reflect the change in each state's population. In recent counts the population has not only grown but has shifted toward the South and West of the country. This trend continued with the 2000 census. Because the number of seats in the House is limited by law to 435, states in the northeast lost seats while the so-called Sunbelt gained congressional members. Florida, Georgia, Arizona, and Texas gained two congressional seats, while New York and Pennsylvania lost two apiece. Several midwestern and northern states lost one each, while a number of southern and southwestern states gained one. (See Figure 4.1.)

The redistricting following the 2000 census was as partisan as ever with each party seeking an advantage in the states they controlled. Overall the Republicans were considered the winners with a seven-seat gain in the House resulting from redistricting, according to some

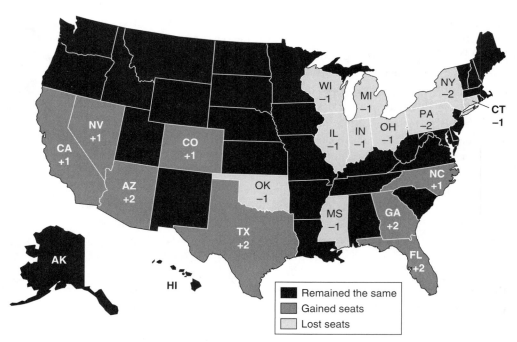

FIGURE 4.1
State Gaining and Losing Congressional Seats following the 2000 Census.
Source: U.S. Bureau of the Census, "News release," December 28, 2000

experts. However the key result from this recent redistricting was to solidify incumbents. These incumbents looked after their own interests rather than those of their party. House races were made less competitive and more immune to change. In New Jersey in 2002, only one of 13 congressional races was won with less than 60 percent of the vote; in California, all but four of the 53 Republican and Democratic winners took at least 60 percent of the vote.

The House of Representatives which the Constitution designed to be the part of the national government closest to the people, has become the most insulated from election. (Senate races can not be manipulated by redistricting.) This gerrymandering produces more partisan politics by cementing one-party districts dominated by the extreme wings of both parties. It also discourages voter interest and, not surprisingly, low turnout. As Professor Tom Patterson has written, the framers' design has been stood on its head, with House races now the least competitive, with the lowest turnover rate of any freely elected national legislature. (See "The Incumbent Protection Racket.")

The Incumbent Protection Racket

During elections to Congress, the advantages of incumbency (being currently in office) are considerable. Incumbents have wide name recognition, and by issuing "official" statements, they can get free publicity that their opponents would have to pay for. Members of the House have office and staff budgets of approximately $350,000 a year; senators are given at least that and often considerably more if their states are large. Both receive 32 government-paid round trips to their districts each year. Facilities for making television or radio tapes are available in Washington at a low cost. And there is the *frank*, the privilege of free official mailing enjoyed by Congress, under which 200,000,000 pieces of mail, much of it quite partisan, are sent free every year. The local press joins the parade by generally treating incumbents like hometown heroes.

Adding to the advantages of House incumbents is reapportionment. By literally changing the shape of the playing field, the House maximized the number of districts favorable to incumbents. Coupled with the usually low voter turnout in congressional races and the one-party dominance of most congressional districts, it is no wonder that incumbents win bigtime. This "incumbent-protection racket" resulted in 2002 in only four challengers defeating incumbents in the House— the fewest in history. In 2004 five challengers won.

Organization of the House of Representatives

Congress is organized around its parties. The *majority party* in each house is the one with the greatest number of members. The majority party chooses the major officers of that branch of Congress, controls debate on the floor, selects all committee chairs, and has a majority on all committees. Until 1994 the Democrats had controlled both houses of Congress for 40 years, except for the years 1980–1986 when the Republicans ran the Senate. Since 1994 the Republicans have been the majority in both houses, with a brief 18-month interim from June 2001 to January 2003 when the Democrats took back the Senate after a Republican senator left his party.

In the House of Representatives, the majority party, the Republicans, chooses the *speaker of the House* from among its members. He does not have to be the oldest or longest-serving member, but he will certainly be well respected and is likely to have served in other party posts. During some periods, such as 1890 to 1910, the speaker exercised almost dictatorial powers. The speaker still retains power through his control over the majority party. He influences how the committee system operates, including who becomes committee chairman.

The selection of the speaker takes place every two years, at the beginning of Congress. The majority party votes for its leader in its party caucus, and then he becomes their candidate for speaker voted on by the entire House. Since this is one time when party discipline must hold, the leader of the majority becomes the speaker.

In 1994 Newt Gingrich of Georgia became the first Republican speaker of the House since 1954. He led the Republican majority toward achieving a national "mandate for change" to shrink the federal government. Believing that the best place to start this process was within Congress itself, he ushered in many rule changes, cutting staffs, eliminating committees, strengthening party control, and increasing the power of the speaker. Within a few years, the limits of a speaker's powers became more apparent. When Republicans lost five seats in the House in the 1998 elections, after Gingrich had predicted a gain, he was pushed into resigning. Dennis Hastert, from Illinois, emerged as speaker in 1999, pledging more power to committee chairmen and a low-profile tenure in office. Though he began by seeking cooperation with Democrats, in recent congresses as the Republican majority increased, Hastert became a more assertive and partisan speaker. (See "Speaker Dennis Hastert, Coach.")

The *caucus* of each political party in the House or Senate is simply a gathering of all the members of that party serving there. (A "caucus" may also refer to organized groups in Congress such as the farm bloc,

Speaker Dennis Hastert, Coach

When first taking over as speaker from Newt Gingrich in 1998, J. Dennis Hastert of Illinois was reluctant to dictate direction to his party. As a winning high school wrestling coach, he followed the symbolism of his former profession. He saw his job as getting his "team" to pull together, saying, "The job of a coach is to bring others along, and let them be the stars."

Hastert's low-key approach worked better than most predicted. In the 2000 election he helped maintain the Republican majority in the House. While avoiding a high-profile national media role in the election, he made an estimated 655 campaign appearances in 126 House districts and raised more than $40 million for the GOP. In the 2004 election Hastert took on an unusually partisan role for a House Speaker. Beyond raising money, he was described as a pit bull in defending the president and attacking the Kerry campaign.

blacks, women, and Hispanics.) The Republican majority caucus in the House is referred to as the Republican *Conference.* The conference chooses a *majority leader* who is second in command to the speaker. The majority leader works closely with the speaker and schedules legislation for debate on the House floor. Republican Tom DeLay of Texas is majority leader, and is nicknamed "The Hammer" because of his strong right-wing views and an influence that rivals the speaker's.

The speaker and majority leader are assisted by *majority whips.* (The word *whip* comes from English fox hunting, where the "whipper-in" keeps the dogs from running away.) The whips help coordinate party positions on legislation, pass information and directions between the leadership and party members, make sure party members know when a particular vote is coming, try to persuade wavering representatives to vote with the leadership, and conduct informal surveys to check the likely outcome of votes. Being at the center of the congressional process, these party leaders possess more information than other legislators, which adds to their power.

The minority party in the House, currently the Democrats, select in their caucus a *minority leader* and *minority whips.* Like the majority party's leader and whips, their duties are to coordinate party positions. Minority leaders are usually their party's candidate for speaker should it become the majority party. Nancy Pelosi of San Francisco is the Democrats' minority leader. Selected in 2002 following Democratic election defeats, she is the first woman to have a leadership position in either house of Congress.

The Democratic and Republican caucuses in the House run their affairs in slightly different ways. The Republican party chooses a *Steering Committee* to function as an executive committee of the caucus. The Steering Committee helps chart party policy in the House, and assigns Republican members to committees. It also is the key body that appoints committee chairs, who must be approved by the Republican Conference. The Democrats' Steering Committee is divided into two. The *Steering Panel* nominates committee members and ranking minority members, and the *Policy Committee* studies issues, writes bills, and publicizes them. After 1994, the Steering Panel had to adjust to the Democrats no longer controlling committees and was forced to remove members from many committees.

Organization of the Senate

The Senate has no speaker. The *president of the Senate* is the vice president of the United States. He has the right to preside over the Senate chamber, which he does only on significant votes. He is allowed to vote in case of a tie. In the period from January to June 2001 when there was a 50–50 party split in the Senate, the vice president's vote was of unusual importance—it determined the majority party.

The honorary post of president *pro tem* (from *pro tempore,* meaning "for the time being") of the Senate is given to the senator from the majority party who has served longest in the Senate—currently Republican Ted Stevens of Alaska, a senator since 1969. His only power is to preside in the absence of the vice president, but he hardly ever does so. Because the vast majority of Senate work takes place in committees, the job of presiding over a Senate chamber that may be dull and nearly vacant usually falls to a junior senator, who is asked to do so by the Senate majority leader.

The *Senate majority leader* is the closest position to the speaker of the House. However, because the Senate is smaller and not tightly organized, the majority leader has less control over the Senate than the speaker has over the House. The majority leader schedules debate on the Senate floor, assigns bills to committees, coordinates party policy, and appoints members of *special committees*. Dr. Bill Frist, senator from Tennessee and former heart surgeon, became majority leader in 2003. Frist, a strong supporter of President Bush, took over for Trent Lott of Mississippi, who was pressured to resign after making remarks that were widely denounced as racist.

The Republicans regained their position as the Senate's majority party when they picked up two seats in the 2002 election. They had lost their majority a year before when one Republican senator announced that he would leave his party to become an independent. The GOP had barely kept its position as the majority party after the 2000 election when an exact 50–50 split between Republicans and Democrats was broken by the vote of the vice president. The chairmen of all senate committees are now Republican. Both the majority and minority leaders are assisted by a whip and assistant whips who coordinate party positions and floor strategy. The minority leader is now Harry Reid, Democrat of Nevada.

In the Senate the Republicans have a *Committee on Committees,* which assigns members to committees, and a *Policy Committee,* which charts legislative tactics. The party caucus, called the *Republican Conference,* consists of all Republicans in the Senate. Each of these groups is chaired by a leading Republican senator. Senate Democrats are organized in much the same way. A *Steering Committee* assigns members to committees and a *Policy Committee* coordinates strategy. Unlike the Republican organizations, the Senate Democratic leader chairs the Democratic caucus (called the *Democratic Conference*), the Steering Committee, and the Policy Committee.

HOW CONGRESS WORKS

Either the House or the Senate, or both houses at the same time, may introduce legislation. The only exceptions to this rule are money-raising bills, which according to the Constitution must originate in the House, and appropriations (spending) bills, which by custom also begin there. Approximately 20,000 bills are introduced in Congress each year. (See Figure 4.2.) They may be part of the president's program, they may be drafted by individual members or by committees, or they may be the result of alliances between Congress and the executive bureaucracy or lobbyists. Only 5 percent of these bills become law.

With Republicans in control of the executive branch, the Senate and the House of Representatives, the GOP (for *Grand Old Party,* as the Republicans are sometimes called) can give priority to its legislation. However, the Senate and House act separately and may amend

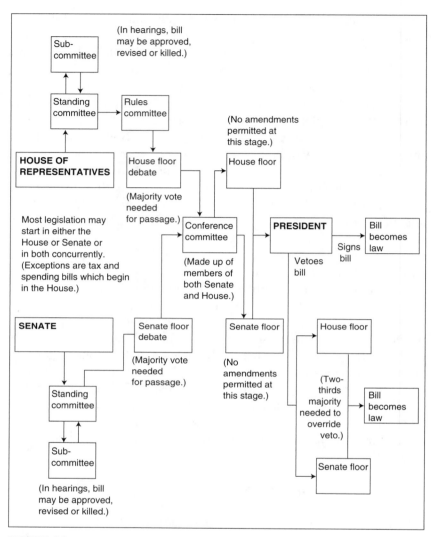

FIGURE 4.2
How a Bill (Rarely) Becomes a Law.

or revise bills as they see fit. For any bill to become law, it must ultimately be passed by both houses of Congress in identical language and approved by the president or passed over his veto.

The Congress operates by division of labor. Most of the work of Congress goes on not on the House or Senate floor, but in committees. House committees may have anywhere from 20 to 50 representatives; Senate committees usually have 10 to 20 senators. If they did not separate into committees, the Senate and House would move even more slowly and deal with far fewer issues because they could consider only one subject at a time. It is difficult to imagine Congress without the committee system.

When a piece of legislation is introduced in either the Senate or the House, it is assigned to a committee. The committee (or, often, one of its subcommittees) reviews the bill and decides whether to recommend it to the whole House or Senate. Between 80 and 90 percent of the bills introduced in Congress die in committee. Because the committee system is central to Congress, a discussion of its operation begins there.

THE COMMITTEE SYSTEM

Congress in session is Congress on exhibition, whilst Congress in its committee rooms is Congress at work.
—Woodrow Wilson

The *Washington Post* reported that on the last week of April 2004, the House of Representatives was in session for two days and one night, an average workweek. On one day they renamed a post office in Rhode Island, and supported "Financial Literacy Month." On another they renamed a Miami courthouse and extended the popular repeal of the tax code's "marriage penalty." That same week, 35 U.S. servicemen died in Iraq and CBS showed shocking pictures of Americans abusing Iraqi prisoners.

In fairness, the floor of the House isn't the whole story. Floor sessions are often little more than a formality designed to make a public record. At the same time, many of the committee rooms would be filled with activity.

How Committees Work

There are four types of committees in Congress: standing, conference, select, and joint. *Standing committees* are the basic working units of Congress. They were started early in the nation's history because Congress found it could do more work faster if it broke down into smaller, specialized groups. There are 19 standing committees in the House and 17 in the Senate, most focusing on one or two general subjects. Representatives serve on one or two standing committees, senators on three or four. Usually these committees break down into subcommittees for a further division of labor. In the 108th Congress, the House had 88 subcommittees and the Senate had 68. This is a dramatic reduction from the number of subcommittees in the last fully Democratic Congress, the

103rd, with 147 in the House and 87 in the Senate.

Before any bill can be sent to the floor for consideration by the entire Senate or House, it must be approved by a majority vote in the standing committee to which it is assigned. A committee's examination of a proposed bill may include holding public hearings in which interested parties, including the executive bureaucracies and lobbyists, are invited to testify. Often the actual work on a bill assigned to a standing committee goes on in one of its subcommittees. If the full committee then approves the bill, it will be sent to the floor of the Senate or House with a report describing the committee's findings and the reasons the committee thinks the bill should be passed. If the bill is not supported by the committee, it will be killed. The bill's sponsors may resubmit it in a later Congress, but if the committee involved continues to reject it, it will fail again.

A *conference committee* is a temporary body including both senators and representatives, created solely to iron out the differences between House and Senate versions of one bill. These differences come about because of amendments attached to the bill by one chamber but not the other, or because the two houses have passed different bills dealing with the same subject. Before a bill can be sent to the president for his action, it must be passed in identical language by both houses.

The speaker of the House and the Senate majority leader have the authority to appoint the members of conference committees. However, in practice they allow the chairs of the relevant standing committees to do this and typically appoint the senior members of these committees. The conference committee engages in bargaining and trade-offs to reach a compromise; once this job is finished, it is disbanded. When (and if) the conference committee reaches agreement, the new substitute bill is then sent back to the House and Senate floors for approval or disapproval. This bill cannot be amended; it must be accepted or rejected as is. If this rule were not in force the bill might be amended again in different ways in the House and Senate, thereby requiring another conference committee, and so on.

Select or *special committees* are temporary panels set up to do specific jobs and usually dissolved after the two-year congressional term. Typically select committees do not have legislative authority and can only study, investigate, and recommend. For example the Senate Special Committee on Whitewater was set up to investigate the Clintons' Arkansas real estate dealings.

Joint committees are permanent bodies including both senators and representatives, usually set up to coordinate policy on routine matters. There are currently two joint committees: one handles the Library of Congress and one is the more important Joint Economic Committee, which reports on the president's annual economic report. The jealousy of the two branches over their separate powers makes joint committees rare.

Committee Chairmen and the Seniority System

By the unwritten rule of *seniority,* the chair of any committee is typically the majority-party member who has served longest (consecutively) on the committee. While the current congressional leadership often follows seniority, acceptance of the party's legislative agenda is also part of the job requirements for any committee chairman.

The important power of committee chairmen was apparent in 2003 when the Republicans again became the majority party in the Senate, allowing them to have a majority on each committee and to appoint all the chairmen. Usually this would mean control of the Senate agenda—the issues it would consider and those it would ignore. But a Republican in the White House limited Senate actions. For example, Senate Foreign Relations Committee Chairman Richard Lugar believed the administration's policies in Iraq were flawed. Yet this respected foreign policy expert never held hearings on Iraq policies. One party's control of both the presidency and congress meant there was little legislative oversight of controversial foreign policies.

Chairmen influence the hiring of majority-party staff, schedule committee meetings and agenda, and have something to say about the appointment of new members to their committees. Chairmen usually can kill legislation they oppose. Even when a majority of committee members supports legislation, the chairman can refuse to schedule a bill for hearings. That stops a bill from moving forward. A chairman's blocking power is stronger in the House than in the Senate.

The tradition of seniority is not written down in the rules of the House or Senate, and yet for most of the twentieth century the custom was almost never broken. Then, starting in the mid-1970s, things changed. A combination of scandals and the desire of the growing number of junior Democrats for a "piece of the action," led to several committee chairs being ousted and an increase in the power of the party caucus.

When the Republicans took power in the House in 1994, party leadership was strengthened at the expense of the committees. The House Republican Conference imposed six-year term limits on chairmen, leading to some early retirements by committee chairs in 2000. In the present Congress the Republican leaders—House Speaker Hastert and Majority Leader DeLay have centralized power and rewarded loyal allies with important chairmanships. The House Republican leaders make the decisions on chairmen with some weight given to seniority. Loyalty to the party and the White House is critical to winning the approval of the House Republican leadership.

While the Republican party leadership in the Senate exercises control over committees, it nearly always defers to the seniority rankings in determining who heads a committee or subcommittee.

The seniority system (on occasion mocked as the *senility system*) lives on in the House and, even more, in the Senate. Attacked as undemocratic, it has allowed members who are reelected to accumulate national power. It also has allowed minorities in the Democratic party and moderate Republicans to gain positions of power. Seniority ensures that an experienced person will become chairman, and has provided a predictable system of succession without constant fights over control of the chair. But party leaders of Congress no longer feel the need to automatically follow a custom that limits their own influence.

Specialization and Reciprocity

Though weakened, two other informal rules, support the power of committees in Congress. The first, *specialization,* is closely related to the second, *reciprocity.* Specialization means that once assigned to a committee or subcommittee, a member of Congress is expected to specialize in its work and become expert in that area. Particularly in the House, members are not expected to follow all legislation in Congress equally, or to speak out on widely varying issues. The result of this system is that committees and their individual members become experts in their own work but may not know much about other areas.

This potential problem is resolved through the practice of reciprocity. Here members look for guidance in voting on legislation outside their committee's field to members of committees that do specialize in it. Legislators tend to vote the way their party's representatives on the most closely concerned committee tell them to vote, because that committee knows most about the legislation and because the members want the same support when their committee's business is involved. Specialization and reciprocity, then, are two sides of the same coin. You develop expertise in an area and other members follow your lead in that area. You, in turn, follow the lead of others more knowledgeable than you in areas outside your expertise.

Recently greater party control of the legislative agenda has reduced the ability of the committees to take the lead in their fields. Still, the two general practices operate, if somewhat diluted, both in the Senate and the House. Because senators commonly serve on three or four committees, their areas of specialization are more varied and less intense.

Assignment to a committee or subcommittee are vital to a legislator's power. These patterns of influence tend to keep committees stable and discourage "hopping" from one to another. Once members of Congress have been assigned to a committee, they will not be removed against their wishes unless the ratio between the parties should shift, including a change in the majority party as happened when the Republicans won control of the Senate in the 2002 elections.

Floor Debate in the House and Senate

Once it has been approved by committee (and in the House by the Rules Committee), a bill is sent to the House or Senate floor for debate. There it is placed on a calendar. *Calendars* are the business agendas or schedules in Congress. Certain calendars are for routine or minor legislation, others for more important bills, and one in the House, the "discharge calendar," can be used to try to force a bill out of committee against the committee's wishes. The campaign reform bill was a rare successful example of the use of a discharge. (See Case Study, "Campaign Finance Reform," p. 115.)

In the House, floor debate is controlled by the Speaker. He schedules bills for consideration and then makes sure the committees deliver their bills in the correct form and at the right time. He has the right to preside over debate. House members are commonly restricted to a few minutes of talk each. The Senate, being smaller, is able to operate more informally and senators can speak longer. Power is more widely distributed in the Senate than in the House. Even junior (new) senators often chair subcommittees. The Senate majority leader schedules bills for debate, but his control during debate is much less than the House speaker.

When debate on a bill has ended, it is put to a vote. A majority of the legislators present is needed for passage. Whether a bill begins in the Senate or the House, it must sooner or later be submitted to the other chamber, where the whole procedure of committee review and floor action will be repeated. Then, any differences between the House and Senate versions of a bill must be eliminated before it can be sent to the president for his signature or veto.

Both in committees and on the floor of Congress, members of the same political party do not always vote together. In the fights over the North American Free Trade Agreement (NAFTA), which President Clinton strongly supported, most Republicans were behind the measure, and the Democrats were divided, with most opposing it. Regional coalitions of Republicans and Democrats have united to prevent the closing of local military bases.

More often, especially with the more unified Republican party, President Bush got almost total support from his party for his tax reform measures as well as his foreign policy positions. The Democrats generally voted against the president's tax cuts and energy proposals, and were divided over his aggressive stance toward Iraq. But most Democrats supported his education bill that paralleled many of their party's proposals. The most frequent division in Congress remains that between Republicans and Democrats. (See Table 4.1.)

In recent Congresses, party loyalty has increased in both parties. The majority of the two parties oppose each other more often. Members now vote with their party about 80 percent of the time, whereas 25 years ago loyalty was only seen in 70 percent of the votes. The parties are more united and more different. As the Democratic party continues to lose its more conservative members from the South, and as the number of conservative Republicans has increased, the parties have become more polarized—there are now fewer liberal Republi-

TABLE 4.1   MAJOR DIFFERENCES BETWEEN THE HOUSE AND THE SENATE

HOUSE	SENATE
Larger (435)	Smaller (100)
Shorter term of office (2 years)	Longer term of office (6 years)
More procedural restraints on members	Fewer procedural restraints on members
Narrower constituency	Broader, more varied constituency
Policy specialists	Policy generalists
Less media coverage	More media coverage
More powerful leader	Less powerful leaders
Less prestigious	More prestigious
Briefer floor debates	Longer floor debates
Less reliant on staff	More reliant on staff
More partisan	Less partisan

Nastiness on Capitol Hill

Thomas Jefferson recognized the importance of polite behavior in the legislature. He hoped the Senate would cool the passions of the more populist House and outlined rules to reduce personal attacks. Jefferson saw no reason that partisanship should undercut civility among legislators. But with Clinton's impeachment in late 1998, followed by the election crisis of 2000, Congress has become increasingly nasty. By 2004, the Senate floor witnessed Vice President Cheney grunting an obscene command to a Democratic senator to contort himself into an impossible sexual position. (As in "Go F—k Yourself.")

The House seemed worse with Democrats and Republicans barely talking to each other, but the Senate wasn't far behind. The Republican Chairman of the House Ways and Means Committee evicted Democrats from a library where they were meeting, leading to a round of accusations. A Senate Democrat denounced the Republican majority as the most "amateur leadership" he had seen in his 21 years in Congress. And the polarized politics on the Hill led to the decline of a bipartisan middle that might bridge the social and political distance between the parties. One leading political scientist, Burdett Loomis remarked that this partisanship hurt good policy making, "There seems to be almost no shame. Everyone is just completely righteous right now."

Source: New York Times, November 30, 2003.

cans, fewer conservative Democrats, and fewer moderates in both parties. As a result, recent Congresses have become harsher and more partisan. (See "Nastiness on Capitol Hill.")

This change in the parties has left Congress with fewer mavericks. *Mavericks* are members who show less loyalty to their party and do not abide by the informal rules. Usually mavericks represent constituencies that are not like the typical voters of their party: for example, conservative Democrats from Republican-leaning districts or liberal Republicans from Democratic-leaning states. Mavericks may be popular in their home state and in national opinion that is more moderate than the parties. But mavericks are less popular with their party leadership—as shown by Republican Senator John McCain, who frequently butted heads with the Bush administration. Former Speaker Sam Rayburn was fond of saying to new members of Congress, "To get along you've got to go along."

Filibuster

In the Senate, except under very unusual circumstances, debate is unlimited. Senators may talk on a subject for as long as they wish, and they will not be cut off. Never-ending talk by one or a number of senators designed to delay or block action in the Senate is called a *filibuster.* The original filibuster was a type of pirate ship. Its current meaning probably comes from the image of a lone individual defying the rules. Senators engaged in a filibuster usually talk for several hours at a time (sometimes reading the Bible or the Washington phone directory) before giving up the floor to an ally. Former Senator Strom Thurmond of South Carolina set the individual filibuster record in 1957 by speaking against a civil rights act for 24 hours and 18 minutes nonstop. (See "A National Town Meeting?")

Rule 22 (of the Senate Rules—a set of regulations governing Senate behavior) protects the filibuster unless three-fifths of the Senate votes for an end to debate. This is the only vote in Congress based on the total number of legislators. All other votes in both the Senate and House are based on the number of members who are present and voting. Voting to end debate is called *cloture.* Because many senators, especially those of the minority party, see advantages in having the option of a filibuster available, cloture is rarely successful.

Filibusters are most effective late in a session of the Senate when legislation has piled up. Senators are eager to adjourn, and they feel

A National Town Meeting?

The Cable Special Public Affairs Network (C-SPAN), which started on the air in 1979, expanded as the public's apparent appetite for raw, unedited views of government in action grew. Beginning with the House, C-SPAN later added coverage of the Senate in 1986. The federally supported C-SPAN televises uninterrupted coverage of the proceedings of both bodies on the floor and in committee. It also broadcasts other public interest events and viewer call-in interviews with public figures. Starting with less than a million dollars, C-SPAN grew to a $20 million operation that is carried by cable systems serving 60 million households. The initial fear that members would grandstand in front of the camera gave way to an appreciation among members of Congress of the value of free TV exposure for incumbents' reelection hopes.

the pressures of any delaying tactic. If 60 senators cannot be found to invoke cloture, a compromise is likely. The minority party frequently uses the threat of a filibuster to prevent majority actions. Democrats were heard bragging after the 2002 and 2004 elections that they could still stop the Republican majority because the GOP lacked 60 votes in the Senate. And there was a notable slowdown in legislation, including a mammoth energy bill, that easily passed the House and then stalled in the Senate. The House, being larger and harder to manage, has decided it cannot afford the luxury of unlimited debate. Hence, filibusters are not allowed in the House.

Presidential Veto

Even after it has been approved by both the House and Senate, a bill may still be killed by a presidential veto. The president may veto any legislation he wishes. The threat of a veto allows a president to bargain with congressional leaders while legislation is still being drafted.

A president may not veto only part of a bill. He must veto it all or accept it all. But of course, Congress has the last word: If Congress *overrides* a veto, the bill becomes law. To override a veto requires two-thirds approval of each house of Congress. Vetoes are rarely overridden. But lately they have been rarely issued—witness President Bush's zero vetoes.

The president must act on a bill within ten working days. If he does not sign it within that period while Congress remains in session, the bill becomes law without his signature. If Congress adjourns before the ten days are up and the president does not sign the bill, it does not become law—this is called a *pocket veto.*

Because the item veto was declared unconstitutional by the Supreme Court in 1998, Congress retains the advantage of *riders* in any confrontation with the president. A rider is a piece of legislation attached as an amendment to another bill, which may deal with a totally different issue. Commonly, the rider contains provisions that the president does not like, whereas the "parent" bill to which the rider is attached is favored by the president. Either he vetoes the rider he does not like and thus also the main bill that he wants, or he accepts the unwanted rider in order to get the rest of the bill. These riders helped increase government spending, and for this reason many Republicans supported the item veto, even for a Democratic president. (See "The White House Trades for China Trade.")

Finally, passing legislation does not automatically make anything happen. If money is needed for the government's wishes (as expressed in a bill) to be carried out, the entire legislative process

The White House Trades for China Trade

To get congressmembers to agree with the White House often requires appealing to the interests of their district. In 2000 a bill to allow free trade with China came before Congress. It was strongly backed by the Clinton administration and eventually passed both houses. But before that could happen the White House had to offer local deals for this national issue.

House Democrats, who generally opposed the trade agreement, were swayed by other considerations. Democrat Robert E. "Bud" Cramer voted "yes" after the Commerce Department promised to reconsider closing a weather station in his tornado-prone Alabama district. Martin Frost, a Texas Democrat, supported the bill when Northrop Grumman Corp., a major defense contractor, decided to stay in Dallas after reaching an agreement with the Navy. And three other Texas congressmen supported the administration when EPA promised to quickly complete its required environmental review that was holding up the opening of a gas pipeline across southern Texas.

Source: CQ Weekly, May 27, 2000, p. 1250.

must be gone through *twice*—once to pass a bill authorizing the activity, and a second time to pass a bill appropriating the money to do it. The goals of the authorizing bill will not come into effect if the appropriations process does not provide the funds. And that brings us to the budget process.

The Budget Process

The "power of the purse" is a basic constitutional power of Congress. Historically, the *authority* to control government spending and taxes has not meant the *ability* to control them. Congress has traditionally not acted coherently on the budget. The numerous committees and decentralized power bases in Congress has meant that overall spending (expenditures) was seldom related to taxes (revenues), and neither fit into a national economic policy. The responsibility for putting together a comprehensive government budget and national economic policy thus fell to the president. For the last 30 years, Congress has struggled to change this.

In 1974 Congress passed the Budget Act (the Congressional Budget and Impoundment Control Act) which allowed Congress to propose an alternative to the president's budget. Congress could now examine

all spending and tax measures, and evaluate them in terms of the overall needs of the economy. The Budget Act did this in several ways.

The act set up House and Senate Budget Committees. The House Budget Committee members are drawn mainly from the Ways and Means and Appropriations committees, with one member from each of the other standing committees. Members and the chair are rotated periodically without regard to seniority. Members of the Senate Budget Committee are selected in the same way as members of other committees in the Senate. The committees guide the Congress in setting total spending, tax, and debt levels. Aiding the two budget committees is a *Congressional Budget Office (CBO)*. The nonpartisan CBO's experts analyze the president's budget proposals and match Congress's spending decisions with the budget targets.

The budget works its way through Congress on a series of deadlines. The goal is to have a completed budget by the beginning of the government's fiscal year, October 1. The process starts when the president submits his budget to Congress in January. All the committees in Congress then submit their estimates and views of the budget to the budget committees, which gather them in a first resolution. Congress must vote on this resolution, which sets overall spending and tax levels, by April 15. The various parts of this first resolution then go back to the standing committees concerned with the particular subject or program. By mid June the standing committees' recommendations have gone back to the budget committees, which draw up a reconciliation bill that is then voted on by Congress. This part of the process is called *reconciliation* because it attempts to balance the separate standing committees' decisions with the targets set by the first resolution.

Throughout the 1980s the budget deficit skyrocketed into the 100s of billions while various Congressional efforts to control it failed miserably. In 1993 President Clinton introduced an ambitious deficit-reduction package that promised to reduce the deficit by $500 billion. The White House claimed that half of the reduction would come from tax increases (mostly on the wealthy) and half from cutting government spending. Republican opponents charged the bill's numbers were suspect and that it was too "tax heavy." After considerable debate and changes by Congress, the bill was passed in August 1993.

With the rise of Republican majorities in both houses, balancing the budget became a major political goal. Failed attempts to pass a balanced budget constitutional amendment moved Republican leaders to the practical task of actually balancing the budget. The Republicans did what the Democrats charged they could never do—actually spell out their cuts in government spending. President Clinton's own balanced budget called for fewer tax cuts and fewer reductions in popular programs like Medicare. Disagreements over the budget between the president and Congress led to a government shutdown in late 1995 and early 1996.

The prosperity of the late 1990s increased tax revenues beyond all predictions and aided in producing balanced budgets in 1998, 1999, 2000, and 2001. It had been 50 years since the U.S. government had this many consecutive years of national debt reduction. It didn't last. President George W. Bush pushed through a $1.35 trillion tax cut that slashed government revenues, the stock market cratered, the recession continued, and the war on terrorism and Iraq led to increased spending for defense. By 2004, the Bush administration was estimating that the year's federal deficit would hit a record $521 billion, roughly 4.25 percent of the total economy. It was a blunt contrast with the *surplus* of $236 billion in fiscal 2000.

Major Committees in the House

In the old days, power came through seniority to all committee chairmen. Committees and their chairmen ran the House. Power is now concentrated in the House leaders of the majority party and in the senior majority party members of a few elite committees. Since the 1994 GOP takeover, party leaders have increasingly directed the shape of legislation in the committees, usually at the direction of the Republican administration. However, there remain key committees, usually dealing with the budget. These House committees, besides Budget, are Rules, Ways and Means, and Appropriations.

Almost all legislation approved by committees in the House must pass through the Rules Committee before reaching the House floor. The Rules Committee's name comes from its function: If the committee approves a bill for transmission to the House floor, it assigns a "rule" to that bill setting the terms of a debate. The Rules Committee can, for example, assign a "closed rule," which forbids any amendments and forces the House into a "take it or leave it" position. Thus the Rules Committee acts as a traffic cop. It has the power to delay or even stop legislation; it can amend bills or send them back to committee for revision; and it can decide in cases where two committees have bills on the same subject, which one gets sent to the floor. In recent congresses this powerful committee has been largely directed by the majority party leadership.

The Ways and Means Committee deals with tax legislation, or the raising of revenue for the government. A former powerful chairman, Dan Rostenkowski, called it "the cadillac of committees." Because all money-raising bills begin in the House, any tax legislation goes first to Ways and Means, making this committee a central power in Congress. The Committee was key in moving much of the Bush administration's tax cut legislation through the House. Ways and Means has been the central committee on issues such as welfare reform, and proposed changes in the Social Security system. In "reconciliation," it and the Senate Finance Committee are important in deciding where the Budget Committee's spending cuts will fall.

The Ways and Means Committee raises money; the Appropriations Committee deals with how government spends that money. When the federal budget is presented to Congress by the president each year, it is first sent to the House Appropriations Committee and its 11 subcommittees. Because the power to tax and spend is the power to make or break programs, industries, and interest groups, and because specialization and reciprocity nudge Congress to follow the lead of its committees, the importance of Ways and Means and Appropriations is clear. While Appropriations is limited by the budget process on its overall spending, it can still decide where it will spend money or make cuts. It has become the place for doing favors for other members, such as passing their *pork-barrel bills*—legislation designed to produce visible local benefits, like highways and post offices. (See "The Prince of Pork.")

Major Committees in the Senate

The most important committees in the Senate (besides Budget) are Appropriations, Finance, and Foreign Relations. The Senate Appropriations Committee receives spending bills after they have been passed by the House. Its procedures are very much like those of its House counterpart, with the important distinction that the Senate committee tends to act as a "court of appeals," adding money to or subtracting it from the amounts granted by the House. If passed by the House, tax legislation then goes to the Senate Finance Committee,

The Prince of Pork

On reelection night 2000 the senior senator declared, "West Virginia has always had four friends: God Almighty, Sears Roebuck, Carter's Liver pills and Robert C. Byrd." Years earlier Senator Byrd had happily set his goal: "I want to be West Virginia's billion-dollar industry." In delivering pork to his poor state in the form of federally funded projects, the senator has accomplished his goal and earned the title, "Prince of Pork."

These "Byrd Droppings" fill the state, often with the senator's name attached. There is the Robert C. Byrd Locks and Dam project and the Byrd Green Bank Telescope, both with statues of the senator to greet visitors. There are two Robert C. Byrd U.S. Courthouses, four Byrd stretches of highways, a Robert C. Byrd Bridge and two Robert C. Byrd interchanges. The senator's name graces a Lifelong Learning Center, Hardwood Technology Center, Health and Wellness Center and an Institute for Advanced Flexible Manufacturing. One newspaper counted more than 30 projects named for the senator and far more that he brought to the state without his name. One critic surmised, "What next—West Byrdinia?"

As chairman of the Senate Appropriations Committee the senator in 2001 brought home ten times the national average of legislative pork or $236 per resident. He won reelection the year before with 78 percent of the vote.

Source: New York Times, May 4, 2002.

the Senate's equivalent to Ways and Means in the House. Republicans and Democrats on Senate Finance were key in reaching a compromise that allowed President Bush's 2001 tax cut to become law.

The Senate Foreign Relations Committee is a watchdog over the president's dominant position in foreign policy. Its importance comes from the Senate's role in confirming appointments of ambassadors and approving or disapproving treaties. In the past under conservative leadership it has pushed for cutting foreign aid (which is less than 1 percent of the federal budget), for reorganizing the foreign affairs bureaucracy, and to halt high-level foreign policy appointments needing Senate approval. Senator Richard Lugar of Indiana is the present chairman of Foreign Relations and, as a moderate Republican, frequently dissented from administration foreign policies.

The Senate also has a Rules Committee, but it is much less important than its House counterpart. With fewer than one-fourth as many members as the House, the problem of coordination is not as great. The Senate decided that it did not need a strong "traffic cop" to screen legislation. (See "Congressional Staff.")

OTHER POWERS OF CONGRESS

Besides these legislative powers, Congress also has several nonlegislative powers. Among them are *oversight* of the executive branch and *investigation* which are more important when different parties control the two branches. Congress created the executive agencies and departments and specified their duties. It can change them at any time. Congress appropriates the funds those agencies need to perform their jobs. These powers give Congress an interest in what the executive branch is doing and the means to find out. For example, Congress can decide who will and who will not receive food stamps, and judge who will be allowed to use federal lands. In short, the annual appropriations process gives Congress the chance to ask what the bureaucracies are doing; tell them what they ought to be doing; and, finally, give money for what Congress wants and withhold money for what it doesn't want.

Congressional Staff

Despite recent efforts to shrink staff, the U.S. Congress remains the most heavily staffed legislature in the world, with over 35,000 employees. In 1995 the Republican House reduced its committee staff from 2,100 to 1,407. The Senate followed, lowering its number of committee staff from 1,185 to 950. However, personal staffers for members of Congress have gone untouched. Even junior representatives can have 18 full-time staffers and 4 part-time employees. By comparison, the 650 members of the British House of Commons get by with about 1,000 employees.

Congress found it difficult to cut staff further because, other than voting, a member's staff is likely to do everything he or she does. Staffers will organize hearings, negotiate agreements with other members' staffs, research proposals, speak with voters, and promote legislation. Staffers will often initiate policies and then "sell" them to their bosses. Lobbyists understand the importance of the staff and spend much of their time cultivating relationships with them. Because staff influence is best exercised quietly, it may not be visible yet it is always present.

The *General Accounting Office (GAO)* is an agency created by Congress to help with its oversight function. Congress uses the GAO to examine certain government programs or departments. Many of the stories about scandals in government that appear on shows like *60 Minutes* start as GAO reports.

In addition, Congress has the power to investigate. If Congress, or a committee (or a committee chair), decides that something is not being done properly, an investigation may be launched. The subject might be the abuse of prisoners in Iraq, a price rise in gasoline, or campaign contributions by Asian businesses. In other words, Congress can investigate whatever it wishes.

Congressional investigations are not welcomed by the executive. On June 4, 2002, the House and Senate Intelligence Committees began joint hearings to investigate "why the Intelligence Community did not learn of the September 11th attacks in advance." To divert attention from Congress's action, the president announced on June 6 in a nationally televised speech his proposal to create a Cabinet-level Department of Homeland Security. Though not happy about the congressional probe, the president was even more opposed to the Democrats' push for an independent commission from outside of government to investigate these intelligence failures. Only later in the year did the president reluctantly agree to such a probe, and still later, and even more reluctantly, agree to testify to the 9/11 commission.

Congressional investigations have sometimes proven dangerous to civil liberties. In the 1950s, Republican Senator Joseph McCarthy's Permanent Investigations Subcommittee and the House Un-American Activities Committee ruined the reputations of many innocent people, forced able persons out of government service, and whipped up fear throughout the country with charges of disloyalty and communist sympathies.

The Senate also has the power to approve or reject most presidential appointments, including ambassadors, cabinet members, and military officers. Many presidential appointments within the executive branch are routine, and there is a tendency in the Senate to agree that the president has a right to have the persons he wishes working with him. Still, John Ashcroft, President Bush's nominee for attorney general, was only confirmed by the Senate in a 58–42 vote with most Democrats opposing his conservative positions. The "behind-the-scenes" pressure of Senate dissatisfaction undoubtedly causes presidents not to make certain nominations in the first place. The Senate often takes a more active role in presidential appointments to the independent regulatory commissions and the Supreme Court, as shown by the close Senate vote in October 1991, following televised committee hearings on Clarence Thomas's nomination to the Supreme Court.

Congress also has certain judicial functions. The House of Representatives can *impeach* (bring charges against) a federal official by a simple majority vote. Then, the Senate holds a trial on these charges. In the case of impeachment of the president the chief justice of the Supreme Court presides. If two-thirds of the Senate votes to uphold the charges and to convict the official, that official is removed from office.

Impeachment is difficult, slow, and cumbersome. Several federal judges have been impeached and convicted in the past. Only two presidents were ever impeached, Andrew Johnson in 1868 and Bill Clinton in 1998. Neither was convicted by the Senate. Richard Nixon resigned the presidency in 1974 (the only president ever to do so) in the face of almost certain impeachment by the House and conviction by the Senate.

The failed 1998–1999 attempt to remove President Clinton illustrated the political and constitutional obstacles to impeachment. Acting on the report of Independent Counsel Kenneth Starr, the House of Representatives in the fall of 1998 took up the question of whether the president should be impeached. Accused of perjury for lying before a grand jury about his affair with Monica Lewinsky and then of obstructing justice by trying to cover it up, the president benefited from high popularity and national prosperity throughout the scandal. Voting almost entirely on party lines, a majority of the House voted to impeach the president shortly before Christmas. But on February 12, 1999, the GOP, lacking Democratic support, could not get a two-thirds vote for conviction in the Senate. His accusers could never quite convince either Democrats or the public that the president's sleazy behavior rose to the level of the "high crimes and misdemeanors" that the Constitution requires for impeachment.

Despite its difficulty, impeachment remains an ultimate check over the executive in the hands of the legislature.

CASE STUDY

CAMPAIGN FINANCE REFORM

Despite calling it "flawed," President Bush signed the legislation on March 27, 2002, with little ceremony. He then left Washington to raise $4 million for Republican candidates. The *New York Times* editorialized that it was "the biggest election reform in a generation" and "a victory for all Americans." Senate opponents declared that the bill infringed on free speech and vowed to take it to the Supreme Court to have it declared unconstitutional.

The Campaign Finance bill also known as McCain-Feingold after its two longtime Senate sponsors, John McCain (R-Arizona) and Russell Feingold (D-Wisconsin), had two major reforms in it. One was to ban unregulated, unlimited "soft money" contributions to national parties. The second was to bar corporations, unions and nonprofit groups from broadcasting "issue ads" that mention a federal candidate within 60 days of a general election or 30 days of a primary. Any such ads would have to be regulated as a campaign contribution.

In its seven-year uphill battle the reform bill had picked up several moderating elements. Soft money up to $10,000 was allowed for state and local parties. Hard money contribution limits by individuals were doubled from $1000 to $2000 as a way of replacing soft money funding. Review by the Supreme Court was speeded up, although the legislation provided that the court could strike down parts of the bill without invalidating the entire law. And the reforms themselves were delayed until after the November 2002 elections giving incumbents the benefits of the existing laws.

A Legislative Marathon

Even with its compromises the bill represented an overhaul of the campaign finance system that many thought would never become law; lawmakers would never risk changing a system that elected them in the first place. There were three reasons behind a victory that had stretched over years of debate and hundreds of votes. They could be summed up as *elections, scandals, and pragmatic legislating.*

Recent presidential elections highlighted the problem of campaign fundraising and aroused public concern about it. Soft money contributions had grown into huge unregulated amounts that made the restrictions on money in elections more loophole than law. (See Chapter 7, "Soft Money" p. 000.) During the 1992 campaigns the two parties raised about $86 million in soft money. Four years later the figure was $262 million, and by the 2000 elections it was $495 million. Much of this money went to issue-advocacy ads that, while supposed to inform voters about issues, looked more like typical campaign commercials.

But the 2000 elections also provided a stage for boosting reform. Senator John McCain, a former Vietnam prisoner of war, ran as a reformer for president and gave George W. Bush an unexpectedly strong challenge for the Republican nomination. This energized campaign reform as other candidates recognized its popularity among voters. In the same election four GOP senators who opposed the bill were replaced by four Democrats who supported it. This gave the bill critical backing in a closely divided senate. After his battle with McCain, the new president was reluctant to veto a reform he had opposed. He declared neutrality, which would prove critical to the bill's success.

Scandals played a role in the president's hands-off approach. The 1996 elections were spiced up by Lincoln Bedroom sleepovers for wealthy donors to the Clinton campaign, and Asian contributors increasing the momentum for reform. The Enron scandal in 2002 became, in the words of a *Washington Post* headline, the "Last Push in Battle for Reform." It was Enron's collapse that made it politically impossible for the president to oppose the bill. The Texas energy company had a vast network of political influence underwritten by $3.6 million in soft money, which included being the largest donor to President Bush's political career. Earlier Senator McCain had correctly prophesized, "It would take a scandal—might take more than one scandal—but we would prevail."

Legislative Pragmatism

The law that emerged was far different than the campaign finance bill first introduced in 1995. Supporters reshaped the legislation, made compromises, dropped parts of the bill that were politically unacceptable, and refined others to gain support. In the process a reform that one opponent described in 1997 as "not going to pass now, is not going to pass tomorrow, is not going to pass ever," became inevitable.

McCain and Feingold teamed up in 1995 to introduce an ambitious campaign finance reform. This first bill in addition to eliminating soft money had banned contributions from political action committees (PACs), limited overall spending in political campaigns, and provided public funding and free television time to candidates who accepted voluntary spending limits. But this maximum position was later admitted by its backers to be politically unrealistic. Free television time couldn't overcome the broadcasters' lobby, and abolishing PACs had constitutional problems. Over the years the sponsors scrubbed their bill, dropped many provisions, and pragmatically focused on banning soft money and limiting issue-advocacy ads.

In 1998 and 1999 the House approved their own revised version of campaign reform. Support for the bill was made easier for many in the House because they assumed the reform would never pass the Senate. However, in the process of going on the record many lukewarm supporters boxed themselves in. Backing away from legislation they had publicly voted for became politically difficult. But the Republican leadership in both chambers opposed the reform and it was blocked in the Senate by filibusters.

But as the more controversial provisions were removed it became more difficult to attack. One Republican senator changed his mind after the flood of money in the 2000 election convinced him that the influence of soft money was overwhelming other campaign activities. Another, noting that Republicans do better than Democrats in raising hard money, changed when the limits on hard money were raised in the bill. During the debate in the Senate, an exemption was added to the soft-money ban that allowed $10,000 contributions to state and local parties. Additional modifications aided incumbents.

Reformers laid siege to opponents' stalling tactics. In the House in 1998, a rarely successful discharge petition was used to overcome strong leadership opposition. Under the discharge petition 218 House members (a majority) forced the bill out of committee to a vote on the floor where it passed 252–179. But once again it was blocked in the Senate by a filibuster. Not until after the 2000 election and the Democrats gaining control of the Senate in 2001 were there enough votes—60—to support "cloture" to limit debate and eventually secure final passage of the legislation in the following year.

Opponents vigorously maintained that the bill infringed on the bill of rights protections for political speech. Former supporters of the original reform now criticized the bill as being "riddled with loopholes" and objected to doubling the limits on hard money contributions. Nonetheless it passed the House on Feb. 15 and the Senate by 60–40 on March 20, 2002.

Deforming Reform

Would the reform limit the role of money in elections? The evidence from the 2004 elections seemed to cast doubt on its impact. Both presidential nominees opted out of public financing of their preconvention campaigns, in part because the increase in hard money limits and the use of Internet fundraising blew the roof off the amounts they could raise. The presidential nominees and congressional candidates were raising much more money than they had before. And now unregulated big bucks that could no longer be given as "soft money" were channeled into "527" organizations. These advocacy groups (like MoveOn.org), while supposedly independent of the parties, were headed by close allies of the presidential candidates. They raised huge amounts, and ran expensive ads attacking the other side.

The reforms did restrict federal officials from soliciting large donations. Instead it was being done by their close associates. Even though the Supreme Court largely upheld the reform, the results as seen in the 2004 elections were not reassuring for supporters. For now the negative unintended consequences of campaign reform seemed to outweigh the positive results.

WRAP-UP

The U.S. Congress consists of two houses, the Senate and the House of Representatives. Two senators are selected from each state, and they serve for six years. Representatives are allocated to states according to population; they serve for two years. The Senate, with 100 members, is smaller, more informal, and more prestigious than the House, with its 435 members. The House, because it is larger, is more tightly controlled by the majority party leadership.

The House and Senate operate separately, but before any legislation can be sent to the president for signing, it must be passed in identical language by both branches. In the House floor debate, the agenda for legislation, and even committee priorities, are controlled by the leadership elected by the majority party. The speaker of the House works closely with the majority leader and whips. The Senate has no speaker; floor debate is managed by the Senate majority leader. Each branch also has minority leaders and minority whips.

While much of the work of the House and Senate goes on in committees and subcommittees, party leadership has generally become more important. The committee chairmen (who are always from the majority party) exercise considerable power, especially in the House. Despite some recent exceptions, chairmen are usually chosen on the basis of seniority—longest consecutive service on the committee. The Republican majority leadership in the House has become influential in this decision, but the Republican leaders in the Senate defer to seniority. The attention to the budget, and the willingness of members to follow specialization and reciprocity, has increased the importance of the taxing and spending committees.

All legislation other than revenue-raising and appropriations bills (which must start in the House) can be introduced in either the House or the Senate. It is then assigned to the relevant committee for examination and change. If approved by committee, a bill is sent to the floor of the House or Senate (going through the Rules Committee in the House). When approved there, the bill goes to the other chamber for a similar process. If the House and Senate pass different versions, they will be ironed out by a conference committee. When both branches of Congress have approved the same bill, it is sent to the president. He may sign it, veto it, pocket veto it, or allow it to become law without his signature. If he vetoes it, Congress may try to override by a two-thirds vote in each house. The difficulty of passing any piece of legislation, especially a campaign reform law, was shown in the up-and-down history of Congress's efforts, and the questionable impact of those efforts to control money in elections.

Congressional procedures seem complex and confusing because they are complex and confusing. Congress has been criticized for being slow, unresponsive, and even unrepresentative. Certainly its procedures discussed involve time-consuming duplication. The seniority system, the filibuster in the Senate, and the overall fragmentation of power into committees and subcommittees may sometimes frustrate majority wishes. But they have not stopped Congress from quickly acting on legislation with broad popular support, as seen in the days following the 9/11 attacks.

If Congress is sometimes slow to solve national problems, it may be because the country does not agree on the nature of the problem or the way to fix it. If Congress bogs down in party disputes or struggles to reach a watered-down compromise, it may be because a country as large as the United States includes strongly opposing opinions that the Congress reflects. If special interests receive special treatment from Congress, this may simply be an accurate reflection of these players political power.

Congress was not set up to make government more efficient. It was designed to reflect the wishes of the people governed, to be the political game's democratic centerpiece. Congress acts best not when it acts least, but when it represents the public support on which the United State's government rests.

Thought Questions

---

1. How can Congress be made more responsive to public opinion? Is the political apportioning of congressional districts beyond the public's control. Is nonvoting a reasonable response to 'rigged' elections?
2. Think about the "unwritten rules" of seniority, specialization, and reciprocity. How do these rules help Congress to operate? What are their drawbacks?
3. Congress is generally unpopular, while individual members are popular and usually reelected. Why does the institution suffer while incumbents shine?
4. Does the history of campaign finance reform illustrate that the influence of money is beyond the ability of elected officials to control? Is it a continuing battle between reform and the status quo or are efforts at reform a waste of time?

Suggested Readings

Caro, Robert A. *Master of the Senate: The Years of Lyndon Johnson.* New York: Alfred A. Knopf, 2002.
  The third volume of this masterful biography of Lyndon Johnson dissects the U.S. Senate in the 1950s and LBJ's powerful presence. The first 100 pages is an excellent history of the Senate.
Casper, Barry M. *Lost in Washington.* Amherst: University of Massachusetts, 2000.
  A senate staffer who worked for the late Senator Paul Wellstone tells the inside story of how big money overwhelms reform.

Fenno, Richard E., Jr. *Home Style: House Members in Their Districts.* Boston: Little, Brown, 1978.
Still the classic study of how representatives act in front of their most important audience—the folks back home.

Kennedy, John F. *Profiles in Courage.* New York: Harper & Row, 1956. Pb.
The future president wrote these prize-winning profiles of members of Congress who stood up to the popular pressures of their time and sacrificed their careers to do what was right.

Killian, Linda. *The Freshman: What Happened to the Republican Revolution.* Boulder, Colo.: Westview Press, 1998.
A detailed and chatty narrative on the progress of some Republican congressmen from the class of 1994.

Mayhew, David R. *America's Congress,* New Haven, Conn.: Yale University, 2000.
A leading scholar of Congress takes an historical look at the importance of individual congressional members to our system of government.

CHAPTER 5

The Judicial Branch:
The Supreme Court and
the Federal Court System

The Constitution is brief in providing for the judicial player: "The judicial Power of the United States shall be vested in one Supreme Court, and in such inferior courts as the Congress may from time to time ordain and establish" (Article III, Section 1). Congress, in turn, set up two major levels of federal courts below the Supreme Court—federal district courts and courts of appeals. It also established several special federal courts as the need for them has arisen. The federal court system is responsible for judging cases involving the U.S. Constitution and federal laws.

Paralleling the federal court system are the state courts. Each state has its own judicial system to try cases that come under state law (though it may also deal with cases under the U.S. Constitution and laws). Issues involving the Constitution may be appealed to the U.S. Supreme Court. In this chapter we will focus on the federal court system and particularly the Supreme Court; state courts are set up in much the same way.

FEDERAL COURT SYSTEM

U.S. District Courts

At the base of the federal system are the courts of *original jurisdiction*— the *U.S. district courts*. Except in a few special instances, all cases involving federal law are tried first in district courts. There are 94 district courts in the United States and its possessions, with at least one federal district court in each state. The larger, more populous states have more district courts. New York, for example, has four. Each district has between 1 and 28 judges, for a total of 649 district judges in the country. These judges preside over most federal cases, including civil rights cases, controversies involving more than $10,000, antitrust suits, and counterfeiting cases. The large volume of cases they handle (almost 260,000 in 2000) has led to long delays in administering justice. At one time, it took almost four years to complete a civil case in the Southern District of New York.

Courts of Appeals

Above the district courts are the *courts of appeals* (sometimes called by their old name, *circuit courts of appeals*). These courts have only *appellate jurisdiction;* that is, they hear *appeals* from the district courts and from important regulatory commissions, like the Federal Trade Commission. If you took a civil rights case to your district court and lost, you could appeal the decision and have the case brought

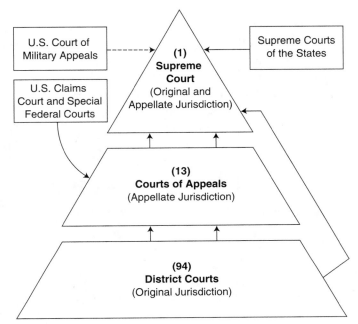

FIGURE 5.1
Federal Court Structure and the Flow of Cases to the
Supreme Court.

before a court of appeals. The United States is divided into 13 courts
of appeals. There are 12 geographic *circuits* (11 plus 1 in Washington,
D.C.), and one U.S. Court of Appeal for the Federal Circuit dealing
with appeals from special federal courts like the U.S. Claims Court.
Each of the 13 appeals courts has between 6 and 28 judges, depending on the volume of work. Usually three judges hear each case. One
hundred and seventy-nine circuit court judges handle almost 55,000
cases annually. These are the final courts of appeal for most cases, but
a hundred or so cases each year are appealed further to the Supreme
Court. (See Figure 5.1.)

Special Federal Courts

Special federal courts have been created by Congress to handle certain cases. The *U.S. Claims Court* deals with people's claims against
government seizure of property. The *U.S. Court of Military Appeals*
(often called the *GI Supreme Court*), composed of three civilians, is
the final judge of court-martial convictions. The U.S. Supreme Court
can review only certain types of military cases.

The Judges

All federal judges, including Supreme Court justices, are nominated to the bench by the president and must be confirmed by the Senate.

Under the Constitution, all federal judges hold office for life "during good behavior" and can be removed only by impeachment. This has rarely happened. However, in October 1989 the Senate removed a Florida judge (who is now a congressman), Alcee Hastings, in a controversial case involving bribery. To further protect them from political pressures, judges' salaries cannot be reduced during their time in office.

Despite these protections, the appointment of judges is a very political matter. Judges almost always are selected on a party basis, usually as a reward for their political services. One commentator called the judiciary "the place to put political workhorses out to pasture." In this partisan spirit, 87 percent of Bill Clinton's appointments to federal judgeships were Democrats, while 89 percent of George Bush, Sr.'s were Republicans.

The Senate's power to confirm all federal judges is also the considerable power *not* to confirm. In recent years, this has led to a "vacancy crisis" in the federal courts as the Senate delayed acting on presidents' nominees to the bench. President Bush in 2002 accused the then-Democratic Senate majority of not filling 88 vacancies in the federal district and appeals courts (representing 10 percent of the 850 positions), and of using the approval of nominations as bargaining chips for other legislation. The Democrats argued that they had approved more nominees than the Republicans had done when they controlled the Senate and Democrat Bill Clinton was in the White House. Of course, both sides could be correct.

Part of the Democrats' argument was that many of these nominees did not yet have the consent of home-state senators. This refers to a custom, *senatorial courtesy,* followed by the Senate in confirming federal judges below the Supreme Court. By this practice, senators will not vote for nominees unacceptable to the senator from the state concerned. This gives the Senate the whip hand in appointing federal judges and makes sure local opinion is heard in the selection process. How the two senators of each state divide up their choices for nominees is left up to them. In the 1960s and 1970s, when the federal courts took the lead in enforcing controversial racial integration, senatorial courtesy made the appointment of liberal judges in the South politically difficult for a president.

This power of the president to influence the makeup of one of the three major branches of the government is extremely important. This influence may be restricted in practice. (See "Presidents and the Court.") Twelve years of Ronald Reagan's and George Bush Sr.'s judicial appointments created a conservative impact on the courts. By 1993 Reagan/Bush judges represented about two-thirds of all appellate court judges with majorities in 9 of 13 appellate courts. By the end of his second term Clinton had appointed 373 federal judges, including 65 of the 179 appellate judges. But with a conservative Republican now in the White House, the new appointees to the federal courts will reflect Bush's politics.

A majority of the Supreme Court has been appointed by Republican presidents. In 1981 President Reagan appointed the first woman to the Supreme Court, Sandra Day O'Connor. When Chief Justice Warren Burger resigned in 1986, the president elevated Justice William Rehnquist to be chief justice and nominated an equally conservative Antonin Scalia to be the first justice of Italian descent. Reagan's 1988 selection of Anthony Kennedy, after the Senate had rejected Robert Bork, was aimed at pointing the Court in a conservative direction. President Bush's 1990 appointment of a moderate New Hampshire judge, David Souter, was later considered a mistake by conservatives.

Presidents and the Court

Supreme Court justices have a way of disappointing the president appointing them. Theodore Roosevelt said of famed justice Oliver Wendell Holmes: "He has the backbone of a banana." President Eisenhower was so angered at Chief Justice Earl Warren's rulings that he called Warren's appointment "the biggest damn-fool mistake I ever made." The controversy set off by the Warren Court's activism led President Nixon to appoint Warren Burger as chief justice to replace Earl Warren when he retired in 1969. Nixon hoped that the four justices he had appointed, including Burger, would inspire greater political restraint in the Court. But the Burger Court, in *U.S.* v. *Nixon* (1974), ruled that President Nixon had to surrender to the special Watergate prosecutor the White House tapes of his conversations about illegal activities. The president, who resigned shortly afterward, was certainly not pleased by this example of the Court's independence.

Once a fairly gentlemanly affair, Senate confirmation of justices got nastier in the late 1980s. President Reagan's 1987 nomination of Robert Bork set off fierce opposition from liberal groups offended by his views on civil rights, abortion, and privacy. After a flurry of personal attacks (now called "borking" by conservatives), Bork was rejected by the Democratic Senate. This unusually public politicizing of the confirmation process continued with President Bush's nomination of conservative Clarence Thomas in 1991. Unlike Bork, Thomas had fewer qualifications, which ironically gave opponents less of a "paper trail" to criticize. Despite the dramatic televised testimony of Anita Hill that he had sexually harassed her, Thomas was confirmed, though by the smallest margin of approval (52–48) in more than 100 years.

Only the two most recent appointees were chosen by a Democrat, President Clinton. When he selected Ruth Bader Ginsburg in 1993, she was labeled a middle-of-the-road judge. Similarly, Stephen G. Breyer was also considered a moderate when he was appointed in 1994. Both justices have consistently voted as part of the Court's liberal wing. They have acted as a brake on the court's more conservative tendencies, including a willingness to restrain individual rights. Justice Ginsburg's main focus has been on gender issues, and she vigorously dissented from the Court's decision to stop the vote recount in the 2000 Florida presidential election.

Jurisdiction

Jurisdiction refers to the matters over which a court may exercise its authority. The jurisdiction of the federal courts falls into two broad categories: In the first group, it depends on the *subject of the case;* in the second, on the *parties to the case,* no matter what the subject. The federal courts have jurisdiction over all subjects related to the Constitution and over treaties of the United States. (Admiralty and maritime cases involving international law are also included.) Jurisdiction determined by parties includes cases involving ambassadors and other foreign representatives, controversies in which the United States is a party, and controversies between two or more states or between a state or citizen of the United States and a foreign citizen or state. The federal court system's last and largest source of cases is suits between citizens of different states.

This definition does not mean that the federal courts have the *only* jurisdiction over such cases. Federal courts have *exclusive jurisdiction* in some cases, such as cases involving crimes against the laws of the United States. But in other cases they have *concurrent jurisdiction,* shared with state courts. For example, some suits between citizens of different states may be heard by both federal and state courts.

U.S. SUPREME COURT

Sitting on the summit of the federal court system is the *Supreme Court of the United States*, composed of a chief justice and eight associate justices. (See Table 5.1.) Congress can set by law the number of justices on the Supreme Court. Although the number has varied from time to time, it has remained at nine since 1869. Though the Supreme Court has some *original jurisdiction* (cases that can be presented first to the court), most of the cases it hears are appeals of lower court decisions, which involve its *appellate jurisdiction*. If your civil rights case lost in both the district court and the court of appeals, you might be able to get it heard by the Supreme Court.

Actually, very few cases ever reach the Supreme Court. Of more than 10 million cases tried every year in American courts (federal and state), some 7,400 petitions for review make it to the Supreme Court. Of these, the Court agrees to consider only about 140 cases in a term. The other petitions are affirmed or reversed by written *memorandum orders*. The majority of the cases that come to the Court do so in the form of petitions (written requests) for a *writ of certiorari* (*certiorari* means to be informed of something). A writ of certiorari is an order to the lower court to send the entire record of the case to the higher court for review. If you lost your civil rights case in a lower court, you could petition for this writ. It is granted when four justices of the Supreme Court feel that the issues raised are important enough to merit a review. Many of these involve constitutional issues. The Court denies between 85 and 90 percent of all such applications. This procedure keeps control over the appeal process in the hands of the

TABLE 5.1 THE SUPREME COURT, 2003			
JUSTICE	DATE OF BIRTH	APPOINTED BY	DATE APPOINTED
William H. Rehnquist, Jr. (chief justice)	1924	Nixon	1971
John Paul Stevens	1920	Ford	1975
Sandra Day O'Connor	1930	Reagan	1981
Antonin Scalia	1936	Reagan	1986
Anthony Kennedy	1936	Reagan	1988
David Souter	1939	Bush	1990
Clarence Thomas	1946	Bush	1991
Ruth Bader Ginsburg	1933	Clinton	1993
Stephen G. Breyer	1938	Clinton	1994

Supreme Court, allowing a maximum number of decisions to come to rest in the lower courts.

The Final Authority?

The prominence of the Supreme Court in American history rests on its "final" authority over what the Constitution means. Yet a ruling of the Court has not always been the final word. The Court itself has reversed its decisions, as will be seen in our Case Study, "Separate but Equal?" at the end of the chapter. If the Court interprets a law in a way Congress doesn't like, Congress often will overrule the Court simply by rewriting the law. In 1990 Congress passed a Civil Rights Restoration Act that extended civil rights protection to all programs of colleges accepting federal aid. The Act overturned a court ruling that limited this protection. Amendments to the Constitution also have reversed decisions by the Court. An 1895 Court decision striking down the federal income tax was overturned by the Sixteenth Amendment in 1913, which allowed such taxes.

The strength of the Court's "final" authority is also tempered by the other branches of government and by public opinion. (See "The Court's Supreme Popularity.") Despite the Court's popularity, the public's acceptance of a decision is not always a given. In civil rights cases like school busing, and in civil liberties cases like school prayer, local communities have ignored the Court's interpretation of the Constitution. Congress and the president have taken their turn in interpreting vague parts of the Constitution to meet the demands of the time and the needs of those in power. The president's right to involve the country in the Korean and Vietnam wars without a declaration of war would seem to fly in the face of the war-making powers given to Congress by the Constitution. Yet without a challenge by Congress, the president's interpretation of the Constitution stood.

Despite this shared role in changing the Constitution, the Supreme Court, by its constant interpretation and reinterpretation of the Constitution through its rulings, breathes life into 200-year-old words. A brief history of the Court will show how.

Early Years of the Court

The Supreme Court did not begin life as the powerful institution we know today. The Court was a neglected infant. No cases at all were brought to the Supreme Court in its first three years. Many leaders, such as Patrick Henry and Alexander Hamilton, refused appointments to the Court; court sessions were held in places like basement apartments. When the federal city was first planned, the Court was

The Court's Supreme Popularity

One of the ironies of American democracy is that the least democratic branch is also the most popular. Other than the president's popularity following 9/11, people consistently show more confidence in the Supreme Court than in either of the two elected branches of government. One explanation for this lies in the very invisibility of the Court's activities. As one scholar of the Court remarked, the public likes its politics done quietly and without an appearance of partisanship. The Court generally does this. Other reasons lie in the popular view that the Court carries out its duties in a disinterested way, that the justices are people of wisdom, and that the Court both protects and represents the Constitution. (See Figure 5.2.)

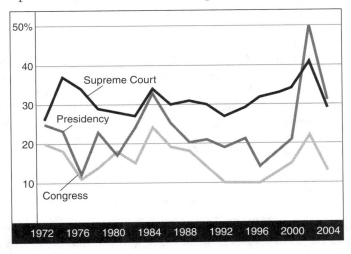

FIGURE 5.2
Public Confidence in the Supreme Court.
A higher percentage of the public has consistently said it has a "great deal of confidence" in the Supreme Court than in the presidency or Congress.
Source: The Harris Poll, www.harrisinteractive.com; Compiled from Harris Poll data by John R. Hibbing and James T. Smith for their article "What the American Public Wants Congress to Be" in *Congress Reconsidered*, seventh edition, Lawrence Dodd and Bruce I. Oppenheimer, editors (Washington: Congressional Quarterly Press, 2001).

completely overlooked with no building or chamber provided to house it.

Under the leadership of John Marshall (who served as chief justice 1801–1835), the Court's influence greatly increased. (See "Chief Justice John Marshall.") Two landmark decisions marked its growth in power.

Chief Justice John Marshall

"Marshall found the Constitution paper and he made it power."
—James A. Garfield

John Marshall served as the fourth, and arguably greatest, chief justice from 1801 to 1835. He applied his genius to a single mission: building the government of a united nation. Raising the prestige and power of the Supreme Court from the low level he found it was necessary so that it could serve that mission. Similarly, he shaped constitutional law so that it too could preserve a strong central government into an unlimited future.

Marshall acted more like a statesman than a judge. In his major decisions on judicial review and national supremacy, he was not strictly interpreting and applying the law. He was establishing principles for a growing nation. Interestingly, his lack of legal training—less than three months of law classes, and poorly attended at that—may have helped him. Rather than deciding cases legalistically, he acted like a legislator breaking with the past. His experience in General Washington's army at Valley Forge may have provided his most important education by reminding him of the price of disunity. For Marshall, the Constitution must serve its goal of creating a lasting union. This underlines his famous phrase, "We must never forget that it is a *constitution* that we are expounding."

Source: See Bernard Schwartz, *A History of the Supreme Court.* New York: Oxford University Press, 1993, chapter 2.

The first proclaimed the Court's *judicial review,* the power not only to declare acts and laws of any state and local government unconstitutional, but also to strike down acts of any branch of the federal government. The second major decision established the principle of *national supremacy,* that the U.S. laws and Constitution are the supreme law of the land and that state laws that are in conflict with federal laws cannot stand.

Judicial Review and National Supremacy

Marbury v. *Madison* (1803) clearly established the principle of judicial review. In this case the Supreme Court, for the first time, struck down an act of Congress. The case shows Chief Justice John Marshall as a shrewd politician.

Shortly before leaving office, President John Adams (who had nominated Marshall to the court) appointed a number of minor judicial officials in order to maintain the influence of his party in the coming administration of his opponent, Thomas Jefferson. When Jefferson took office, he discovered that one of the commissions, that of William Marbury, had not actually been delivered. Jefferson ordered his secretary of state, James Madison, to hold it up. Under a section of the Judiciary Act of 1789, Marbury sued in the Supreme Court to compel delivery of the commission. Marshall was then confronted with deciding a case between his political allies and his enemy, Jefferson, who was president and was determined to weaken the power of the conservative Supreme Court.

What Marshall did was to dismiss Marbury's case, ruling that the section of the Judiciary Act under which he had sued was unconstitutional (the Act allowed the Supreme Court original juris-diction in a case not mentioned by the Constitution). By doing so he clearly asserted that the Supreme Court, on the basis of *its* inter-pretation of the Constitution, could limit the actions of Congress. At the same time, the Court supported Jefferson's argument that he did not have to deliver the commission. How could the president object?

Another early decision established that states could not interfere with the functioning of the federal government. In this case, *McCulloch* v. *Maryland* (1819), the state of Maryland attempted to tax the Baltimore branch of the unpopular Bank of the United States, established by the federal government. Chief Justice Marshall, speak-ing for a unanimous court, ruled that the federal government, "though limited in its powers, is supreme within its sphere of action." He also found that although the Constitution did not specifically allow Con-gress to create a bank, Article I, Section 8 gave Congress the power to make all laws "necessary and proper" for carrying out its authority. *Implied powers* based on this clause were to be used later in broadly expanding the duties that Congress could undertake.

Then in 1857 came the famous *Dred Scott* case (*Dred Scott* v. *Sandford*). Here, the Court ruled that a slave (Dred Scott) was not automatically free merely because his owner had taken him to a state not allowing slavery. Congress, the Court said, had no right to inter-fere with property rights guaranteed by the Constitution. The Court went on to say that the Missouri Compromise (1820), which had attempted to resolve the slavery issue by dividing the new western territories into slave and free parts, was invalid. In terms of constitu-tional development, this unpopular decision was the first time an act of Congress of any great importance was struck down by the courts. As such, the *Dred Scott* case marked a critical expansion of judicial powers. Many concluded that the Court had gone too far.

The Court After the Civil War

The end of the Civil War signaled the end of the major political conflict that dominated the first 75 years of the Republic—*states' rights* versus *federal powers*. With federal unity achieved, rapid national growth began. The resulting economic expansion and the unrestrained growth of giant monopolies created a new demand for government regulation of the economy. The Supreme Court became more active, and judicial power was greatly enlarged. In just 9 years (1864–1873), ten acts of Congress were struck down, compared with only two acts in the previous 74 years.

Not only was the Court more active, but it also was more conservative. In the view of many, the Court became an instrument for protecting the property rights of the rich and ignoring popular demands for government regulation.

This trend continued into the twentieth century, when the Court found itself up against the growing power of the executive branch. The presidency was widely felt to be the most effective place in the government to regulate the social and economic changes brought about by the post–Civil War industrialization. But the Supreme Court continued to resist the expansion of state and federal regulatory power, even though much of the legislation it struck down (such as minimum wage and child labor laws) was widely popular. Between 1890 and 1936, the Court declared 46 laws unconstitutional in full or in part.

It was President Franklin D. Roosevelt who caused the Court's policy to change. He fought the Court's opposition to his New Deal measures by threatening to expand the Court with new judges of his own choosing, the so-called *court-packing* bill. Although Roosevelt's plan was unsuccessful and aroused a storm of public and congressional opposition, it may have accomplished FDR's purposes. In 1937 the Court backed down—the famous "switch in time that saved nine"—and turned away from economic policy making.

Modern Courts

Since 1937, Supreme Court decisions have shown three major trends. These trends peaked in the decisions of the Warren Court (led by then–Chief Justice Earl Warren) in the 1950s and 1960s and have been less apparent, even undermined, in the decisions of the current Rehnquist Court.

First, the Court has invalidated much less federal legislation than it had in the 50 years before the New Deal. Generally only a few federal laws have been held unconstitutional, and in most of these cases the legislation struck down was not very significant. In a second area, the Court has avoided protecting private property rights. The Court, until recently, has not been greatly concerned with guarding economic interests from government policy making.

A third area in which the Court has shown more positive interest is increased judicial protection for civil liberties. While reducing property rights in importance, the Court has sought to preserve and protect the rights of individuals against the increased powers of the government. First Amendment freedoms of speech, press, religion, and assembly have been developed and expanded by modern Supreme Courts. With Earl Warren as chief justice (1953–1969), the Supreme Court moved in the areas of reapportionment, racial discrimination, and the rights of defendants in criminal cases.

In decisions dealing with reapportionment, beginning with *Baker* v. *Carr* (1962), the Warren Court established the principle of "one man, one vote" for election districts. The Court ruled that districts should be drawn based on equality of population so that each citizen's vote would count as much as another's. In moving to eliminate racial discrimination, the Court was a leading force in cutting away racism in schooling, voting, housing, and the use of public facilities.

Another major interest of the Warren Court, the rights of criminal defendants, saw the Court throw the protection of the Bill of Rights around people accused of crimes by state and federal authorities. The Court insisted on an impoverished defendant's basic right to a lawyer; declared that illegally seized evidence cannot be used in state criminal trials; and held that suspects must be advised of their constitutional right to silence and to have a lawyer, before questioning. This last area, summed up as the *Miranda* decision (*Miranda* v. *Arizona,* 1966), is familiar to all fans of TV detective series. (See "Miranda: Pop Culture and the Court.")

The Supreme Court under Warren Burger (1969–1986) was less activist than the Warren Court, but not as conservative as some had expected. On the liberal side, the Burger Court legalized abortions except in the last ten weeks of pregnancy, declined to stop publication of the Pentagon Papers (official papers on the government's planning for the Vietnam War unofficially leaked to the press), and severely limited capital punishment. The Burger Court also declined to interfere with busing to integrate schools in cities like Boston and Los Angeles.

This was not the whole story of the Burger Court. In more conservative directions, the Court allowed local communities, within limits, to define obscenity and ban those works considered pornographic.

The Court Examines Porn

The following is an account of how the Burger Court researched a decision on pornography:

> The Justices take their obligation to research opinions so seriously that in one area of law—obscenity—the result has led to a lot of snickering both on and off the bench. Since 1957, the Court has tried repeatedly to define obscenity. The subject has become so familiar at the Supreme Court building that a screening room has been set up in the basement for the justices and their clerks to watch the movies submitted as exhibits in obscenity cases. Justice Douglas never goes to the dirty movies because he thinks all expression—obscene or not—is protected by the First Amendment. And Chief Justice Burger rarely, if ever, goes because he is offended by the stuff. But everyone else shows up from time to time.
>
> Justice Blackmun watches in what clerks describe as "a near-catatonic state." Justice Marshall usually laughs his way through it all. The late Justice Harlan used dutifully to attend the Court's porno flicks even though he was virtually blind; Justice Stewart would sit next to Harlan and narrate for him, explaining what was going on in each scene. Once every few minutes, Harlan would exclaim in his proper way, "By George, extraordinary!"

Source: From Nina Totenberg, "Behind the Marble, Beneath the Robes," *The New York Times Magazine,* March 16, 1975. Copyright © 1975 by The New York Times Company. Reprinted by permission.

(See "The Court Examines Porn.") Perhaps the most important changes the Burger Court made were in the rights of the accused. Here the Court allowed the police broader powers in searching without a warrant—deciding, for example, that persons detained on minor charges (like traffic violations) may be searched for evidence of more serious crimes (like possession of drugs)—a decision strengthened in 1996 by the Rehnquist Court. The Court also permitted illegally obtained information to be used at a trial and allowed the police to continue their questioning after a suspect has claimed the right of silence. However, the Burger Court left the *Miranda* decision in place.

The Rehnquist Court (1986–)

The current Rehnquist Court has embraced judicial activism often in support of federalism. Led by their conservative, activist chief justice, the Rehnquist Court has overturned acts by other branches of the federal government, and has invalidated twice as many federal laws as

Miranda: Pop Culture and the Court

"You have the right to remain silent" is how the Miranda warning begins. It was also how Chief Justice Rehnquist began his decision upholding Miranda. The chief justice was reflecting the fact that TV had made Miranda a part of pop culture. Detective shows starting with Sgt. Joe Friday in *Dragnet* had repeated this warning endlessly. When the series began its last run on TV in 1967, the year after the Court's original decision (*Miranda* v. *Arizona*), Sgt. Friday never missed a chance to rattle it off. It was delivered so frequently that these by-the-book cops made it a bit of a joke.

But when the Supreme Court had to rule on Congress's effort to overturn Miranda, it had to deal with a warning that had become part of the nation's culture. In *Dickerson* v. *United States* (2000), Chief Justice Rehnquist, speaking for a 7 to 2 majority, ruled that Miranda "announced a constitutional rule," which Congress was not free to replace with a case-by-case test. The Court was not unmindful that Miranda had become an accepted national norm for making an arrest legitimate. It was difficult for the justices to overturn both the Constitution and the culture.

the Warren Court. In recent terms, the Court has swept away both conservative and liberal actions. It has struck down "conservative" positions by prohibiting the execution of mentally retarded offenders and forbidding judges (as opposed to juries) to make the decision between life imprisonment and death. The Court overruled "liberal" positions by allowing random drug tests of high school students in extracurricular activities, and by halting further vote counts in Florida in the 2000 presidential election. (See "*Bush* v. *Gore*.")

The 1986 appointment of William Rehnquist as chief justice came from the Reagan administration's hope for a more conservative, more restrained court. In its first years, the Rehnquist Court, lacking a conservative majority, did not dramatically break with past Court rulings. In some areas, like civil liberties, the Court zigged and zagged with little of the clear direction that Rehnquist's Republican backers had hoped for.

Bush v. Gore

The reaction was almost as extraordinary as the decision itself. "Judicial lawlessness," said a writer in *The Washington Post;* "Comparable to Dred Scott," thundered both Alan Dershowitz of Harvard Law and Jesse Jackson. A Columbia law professor predicted increased cynicism about the courts. What the Supreme Court had done in their December 12, 2000, decision, *Bush* v. *Gore,* was to decide the outcome of the presidential election. Five Republican-appointed justices decided that Republican George W. Bush was to be the next president of the United States.

By a 5–4 decision the Supreme Court, in a reversal of their usual federalist support of state rulings, overturned the Florida Supreme Court and halted further counting of the state's disputed presidential votes. This effectively ended 35 days of arguments in the nation's closest presidential election, which had focused on whether to allow hand recounts of Florida's vote. Bush, who had narrowly won the state votes, resisted further counts. Al Gore, who had won the nation's popular vote, thought recounting votes overlooked by machines would give him Florida's electoral votes and the election. The legal fights in the lower courts had brought the case to the Supreme Court.

The majority ruled that the different standards in Florida counties for counting punch-card ballots (remember "hanging and dimpled chads"?) created problems of due process and equal protection of the law. In other words, a valid vote in one county wouldn't necessarily be valid in another one. Some of the dissenting justices agreed that there were problems but thought they could be corrected and the counting resumed. The majority recognized the limits in their opinion when they added that it would only apply in this case. The dissent by John Paul Stevens implicitly criticized the majority for serving partisan interests: "Although we may never know with complete certainty the identity of the winner of this year's presidential election, the identity of the loser is perfectly clear. It is the nation's confidence in the judge as an impartial guardian of the rule of law."

In its abortion rulings, for example, the Court placed few limits on the practice while affirming the basic right to an abortion.

In major decisions affecting race and religion, the Court has been cautiously conservative. In three 5–4 decisions, the Court narrowed the use of race in hiring minority contractors for government programs, in attracting suburban students into city schools, and in drawing boundaries for congressional districts. Yet in its 2003 decisions on affirmative action at the University of Michigan, it narrowly upheld the practice in college admissions. (See "University of Michigan and Affirmative Action" in Chapter 6.) In another 5–4 decision, the Court ruled that a state university could not refuse funds for a student-run Christian magazine (*Rosenberger* v. *Rector and Visitors of University of Virginia* (1995)), marking the first time the Court had approved government funding for a religious activity. The Court's controversial 2002 decision (*Zelman* v. *Simmons-Harris*) allowed government vouchers that parents could use to pay for private school. This removed First Amendment barriers to spending government money on religious education.

Perhaps the Rehnquist Court's most important rulings concern federalism. The Court's so-called federalism revolution limited the power of Congress while protecting the rights of the states. In *United States* v. *Lopez* (1995), the Court ruled that Congress had exceeded its authority to regulate interstate commerce by passing a law intended to keep guns out of schools. This marked the first time in 60 years that the Court had limited Congress's power to regulate interstate commerce. By a 5–4 decision in the 2000 term, the Court threw out a congressional law that allowed victims of violence to sue in federal court against their assailants. In this case (*U.S.* v. *Morrison*), the Court found the matter so clearly noncommercial that it remained a state issue that Congress lacked the power to punish. Previous courts for most of the nineteenth-century and since the New Deal had used the Commerce Clause to expand federal power. (*Federal Maritime Commission* v. *South Carolina Ports Authority.*) (The Commerce Clause—Art. I, Sect. 8—is where the Constitution delegates to Congress the power to regulate trade with foreign nations and 'among the several States'.) In a 2002 ruling in support of states rights, a 5–4 Supreme Court declared that federal agencies may not hear complaints by private parties against states. This made it harder to hold states accountable when they discriminate. All these rulings were significant restraints on the federal government by an activist court.

Many of these decisions reflected a thin 5–4 majority in which two moderate justices, O'Connor and Kennedy, joined a conservative core of Rehnquist, Scalia, and Thomas. But the Court has also shown a pragmatic ability, as one law professor put it, "to split the difference and avoid drawing bright lines." This has led varying majorities in the Court to overturn student-led prayers at public high school football games and to allow partial-birth abortions because they may be the most medically appropriate way of terminating some pregnancies. The Court has also ruled that Congress was not free to replace the famous Miranda warning. (See "Miranda: Pop Culture and the Court.")

The Court has emerged as a conservative activist in areas where it is most interested. These are less in the areas of race and individual rights, where modern Courts have historically been assertive. Now the focus of the Court seems to be on a federal government—including Congress—that it views as too big, too powerful, and too incompetent. Whether this direction is pushed further or changed will depend on retirements. With four justices over 70, including Rehnquist (who is ailing and has served over 30 years on the Court), their replacements will determine how the Court evolves in the next few years. If Republicans continue to be in charge of both the legislative and executive branches, it's a good bet that the successors to these conservative justices will hold similar views.

STRENGTHS AND WEAKNESSES OF THE SUPREME COURT

The Supreme Court has been called "the least dangerous branch of government." Is it? Despite its great power of judicial review, as shown in its decision that determined the 2000 presidential election, it remains the weakest of the three branches. It must depend on the other parts of the government to enforce its decisions. Its authority to cancel actions of the other branches of the federal government is seldom used and strictly limited. These limits are found both within the Court and in the political system.

Internal Limits on the Court

Most of the limits on the power of the Court are found in the traditional practices of that Court. For one thing, a long-held interpretation of the Constitution requires that an actual case be presented to the Court for it to exercise judicial review. The Court cannot take the lead in declaring laws unconstitutional. It cannot give advisory opinions. Justices must wait for a real controversy brought by someone actually injured by the law to make its way through the lower courts. Years may pass after a law is put on the books before the Court can rule on it. (The Supreme Court's *Dred Scott* decision struck down a law—the Missouri Compromise—passed 37 years before.)

Its refusal to resolve political questions is another important limit on the Court. A *political question* is an issue on which the Constitution or laws give final say to another branch of government, or one the Court feels it lacks the capability to solve. Political questions often crop up in foreign relations. The justices of the Court lack important secret information, they are not experts in diplomacy, and they recognize the dominance of the presidency over the conduct of foreign affairs. Consequently, a federal court in December 1990 used the doctrine of political questions to avoid deciding whether President Bush Sr. could use force against Iraq without congressional approval. Similarly, 12 years later the courts were equally unlikely to interfere with his son's decision to go to war with Iraq.

The Court has narrowed or expanded its definition of a political question at various times. For many years, the Court used this doctrine of political questions as grounds for refusing to consider reapportionment of state legislatures and congressional districts. In 1962 the Court reversed its position forcing state legislatures to draw boundaries to create districts with more nearly equal populations (*Baker* v. *Carr*). In the 2000 presidential election, the Court could have avoided deciding the case by declaring that it was more appropriate for state courts or Congress to resolve—a position consistent with the Court's support for federalism. But it didn't. A political question, then, is whatever issue the Supreme Court wants to avoid.

Just as the Court avoids political questions, so too it avoids *constitutional issues*. The Court will not decide a case on the basis of a constitutional question unless there is no other way to dispose of the case. The Court will not declare a law unconstitutional unless it clearly violates the Constitution. In general, the Court will assume that a law is valid unless proved otherwise. Although we have stressed the role of the Court in applying the Constitution, the vast majority of cases it decides deal with interpretations of less important federal and state laws.

A final internal limit on the Court is that of *precedent* or *stare decisis* ("to stand by the decision"). Justices generally follow previous Court decisions in cases involving the same issue. Recent abortion cases have illustrated the reluctance of the Court to reverse precedents, in this instance *Roe* v. *Wade* (1973). Yet, as the conservative majority on the Rehnquist Court has shown, at times the Court will not follow precedent if they feel the prior cases did not follow the Constitution or the justices' own leanings. The Court likes to appear consistent with precedent even when changing the law.

What these limits on its power mean is that the Court avoids most of the constitutional questions pressed upon it. "Delay" is the Court's favorite tactic when, for both political and legal reasons, the Court wants to duck an issue that is too controversial, on which the law is uncertain, or where there is no political consensus. It may simply not hear the case, or it may decide it for reasons other than the major issue involved. A recent example of this judicial avoidance occurred in June 2004 when the Court refused to rule on the constitutionality of the phrase "under God" in the Pledge of Allegiance. The Court cited procedural reasons for not deciding on this inflammatory issue in an election year. Knowing the difficulty of enforcing a ruling against strong public opinion, the Court generally avoids such a confrontation.

This self-imposed restraint may make the use of judicial review scattered and long delayed. But the Court has maintained its great authority of judicial review by refusing in most instances to use it.

External Limits on the Court

External limits on the Court come from the duties the Constitution gives to other parts of the government, especially to Congress. Congress has the right to set when and how often the Court will meet, to establish the number of justices, and to restrict the Court's jurisdiction. This last power has been used to keep the Court out of areas in which Congress wished to avoid judicial involvement. For example, the bill establishing the Alaska pipeline excluded the Court from exercising jurisdiction (on possible damage to the environment) under the Environmental Protection Act. Also, Congress may pass legislation so detailed that it limits the Court's scope in interpreting the law. Finally, the Senate has the duty of approving the president's nominations to the bench, and Congress has the seldom-used power to impeach Supreme Court justices.

These limits on the Court underscore the real weaknesses of that body. With no army or bureaucracy to enforce its decisions, the Court must depend on the rest of the government to accept and carry out its decisions. (President Andrew Jackson, angrily disagreeing with a Supreme Court decision, once remarked: "John Marshall has rendered his decision; now let him enforce it!") Yet, with few exceptions, the Court's decisions have been enforced and accepted. And when opposed, this weak, semi-isolated branch of government has been able to overcome resistance. Why?

Strengths of the Court

The Court relies on three major supports: (1) its enormous prestige, (2) the fragmented nature of the American constitutional structure, and (3) the American legal profession, which acts like the Court's constituency.

The Court's *prestige* is unquestionable. Despite public dissent to many of its decisions in areas like civil liberties and abortion, the Court retains its high public standing. Opinion polls have shown that the position of a judge is one of the most respected in our society. This respect is due not only to the quality of the people who become judges, but also to the appearance of an elevated judicial process. Anyone who has watched televised criminal trials is familiar with the aspects of theater in the legal process: the judge sitting on a raised platform dressed in robes, the formal speeches addressed to "your honor," the use of Latin phrases, and the oath on the Bible. After the controversial 2000 Florida election decision no justice felt the need to justify the opinion in the press, yet the Court's popularity remained high.

All these customs create a somber impression of dignity, which masks the fact that a judge is simply a public administrator resolving controversies. The Supreme Court, which presides over this judicial system, has added prestige because it is seen as the guardian of the Constitution and often is equated with that document in people's eyes.

Another strength of the Court lies in the *fragmented nature of the American system of government*. With the separation of powers among the branches of the federal government, and federalism dividing power between the states and federal government, conflict is inevitable. This division of power creates a need for an umpire; the Court fills that role.

In acting as an umpire, the Court is hardly neutral. Its decisions may reflect the justices' partisan loyalties. They are certainly political in determining who gets what, when, and how, and to enforce them the Court needs political support. The other political players might not give this support to decisions they strongly disagree with. Consequently, the Court's rulings generally reflect the practices and values of the country's dominant political forces. As an umpire, the Court enforces the constitutional rules of the game as practiced by the political game's most powerful players, of which it is one.

A final source of support for the Court is the *legal profession*. There are almost 1 million lawyers in the United States. Lawyers occupy all the major judicial positions, and more lawyers than any other occupational group hold offices in national, state, and city governments. Between 1972 and 1994 the number of Washington lawyers went from around 11,000 to 63,000. Perhaps the number of lawyers explains why so many political conflicts, including sex scandals and presidential elections, end up as legal issues. Other countries manage with far fewer lawyers and far fewer issues winding up in court. Some scholars argue that lawyers use their domination of elected offices to pass laws and regulations that create new demands for their skills. The American Bar Association (ABA), with about half the lawyers in the country as members, reviews nominees to the bench, and its comments on a candidate's fitness influence whether he or she is appointed. Because of their own commitment to law, as well as some similarity in educational and social backgrounds, lawyers generally back the Court.

THE COURT AS A POLITICAL PLAYER

The Supreme Court is a political institution that sets national policy by interpreting the law. In applying the Constitution and laws to the cases before it, the Court clearly makes political choices. In arriving at decisions on controversial questions of national policy, the Court is acting in the political game. The procedures may be legal, the decisions may be phrased in lawyers' language, but to view the court solely as a legal institution is to ignore its important political role.

"We are under the Constitution, but the Constitution is what the judges say it is," declared former Chief Justice Charles Evans Hughes. In interpreting the meaning of the Constitution, each Supreme Court must operate within the political climate of its time. Judges not only read the Constitution, but they read the newspaper as well. The Court must rely on others, especially the executive branch, to enforce its rulings. The Court cannot ignore the reactions to its decisions in Congress or in the nation, because as a political player, its influence ultimately rests on the acceptance of these decisions by the other political players and the public. Nor, generally, are the Court's

The Court Waits for an Election

Civil rights decisions have never been far removed from politics. Here is an example of the Court keeping an eye on the political arena in a landmark case:

"Why doesn't the Supreme Court pass the school desegregation case?" asked one of Chief Justice Vinson's law clerks in 1952. *Brown* v. *Board of Education of Topeka, Kansas,* had arrived on the Court's docket in 1951, but it was carried over for oral argument the next term and then consolidated with four other cases and reargued in December 1953. The landmark ruling did not come down until May 17, 1954.

"Well," Justice Frankfurter explained, "we're holding it for the election"—1952 was a presidential election year.

"You're holding it for the election?" the clerk persisted in disbelief. "I thought the Supreme Court was supposed to decide cases without regard to elections."

"When you have a major social political issue of this magnitude, timing and public reactions are important considerations, and," Frankfurter continued, "we do not think this is the time to decide it."

Source: David M. O'Brien, *Storm Center: The Supreme Court in American Politics.* New York: W.W. Norton, 1993.

opinions long out of line with the dominant views in the legislative and executive branches. (See "The Court Waits for an Election.")

Judicial Activism Versus Judicial Restraint

The question of how the political and legal power of the Court should be applied has centered on the use of judicial review. Should judicial authority be active or restrained? How far should the Court go in shaping policy when it may conflict with other branches of the government? The two sides of this debate are reflected in the competing practices of *judicial restraint* and *judicial activism.*

Judicial restraint is the idea that the Court should not impose its views on other branches of the government or on the states unless there is a clear violation of the Constitution. Judicial restraint (often called *self-restraint*) calls for a passive role in which the Court lets the elected branches of the government lead the way in setting policy on controversial political issues. The Court intervenes in these issues only with great reluctance. Felix Frankfurter and Oliver Wendell Holmes Jr. are two of the more famous justices of the Supreme Court identified with judicial restraint. Frankfurter argued that social improvement should be left to more appropriate parts of the federal and state government chosen by the voters. The Court, he declared, should avoid conflicts with other branches of the federal government whenever possible.

Judicial activism is the view that the Supreme Court should be an active, creative partner with the legislative and executive branches in shaping government policy. Judicial activists seek to apply the Court's authority to solving economic and political problems ignored by other parts of the government. In this view, the Court is more than an umpire of the American political game: It is an active participant as well. The Supreme Court under Earl Warren practiced judicial activism. In its rulings on reapportionment, school desegregation, and the right to counsel, the Warren Court broadly and boldly changed national policy.

It is important not to confuse judicial activism versus restraint with liberal versus conservative. Although many modern activist justices, such as Earl Warren and Thurgood Marshall, have taken liberal positions on issues like school integration and toleration of dissent, this wasn't always so. John Marshall's court was both activist (in establishing judicial review) and conservative (in protecting private property rights). The conservative Supreme Court during the 1930s attempted to strike down most of Franklin D. Roosevelt's New Deal program as unconstitutional. And the recent Rehnquist Court decisions limiting federal authority over the states and halting the vote count in the 2000 Florida election were seen as activist conservative reversals of liberal policies. On the restraint side, justices Frankfurter and Holmes were political liberals. Yet both believed it was not wise for the Court to dive into the midst of political battles to support positions they may have personally backed.

CASE STUDY

SEPARATE BUT EQUAL?

The Supreme Court's political role can be clearly seen in the evolution of "separate but equal." By first approving racial segregation late in the nineteenth century and later abolishing it in the mid-twentieth century, the Court played a central role in establishing national policy that governed relations between the races. The changing but always powerful position of the judiciary in the history of racial segregation demonstrates the influence of the Court in national politics.

Political Background of Segregation

The end of the Civil War and the emancipation of the slaves did not offer black people the full rights of citizenship, nor did the passing of the Thirteenth Amendment in 1865 (which outlawed slavery), the Fourteenth Amendment in 1868 (which extended "equal protection of the laws" to all citizens), or the Fifteenth Amendment in 1870 (which guaranteed the right to vote to all male citizens regardless of "race, color, or previous condition of servitude").

Between 1866 and 1877, the "radical Republicans" controlled Congress. Although the sometimes corrupt period of *Reconstruction* partly deserves the bad name it has gotten in the South, it was a time when blacks won a number of political rights. In 1875 Congress passed a civil rights act designed to prevent any public form of discrimination—in theaters, restaurants, transportation, and the like—against blacks. Congress's right to forbid a *state* to act contrary to the Constitution was unquestioned. But this law, based on the Fourteenth Amendment, assumed that Congress could also prevent racial discrimination by private individuals.

The Supreme Court disagreed. In 1883 it declared the Civil Rights Act of 1875 unconstitutional. The majority of the Court ruled that Congress could pass legislation only to correct *states'* violations of the Fourteenth Amendment. Congress had no power to enact "primary and direct" legislation on individuals—that was left to the states. This decision meant the federal government could not lawfully protect blacks against most forms of discrimination. In other words, white supremacy was beyond federal control.

American Apartheid

Throughout the South during the late nineteenth and early twentieth centuries, Jim Crow laws (taking their name from a blackface minstrel song) were passed to prohibit blacks from using the same public facilities as whites. These state laws required segregated schools, hospitals, prisons, restaurants, toilets, railways, and waiting rooms. Some communities passed "sundown ordinances" that prohibited blacks from staying in town overnight. Blacks and whites could not even be buried in the same cemeteries.

There seemed to be no limit to the absurdity of segregation. New Orleans required separate districts for black and white prostitutes. In Oklahoma, blacks and whites could not use the same telephone booths. In North Carolina and Florida, school textbooks used by black children had to be stored separately from those used by white children. In Birmingham, Alabama, the races were specifically prohibited from playing checkers together.

With this blessing from the Supreme Court, the southern states passed a series of laws legitimizing segregation. These laws included all-white primary elections, elaborate tests to qualify for voting, and other racial restrictions. (See "American Apartheid.")

Separate but Equal

Segregation was given judicial approval in the landmark case of *Plessy v. Ferguson* (1896). Here, the Court upheld a Louisiana law requiring railroads to provide separate cars for the two races. The Court declared that segregation had nothing to do with the superiority of the white race,

and that segregation was not contrary to the Fourteenth Amendment as long as the facilities were equal. The doctrine of "separate but equal" in *Plessy v. Ferguson* became the law of the land in those states maintaining segregation.

In approving segregation and establishing the "separate but equal" doctrine, the Court was undoubtedly reflecting white attitudes of the time. To restore the South to the Union, the new congresses were willing to undo the radicals' efforts to protect blacks. It was the southern black who paid the price—exile halfway between slavery and freedom. And just as the Court was unwilling to prevent these violations of civil rights, so too were the executive and legislative branches.

Plessy v. *Ferguson* helped racial segregation continue as a southern tradition. For some 40 years, the "separate but equal" doctrine was not seriously challenged. "Separate" was strictly enforced; "equal" was not. Schools, government services, and other public facilities for blacks were clearly separate from tax-supported white facilities but just as clearly inferior to them. The Court did not even support its own doctrine during this period.

By the late 1930s, the Court began to look more closely at so-called equal facilities. In *Missouri ex. rel. Gaines* v. *Canada* (1938), the Court held that because Missouri did not have a law school for blacks, it must admit them to the white law school. In *Sweatt* v. *Painter* (1950), a black (Sweatt) was denied admission to the University of Texas Law School on the grounds that Texas was building a law school for blacks. The Court examined the new school carefully, found that it would in no way be equal to the white one, and ordered Sweatt admitted to the existing school.

Thus the *Plessy* doctrine of "separate but equal" was increasingly weakened by judicial decisions. By stressing the "equal" part of the doctrine, the Court was in fact making the doctrine impractical. (Texas was not likely to build a law school for blacks equal to its white one.) These decisions also reflected the Court's change in emphasis after 1937 from making economic policy to protecting individual rights.

Still, the Court did not overrule *Plessy* in this period. The Court was following precedent. Paralleling the rulings of the Court were the actions of the executive branch and some northern states that were increasingly critical of racial segregation. In 1941 Roosevelt issued an executive order forbidding discrimination in government employment. And Truman abolished segregation in the army in 1948. Congress, however, dominated by a conservative seniority system and blocked by southern filibusters in the Senate, was unable to pass civil rights measures. Nonetheless, public attitudes toward segregation were changing, and the Supreme Court's rulings were reflecting that change.

The End of Separate but Equal

In 1954 the Supreme Court finally reversed *Plessy* v. *Ferguson* in *Brown* v. *Board of Education,* even while denying it was overturning the precedent. The Court held that segregated public schools violated the "equal protection of the laws" guaranteed in the Fourteenth Amendment. "Separate but equal" had no place in public education, the Court declared. Drawing on sociological and psychological studies of the harm done to black children by segregation, the Warren Court's unanimous decision stated that in fact separate was "inherently unequal." This finding was the beginning of the end of *legal segregation*.

The Court backed up its new equal protection stand in areas other than education. In the years following the *Brown* decision, it outlawed segregation in interstate transportation, upheld legislation guaranteeing voting rights for blacks, reversed convictions of civil rights leaders, and often protected civil rights demonstrations by court order. These decisions, though they stirred up opposition to the Court (including demands to impeach Earl Warren), helped a political movement apply pressures to wipe out racial discrimination. Civil rights groups were active in these cases, which shows how results sometimes can be gotten from one part of government (the courts) if another part (the Congress) is unwilling to act.

Congress finally joined in by passing civil rights acts in 1957, 1960, and 1964. Both political parties had gained a heightened appreciation for the black voter, especially the large numbers who voted in northern cities. The 1964 act, coming after continuing pressure and agitation by civil rights activists, was the first comprehensive legislation of its kind since 1875. The act prohibited discrimination in those public accommodations (such as hotels, restaurants, and gas stations) involved in interstate commerce and in most businesses, and enforced equal voting rights for blacks.

The Court acted to encourage and to force all levels of the government—federal, state, and local—as well as the private sector to move toward full equality. The Court's support of busing to end the segregation of schools caused by housing patterns aroused opposition in northern cities like Boston. By the 1980s President Reagan was calling *affirmative action* "reverse discrimination" against white males. Yet affirmative action expanded beyond remedies for discrimination against African Americans to include vague goals of cultural diversity and racial "balance." It was also applied to groups from the Middle East and Latin America, with little historical claim to its benefits. As the programs spread, judicial and public support for affirmative action waxed and waned. In recent decisions the Supreme Court has narrowed and upheld affirmative action programs that fell under its strict scrutiny. (See "University of Michigan and Affirmative Action," Chapter 6.)

Still, racism remains. And for this the Supreme Court as well as the rest of the political system must share responsibility. For it was the Supreme Court that struck down Civil Rights Acts of the Reconstruction Era and failed to protect the rights of African Americans between 1883 and 1937 when they were most trampled on. And it was the Court that made "separate but equal" the legal justification for white supremacy. Even today the Court has viewed housing patterns—a major cause of segregated public schools—as largely beyond its influence. The Court's effort to put equal rights before the eyes of the nation was in many ways merely an undoing of its own past mistakes.

Throughout this history of the "separate but equal" doctrine, the Court acted politically as well as legally and morally. At times the Court held back efforts at social and political reform, at other times it confused the efforts, and at still others it forced political and social changes more rapidly than some would have preferred. Yet as the history of "separate but equal" makes clear, whether we agree or disagree with the Court's stand, it is never removed too far or for too long from the positions dominating the political game.

WRAP-UP

The federal court system consists of U.S. district courts, courts of appeals, special federal courts, and the U.S. Supreme Court. Although very few of the cases tried in the United States ever reach the Supreme Court, it retains its position as the "final authority" over what the Constitution means. Yet the Court's decisions often are changed over the years, usually by the Court itself, in part reflecting the changing political climate. Our brief history of the Court showed this, as did the case study of "separate but equal," where the Court first allowed racial segregation and then gradually reversed its position.

The practices of judicial activism and judicial restraint are two sides of the debate over how far the political involvement of the Court should go. The Court is limited by a number of its own practices and, most important, by its dependence on other parts of the government to enforce its decisions. The Court's respect for these limits, as well as its own great prestige, have given it the strength to overcome most resistance. In recent years there has been frequent criticism of its decisions on abortion, federalism, and election procedures. This criticism has run up against solid support for the Court.

Secure within its limits and resting on public respect, the Supreme Court of the United States remains a unique political player. No other government can boast of a long-held tradition that gives "nine old men" (and women, now), nonelected and serving for life, the duty of overturning the acts of popularly elected officials. Through this power of judicial review, the Court is deeply involved in making national policy, setting limits on how the political game is played, and bringing pressing social issues to the attention of the people and their leaders. Whether the Court protects individual liberties or partisan interests will depend on who the justices are, how they interpret the law, and which political forces prevail across the nation.

Thought Questions

1. How did the Supreme Court become so important to our system of government? Would John Marshall be pleased, or surprised?
2. Is the Supreme Court influenced too much by partisan loyalties and by public opinion? Give recent examples.
3. Why did the courts take the lead on civil rights for minorities? Isn't this issue more appropriate for the elected officials of the government?
4. Do judges deserve more respect than other government officials? Why or why not?

Suggested Readings

Branch, Taylor. *Parting the Waters: America in the King Years, 1954–1963.* New York: Simon & Schuster, 1988.
The Pulitzer Prize–winning account of the civil rights movement with a focus on Martin Luther King Jr.

Jacob, Herbert. *Law and Politics in the United States,* 2nd ed. New York: HarperCollins College Publishers, 1995. Pb.
Expertly describes the legal system—from courts to cops—and its gatekeeping role to the political game.

Lewis, Anthony. *Gideon's Trumpet.* New York: Vintage Books, 1966. Pb.
A short story that traces the development of a case from a Florida jail to the U.S. Supreme Court.

Phelps, Timothy M., and Helen Winternitz. *Capital Games: Clarence Thomas, Anita Hill and the Story of a Supreme Court Justice.* New York: Hyperion, 1992.
Eyewitness account of the controversial confirmation hearings of Justice Clarence Thomas by the reporters who first leaked Anita Hill's story.

Schwartz, Bernard. *Decision: How the Supreme Court Decides Cases.* New York: Oxford University Press, 1997.
A legal scholar shows how some major decisions of the Supreme Court were reached, including *Roe* v. *Wade.*

Tushnet, Mark. *A Court Divided: The Rehnquist Court and the Future of Constitutional Law.* New York: W.W. Norton, 2005.
An indepth look at the Rehnquist Court by one of the country's leading legal scholars.

CHAPTER 6

Civil Rights and Liberties: Protecting the Players

Civil Rights and Liberties

Civil rights and liberties protect the political players, as well as the rest of us. They restrict government conduct (e.g., due process of law) and describe some of the goals of politics (e.g., freedom of speech). They have given our citizens protections regarding gender, age, sexual preference, and race that they didn't have a half century ago. The United States' government was defined by the Constitution and Bill of Rights so that certain rules govern the relationships between people and their government, and other rules govern the relationships between groups of citizens. These rules rest on two principles: The government must not violate the civil rights and liberties of the people; the government must protect people from the actions of those who would violate their rights.

This chapter focuses on how the courts and other players protect civil rights and liberties. We will see what these rights and liberties are, and how the protections in the Bill of Rights have expanded down through American history. We will discuss the different players involved in applying these protections. A case study on terrorists and due process shows these civil liberties under pressure (See "Fighting Terror, Guarding Liberties").

WHAT ARE CIVIL LIBERTIES AND RIGHTS?

Civil liberties are protections against government restrictions on freedom of expression, such as freedom of speech and religion. Civil liberties are those First Amendment rights of freedom of speech, petition, assembly, and press that protect people against government actions that would interfere with their participation in democratic politics. This definition includes Fifth Amendment and Fourteenth Amendment guarantees of due process of law in courtroom proceedings and government agencies. The underlying principle here is that ours is a government of laws rather than of arbitrary, unfair action.

Civil rights are protections for some groups, which because of their race, religion, ethnicity, or gender may be discriminated against by others. Civil rights involve the protections granted in the Fourteenth Amendment to the Constitution recognizing that all citizens are entitled to be treated equally under the law. No members of a racial, religious, or economically privileged group may claim or receive privileged treatment by virtue of group membership, nor may any group be discriminated against by other groups or by government officials.

Examples of civil rights and liberties issues are present in our daily lives. Civil liberties involve your rights as a college student: Can school authorities censor the student newspaper? Suspend a student for making nasty remarks about homosexuals? Establish a "civility" code barring "hate speech"? Other issues involve your rights as a member of the public to be informed: Can the government prevent a newspaper from publishing a story on "national security" grounds? Can it require reporters to reveal their sources to a grand jury investigating a crime? Can the government restrict information on making bombs sent over the Internet? (See "Codes, Colleges, and Free Speech After 9/11.")

Codes, Colleges, and Free Speech After 9/11

University attempts at speech codes are a common part of twenty-first-century college campuses. After September 11, new conflicts arose at colleges over speech that might violate codes aimed at avoiding offense to minorities. One of the more bizarre incidents occurred in the library of San Diego State University.

On September 22, 2001, an Ethiopian-born student, Zewdalem Kebede, overheard a discussion in Arabic among three Saudi Arabian students. According to Kebede, they expressed delight at the success of the terrorist attacks. The Ethiopian, a naturalized American, became furious and confronted them in their language, telling them that they "should feel shame" at the barbaric actions of their compatriots. A fourth student, a friend of the Saudis, joined the discussion and asked Kebede if he was threatening them. He said he was not and returned to his table.

A few days later, Kebede was brought up on misconduct charges by the University's Center for Student Rights and Responsibilities. He was told that he could be suspended or expelled under a California Code of Regulations prohibiting "abusive behavior directed toward, or hazing of, a member of the campus community." Kebede was forced to report to an administrator, had to explain his actions in writing, was put on probation, and was warned in a letter, "You are admonished to conduct yourself as a responsible member of the campus community in the future." A university spokesman explained, "[We] feel we have to protect students from feeling threatened."

The Foundation for Individual Rights in Education (FIRE), a civil liberties group, protested the university's action. FIRE wrote to the San Diego State president that no state code can override the protections of the First Amendment. Further the code was directed toward physical abuse such as hazing, not impassioned speech. The so-called victims outnumbered Mr. Kebede four to one. FIRE concluded, "A university in which students and faculty have any fear of reprisal for discussing controversial topics is one that is rendered impotent to address society's most crucial issues." After the warning no further action was taken against Mr. Kebede.

Everyone is affected by civil rights issues: Will you as a woman receive equal pay for equal work? As a Mexican American, will you be discriminated against in hiring and promotion? Will affirmative action programs designed to make up for past discrimination against minorities and women lead to "reverse discrimination" against you as a white male?

These issues have surfaced in national politics. In presidential elections a woman's right to an abortion, gay couples' right to marry, and a gun owner's right to defy local gun control laws have become topics of debate. Congress regularly grapples with civil rights issues: proposals to bar discrimination against the disabled, bills to limit federal funding for abortions in public hospitals, and measures making it easier to prove discrimination against women in employment. To get a handle on some of these current issues, let's look at the past.

EXPANDING THE BILL OF RIGHTS

The Bill of Rights applied only to the activities of the national government when it was added to the Constitution in 1791. The Congress that passed the Bill of Rights had no intention of restricting the activities of state governments. Since the early twentieth century, however, the protections of the Bill of Rights have gradually been extended to cover actions of state and local officials as well as individuals and organizations. In doing this, the federal courts have relied on the *Fourteenth Amendment.* That amendment, ratified in 1868, says in part that "nor shall any State deprive any person of life, liberty or property, without due process of law, nor deny to any person within its jurisdiction the equal protection of the laws." The two key, if vague, phrases are "due process" and "equal protection."

The *equal protection* clause has been used to prevent state officials from discriminating based on race or sex. It has also prevented discrimination by private individuals when that action (1) is aided by state action, such as a law; (2) furthers a state activity such as an election, or the activities of a political party; or (3) involves a fundamental state interest such as education or public safety. Therefore, the equal protection clause has been used to strike down state laws segregating students by race in public schools. It has been used to put an end to the "whites only" primaries that the Democratic parties of southern states used to hold prior to the general elections. It was even used to halt the hand recounting of votes in Florida in the 2000 election when the Supreme Court declared that different methods for counting votes would deprive citizens of equal protection. Though individuals may practice racial or religious or gender discrimination when they decide who to invite to their homes, they cannot discriminate in private schools because education involves a fundamental state interest. And private clubs that serve the public are now considered places of public accommodation. If they discriminate in selecting members on the basis of race or gender, they may lose certain tax advantages.

The *due process* clause of the Fourteenth Amendment applies to state and local governments. But to say that states must act according to "due process of law" raises a basic question: What does "due process" mean? The issue involves the extent that Bill of Rights protections should be "incorporated" into the language of the Fourteenth Amendment so as to apply to the states. On one side of the debate over due process are the *partial incorporationists.* They believe that only some of the Bill of Rights should be included in the meaning of "due process" in the Fourteenth Amendment, mainly those procedures guaranteeing fair criminal trials and First Amendment freedoms of religion, speech, and press. Which rights are to be incorporated? Those that are considered *preferred freedoms,* that is, the liberties necessary for a democracy to function, which, in the words of Justice Louis Brandeis, form the essence of "a scheme of ordered liberty." But not everything in the Bill of Rights is considered fundamental by partial incorporationists.

On the other side of the debate are the *complete incorporationists.* They believe that the entire Bill of Rights was incorporated into the Fourteenth Amendment. Thus, there is no need to consider which rights to apply. When a case comes before them, they incorporate the entire Bill of Rights and use it as a limit against state action.

Consider the case of a prisoner held in a state penitentiary who sues the warden in federal court. The prisoner argues that two months of solitary confinement for a mess hall riot is a violation of the Eighth Amendment prohibition against "cruel and unusual punishment." Partial incorporationists first must decide whether or not the Eighth Amendment should be incorporated into the Fourteenth Amendment as a limitation on state prison officials. They might argue that it applies only to criminal trials in state courts and that prison discipline does not involve any "fundamental rights." Full incorporationists would automatically incorporate the Eighth Amendment into the Fourteenth Amendment: There would be no question that the amendment applied to state prison officials. The judge would decide only the question of whether two months of solitary confinement qualified as "cruel and unusual punishment."

Full incorporation has never been embraced by the Supreme Court. Yet, in the past 90 years, the effect of numerous federal court decisions has been to incorporate almost all of the Bill of Rights into the Fourteenth Amendment. Those that have not been incorporated are not very important.

CIVIL LIBERTIES: PROTECTING
PEOPLE FROM GOVERNMENT

For the framers of the Constitution, the greatest danger to citizens lay in the abuse of government power. For this reason, the most important civil liberties are those that provide protection for citizens from their government. Most of these "preferred freedoms" are derived from the *First Amendment,* which states:

> Congress shall make no law respecting an establishment of religion, or prohibiting the free exercise thereof; or abridging the freedom of speech, or of the press, or the right of the people peaceably to assemble, and to petition the Government for a redress of grievances.

The First Amendment's "rules of the game" are essential to allow democracy to work. They enable people to keep informed, to communicate with each other and with the government without fear. Remove these protections, and it would be difficult for political players to function. The press, interest groups, and even members of Congress would find their ability to "go public" and organize to change government policies restricted. The political party that lost an election might be prevented from getting out its message, making it difficult to contest the next election. The Bill of Rights, along with separation of powers and checks and balances, are designed to protect a people with a historically healthy fear of governmental power.

Supreme Court Justice Oliver Wendell Holmes once wrote that a democratic society needs competition among ideas as much as an economic marketplace needs competition among producers. "When men have realized that time has upset many fighting faiths," he wrote, "they come to believe . . . that the ultimate good desired is better reached by free trade in ideas—that the best truth is the power of the thought to get itself accepted in the competition of the marketplace." Put another way, how can you be sure your opinion is correct unless you are willing to test it against different opinions? And how can wrong opinions ever be changed, even when held by a majority, unless there is freedom for other opinions to be expressed?

Fundamental to Holmes's thinking is the belief that good ideas would drive bad ideas out of the market and that the public will reject the false in favor of the true. Given the awesome power of modern communications, and the lack of knowledge about politics shown by many Americans, these calculations may not always be true. Propaganda sometimes overwhelms reason; the demagogue may defeat the statesman. But it is hard to see how restricting speech can provide better safeguards for democracy.

A look at recent thinking about four of the most important civil liberties—freedoms of speech and religion, the right to privacy, and due process of law—will help us to understand how the Bill of Rights works to protect citizens.

Freedom of Speech

The First Amendment guarantee of freedom of speech has been widened to apply to state governments under the Fourteenth Amendment. "Speech" has also been deepened by court decisions to include not only speaking but also gesturing, wearing buttons and armbands, raising signs, and leafleting passersby. The Supreme Court has upheld laws that make it a crime to conspire to overthrow the government by force. But it has struck down convictions of Communists based on their membership in the Communist Party because the government was infringing on their freedom of association. Just believing in the violent overthrow of the government, or even giving a speech about revolution, is not a crime, nor is membership in an organization that believes in the violent overthrow of the government. The courts insist that if the government puts terrorists in prison, it first proves that they took concrete action to commit violence.

The First Amendment not only protects your right to say what you believe, but it also prohibits the government from forcing you to say what you don't believe. In 1943, during World War II, schoolchildren who were Jehovah's Witnesses refused to say the Pledge of Allegiance, on the grounds that they would be worshipping "graven images" (the flag) against the beliefs of their religion. The Supreme Court overturned their suspension from school by state officials, and Justice Robert Jackson wrote, "No official, high or petty, can prescribe what shall be orthodox in politics, nationalism, religion, or other matters of opinion, or force citizens to confess by word or act their faith therein." As Americans, we have the freedom to refuse to say what we do not believe.

The Supreme Court has protected what is called *speech plus*. This involves symbolic actions, such as wearing buttons or burning flags. In one case, an antiwar student who entered a courthouse with the words "Fuck the Draft" written on the back of his jacket was held in contempt by a local judge. The decision was reversed by the Supreme Court. As one justice pointed out, "While the particular four-letter word being litigated here is perhaps more distasteful than most others of its genre, it nevertheless is often true that one man's vulgarity is another's lyric." (See "Conservative Bake Sales.")

The First Amendment provides no protection to speech that directly leads to illegal conduct or that might be considered illegal conduct by itself. Shouting "fire" in a crowded theater (when there is no fire) is not considered speech, but rather a reckless action that the

Conservative Bake Sales

Conservative student organizations held "affirmative action bake sales" on college campuses across the country in the fall of 2003. Brownies were sold at varying prices: black and Hispanic students were charged less than Asian and white students. Supporters described the sales as satire designed to draw attention to the discrimination involved in affirmative action. Many university administrators were not amused.

At William & Mary, for example, the president denounced the bake sale there as "inexcusably hurtful" and "abusive." The sale was halted because it "did not meet the administrative requirements we routinely impose on such activities." A lawyer for the student group remarked, "One can hardly imagine such tactics being used to shut down a protest that administrators found more to their liking politically." At other campuses, like the University of Washington, the College Republicans holding the sales were attacked by other students.

Elsewhere, universities defended the sales. An Indiana University administrator remarked, "It is exactly the kind of dialogue that should be encouraged on college campuses." Back at William & Mary, after press coverage, a second bake sale was allowed two months after the previous one was halted.

state may punish. Writing or speaking damaging lies about a person (libel and slander) is not protected, and you can be sued. Making or selling child pornography is not protected speech and does not involve freedom of expression, and you go to jail for it. When an individual directs abuse or "fighting words" at someone, particularly a police officer, convictions for disorderly conduct will be upheld by the courts.

Questions of free speech have come online. A few years ago, at the urging of groups like the Christian Coalition, several senators downloaded hardcore pornography from the Internet. The result was the Communications Decency Act of 1996, which punished making "indecent" or "patently offensive" material available to minors over the Internet. But in 1997 the Supreme Court struck down the Act as overly vague (*Reno et al.* v. *ACLU et al.*), ruling that constitutional free speech protections apply just as much to online systems as they do to books and newspapers. (Some pointed out that if the conservative-backed law had remained, the Starr Report on Bill Clinton's behavior with Monica Lewinsky and its graphic descriptions of sexual acts could not have been put on the Internet by Congress.) Since the Court's ruling, computer companies have been pressured to develop

Privacy on the Internet

With traditional communications, like telephone or mail, the courts have been pretty clear what is out of bounds for government snooping. For example, a detective can look at an envelope, but he or she can't read the letter without a search warrant approved by a judge. The Internet introduced entirely new problems both in keeping messages private and in government monitoring of security threats. The USA Patriot Act passed shortly after 9/11 attempted to give law enforcement officials more powers to track down terrorists on the Internet. But three characteristics of the Internet confound any government attempts to deal with individual rights, safety, or privacy:

- *It's global:* On the Internet, a computer across the world can be reached as easily as one across the room. How do you enforce national laws in this environment? One example of a problem lies in the "virtual" gambling casinos that have been set up on the Internet using computers located outside the United States. Parents in the United States have caught their kids gambling on the Internet with their parents' credit cards.
- *It's anonymous:* Disguising your name on the Internet is easy. An occasional contributor to a pornography newsgroup identifies himself as "George W. Bush, the president," although everyone assumes it's not really him.
- *It's huge:* Terabytes, or trillions of bytes, of data are circulating on the Internet at any given moment. As one commentator put it, "Trying to locate illegal or offensive data on the net would be harder than trying to isolate two paired words in all the world's telephone conversations and television transmissions at once."

technological tools to filter information on the Web. Depending on your viewpoint, this filtering technology is either a parental tool for controlling their children without government involvement, or a censoring device limiting this democratic communications medium. (See "Privacy on the Internet.")

Freedom of Religion

The Constitution provides that there will be no religious test for office, and the First Amendment allows the "free exercise of religion" and prohibits the establishment of an official religion by Congress. Yet there has never been a complete "wall of separation" between church and state in the United States. The armed forces have chaplains paid for by Congress; the Supreme Court chambers have a mural of Moses giving the Ten Commandments; the dollar bill proclaims "In God We Trust." This involvement with religions was extended by President George W. Bush who proposed giving government funds to faith-based groups for their charitable work.

The question of freedom of religion inevitably gets mixed up in the constitutional prohibition against the establishment of religion. To allow students to pray in school, a position favored by a large majority of Americans, may seem to be simply an issue of free exercise of religion. But if most children in the class are Protestant, should the prayer be from a Protestant denomination? And if so, which one? Will other children feel like outcasts, even if they are excused from saying the prayer? The Clinton administration tried to clarify the legal limits of religion in public schools and to distinguish between what teachers cannot do, and what students can do. (See "Do's and Don'ts on Religion in Public Schools.")

While Americans strongly support freedom of religion, most believe that the government must not favor one religion over another. Balancing these competing values is very difficult, and the courts have become less rigid in separating government activities from religious practices. In 1995 the Supreme Court ruled against the University of Virginia for refusing to fund a student publication because it had a Christian orientation. In 2002 the Catholic Church argued—unsuccessfully—in court that it was shielded from suits against priests for child abuse by the First

Do's and Don'ts on Religion in Public Schools

Department of Education guidelines on religious activity in schools:

Permitted:

- Student prayer by individuals or groups
- Student-initiated discussions on religions
- Reading the Bible
- Saying grace before meals
- Wearing religious clothing or symbols
- Religious activities before or after school

Forbidden:

- Prayer endorsed or organized by teachers or administrators
- "Harassing" invitations to participate in prayer
- Teaching or encouraging a particular religion, rather than teaching about religion
- Denying school rooms to religious groups

Amendment protection of religious freedom. In 2003 the Alabama chief justice placed a 2.6-ton granite monument to the Ten Commandments in his state building. A federal district court found he had violated the separation of religion and government, and ordered the monument removed. A Gallup poll found that 77 percent of the public disagreed with the decision to remove the monument.

How to recognize the religious sentiments of the people, yet ensure that government does not infringe on religious freedom or favor one group over another, is a delicate matter. As former New York Governor Mario Cuomo observed, "I protect my right to be Catholic by preserving your right to be a Jew, or a Protestant, or a nonbeliever, or anything else you choose."

Rights of Privacy

To what extent do citizens have privacy rights against snooping by government officials or attempts to regulate their intimate social, sexual, and cultural behavior? Though nowhere mentioned in the Constitution, the First Amendment along with the Ninth Amendment are sometimes read by the courts as creating a "zone of privacy" that shields individuals from government intrusion into their homes, phones, computers, and bedrooms.

Some recent privacy issues have centered on sexual conduct. The state, according to the Supreme Court, cannot prevent couples from using contraceptive devices, nor can states forbid abortions in the first trimester of pregnancy. However, state regulations making it difficult for women to use abortion services without informing their spouses or waiting 24 hours after "family counseling" have been upheld. States may not forbid sexual relations between individuals of different races, as some states did to preserve the "purity" of the white race. In a notable 1996 decision, *Romer* v. *Evans,* the Court ruled that Colorado could not single out gays and prohibit local laws designed to end discrimination against them.

The Supreme Court has not required states to recognize homosexual marriages on the same footing as heterosexual marriages (though states and cities are free to do so). In early 2004, President Bush endorsed a constitutional amendment that would restrict marriage to two people of the opposite sex. The president was responding to Massachusetts state court decisions granting marriage rights to same-sex couples, and to the issuing of marriage licenses by mayors, including San Francisco's, to gay and lesbian couples. President Bush's conservative base endorsed his position, but the difficulty of the amendment process made the proposal more of a campaign issue than a likely constitutional change.

Due Process Rights

The Fifth Amendment and the Fourteenth Amendment can be called on to prevent national and state governments from depriving persons of their lives, liberty, or property without due process of law. Due process guarantees involve fundamental procedural fairness and impartial rulings by government officials, especially in (but not limited to) criminal courtrooms. In criminal trials, the right to due process includes the right to free counsel if you cannot afford a lawyer; the right to have your lawyer present at any police questioning; the right to reasonable bail after being charged; the right to a speedy trial; the right to confront and cross-examine your accuser and witnesses testifying against you; the right to remain silent (remember Martha Stewart refusing to testify?); the right to an impartial judge and a jury of your peers, selected without racial bias; and the right to appeal the decision to a higher court if you believe legal errors were committed by the judge.

These rights were granted in federal criminal trials under the Fifth Amendment and the Sixth Amendment. As a result of Supreme Court decisions over the years, these rights also have been established for state criminal trials. In the 1970s the federal courts began to require some of these procedures in noncriminal settings. Students could not be suspended from high schools or public universities without certain kinds of hearings. People on welfare could not be purged from the rolls without receiving "fair hearings." Whether these rights extend to wartime situations and people accused of terrorism is an ongoing debate. (See Case Study, "Fighting Terror, Guarding Liberties.")

Consider the case of a student who has participated in a disruptive campus demonstration against the war in Iraq. She is told by university officials that she has violated rules and will be suspended for a semester. Surely she would want all the due process guarantees she could obtain in order to prove to these officials that they are wrong. Obtaining one due process right often leads to obtaining others. Once the college decides that students are entitled to a hearing, students may demand the right to an attorney. The attorney will insist on written transcripts and an appeals process. The very existence of a fair hearing procedure and the presence of lawyers can encourage informal settlements without a hearing—a money-saving step usually welcomed by all parties.

These due process rights support First Amendment political freedoms. It does little good to give people the right to protest if officials can retaliate by cutting off essential services to protesters. Students or workers who are politically involved need legal protection from unfair action by school administrators or employers. Due process protects them. It also protects officials. By requiring them to meet high standards of fairness and procedure, it helps make their actions appear legitimate.

CIVIL RIGHTS: PROTECTING PEOPLE FROM PEOPLE

Protecting people against state action is only half the game. Civil rights involve the national government in the protection of minorities (or women, who are a majority) against actions by state and local governments or private individuals and organizations.

Civil rights issues involve discrimination based on race, religion, gender, age, sexual preference, or national origin. A group that believes it is being discriminated against may try to obtain satisfaction from elected officials, or it may turn to the judiciary. African Americans may find it difficult to rent apartments because landlords discriminate against them. To combat this, many states and the national government have passed fair housing laws, which make such discrimination illegal. Presidents have signed executive orders banning racial discrimination in public housing and in private housing financed through federal mortgage programs.

Civil rights issues are not always clear-cut. Affirmative action programs sometimes have placed groups in opposition to one another. The woman who supports affirmative action in order to get a job may be in conflict with the African American who believes that these programs were designed primarily to redress wrongs committed against blacks. As the civil rights leader Dr. Kenneth Clark remarked, if women, blacks, Latinos, and Asians are all given affirmative action preferences, almost three-quarters of the population would be protected. These programs also have fueled white resentment against "reverse discrimination."

However valid these critics may be, they have not spelled out alternative policies that would speak to the burdens facing many poor people in minority as well as white communities. Without programs that address poverty, illiteracy, and unemployment, wherever they exist, criticisms of affirmative action can only be half correct—they leave an unfilled space for future efforts that can remedy these ills without the public disfavor of racially based programs. In this evolution the courts, too, will play a role.

Which People Need Protection?
Suspect Classifications

The Fourteenth Amendment sets forth the right to "equal protection of the laws." However, the government may pass laws applying to some citizens and not to others, or applying different criteria to different classes of people. For example, working people with low incomes receive money from the government (in the form of the earned-income tax credit) while people who earn higher amounts of money pay taxes at several higher rates, depending on how much income they receive.

What limits are placed on government classifications of people? Hardly any if the classifications involve wealth and income. The laws dealing with economic issues are routinely approved by the judiciary, under the doctrine of *presumptive legislative rationality*. Courts assume that the lawmakers know what they are doing when they make such classifications. On the other hand, if lawmakers apply racial, religious, or national origin classifications, the courts subject these to "close scrutiny," because these are *"suspect" classifications*. Here the burden of proof is on the government to demonstrate that the classification is not, on its face, unconstitutional.

Governments must, when the law or action touches a "suspect class," prove a compelling state interest for their action. The courts begin their scrutiny with the assumption that the action violates the equal protection guarantee, and it is up to the lawmakers to prove otherwise. Racial classifications always are considered suspect, and almost always are struck down. Gender classifications are not suspect. The court applies a "middle test," which is stricter than standards for wealth and income but looser than standards for race. While courts have struck down many gender classifications, they have upheld some: Women are not registered for the military, and women who volunteer for the armed forces do not serve in combat positions. Women, because they give birth, may be given different medical benefits than men.

Race as a Suspect Classification

In 1896 the Supreme Court supported state actions that segregated the races. In the famous case of *Plessy v. Ferguson*, it upheld the right of Louisiana to require racial segregation in railway cars. "Equal protection of the law" was misshapen into the doctrine of "separate but equal": The African American Plessy would travel in a separate railway car, but would reach his destination at the same time and on the same train as a white person. Then in the 1954 landmark case *Brown v. Board of Education,* the Supreme Court held that schools segregated by race were unequal and violated the Fourteenth Amendment. After *Brown*, courts struck down most laws based on racial categories and made race a suspect classification.

But do racial classifications always violate the Fourteenth Amendment? Are there circumstances in which classification by race is a valid use of governmental power? Courts have upheld racial classifications when used to eliminate prior state-sponsored segregation. In devising plans to desegregate schools, for instance, administrators took into account the race of students attending schools, as well as their teachers. After all, to make desegregation work, one would have to put many blacks into schools that had previously been all white.

Affirmative action programs permit racial classifications. An affirmative action program in schools allows admissions officers to take race and ethnicity into account in awarding places in the entering class. An affirmative action program in employment usually requires employers to make efforts to match the racial and gender numbers in their workforce with the pool of qualified workers in their areas. In 1978, in the *University of California Regents* v. *Bakke*, the Supreme Court upheld the principle of affirmative action, holding that it was a "state interest" to provide for diversity among medical students at the University of California. At the same time, the Court held that the use of numerical quotas for minorities was a violation of the equal protection clause.

The Supreme Court has since grown skeptical of affirmative action programs. In 1986 the court upheld promotion quotas in *Cleveland Firefighters,* but only where the quotas were considered a remedy for a specific violation, rather than to generally promote diversity. *Adarand* v. *Pena* (1995) threw out a federal set-aside program for minority contractors. While still not declaring all affirmative action programs unconstitutional, the Court made clear that there had to be a "compelling interest" to relieve a specific case of discrimination and that the remedy had to be "narrowly tailored." In the recent University of Michigan case, the Supreme Court surprised many by allowing affirmative action programs in university admissions to promote educational diversity. (See "University of Michigan and Affirmative Action.")

Governments have increasingly turned lukewarm toward affirmative action. The Clinton administration's Justice Department issued guidelines for federal agencies stressing that government programs needed to respond to specific discrimination rather than general racism. This led to reducing or eliminating 17 affirmative action programs. President Bush has publicly supported opposition to affirmative action including the cases against the University of Michigan.

University of Michigan and Affirmative Action

In the spring of 2003, the Supreme Court heard arguments about the University of Michigan's admission policies intended to boost minority enrollments. In *Grutter* v. *Bollinger* (and a parallel case in the college), a white student argued that because less qualified minorities were admitted to the law school, she was denied a place.

The university said that race-conscious admissions was a constitutional and limited way of ensuring "educational diversity" in each class. It was the only way of guaranteeing diversity in their selective school. Opponents, including the Bush administration, argued that this was in fact a racial quota and that the goal of diversity could be reached through race-neutral methods, like the Texas plan of admitting the top 10 percent of public school graduates. Using race violated white students' constitutional right to equal treatment under the law.

On June 23, 2003, the Court supported the law school's affirmative action program as a flexible, narrow way of promoting diversity in their student body. At the same time they rejected the undergraduate admissions program that awarded points based on race, regardless of individual merits. The Court supported the *Bakke* decision (1978) that race could be a factor in admissions, but worried that what was once a temporary "catch-up" remedy to discrimination was becoming permanent. But the 5–4 majority seemed more concerned about the briefs filed by 78 of the country's leading institutions stressing their need for affirmative action programs. One influential brief was from U.S. military leaders who, with the war in Iraq raging, pointed to their need for a multiethnic officer corps. The irony of the government arguing against racial preferences that they supported in their own military academies was not lost on the Court.

One member of his administration criticized the "civil rights industry" and denounced affirmative action as "a corrupt system of preferences, set-asides and quotas."

Yet public opinion, which was negative toward the programs a few years ago, seems more mixed today. Polling data are unreliable because the results depend on the wording of the questions. In a 2003 CBS poll, support for affirmative action programs stood at 53 percent. But when mention is made of "preferential treatment" for minorities, support dropped by half. Yet the consequences of eliminating affirmative action also concern the public. The banning in California of the use of race in college admissions led to a drastic 57 percent drop in black applicants and a 40 percent decline in Hispanic high school seniors accepted for admission at Berkeley. This led some opponents of affirmative action to question their criticisms and puzzle over these "unintended consequences." In other arenas, including the military and business, affirmative action programs appear to be a permanent fixture, whatever their popularity.

Is Sex Suspect?

In the nineteenth century, women and children were exploited in factories, where they worked 14-hour days, seven days a week, for low wages and in unsafe conditions. In the late nineteenth century, a coalition of women's rights advocates, labor union organizers, and public health professionals demanded that government provide special protection for women and children in the form of wage and hour regulations. Some states passed such laws, known as *protective legislation*. Many were held unconstitutional by the Supreme Court, which opposed state efforts to regulate industry.

But protective legislation did not stop with factory conditions. State legislatures went further in "protecting" women by restricting their opportunities to enter professions. In 1873 the Supreme Court upheld a decision by the Illinois courts that prevented Myra Bradwell from becoming a lawyer. "The natural and proper timidity and delicacy which belongs to the female sex," a justice wrote, "evidently unfits it for many of the occupations of civil life." Under this reasoning, women were denied the right to enter businesses, serve on juries, make contracts, or work at all if they were pregnant. As former Supreme Court Justice William Brennan observed, this "romantic paternalism" put women "not on a pedestal, but in a cage."

Throughout the twentieth century, these restrictions on women were chipped away. In the 1970s, women's groups attacked the remaining "protective" laws in federal courts. They argued that gender should be considered a suspect classification. The Supreme Court responded by striking down many laws involving gender, but has not held that gender classifications are suspect. The Court has struck down professional and educational requirements that discriminate against women. It has ruled that men have an equal right to sue for alimony, that the drinking age must be the same for both sexes, and that unwed fathers have rights in deciding whether a baby is put up for adoption.

On the other hand, the Court has allowed state laws granting certain tax benefits to widows but not widowers. It upheld a state law permitting men but not women to serve as guards in a maximum security prison. It let stand a lower-court decision permitting single-sex schools to continue to receive federal funds. The Court has also upheld gender classifications when used for approved purposes such as an affirmative action plan. No challenges to single-sex bathrooms have succeeded.

The federal courts do retain one part of the protective movement, and that involves sexual harassment. The Court has recognized a pattern of harassment that exists, which makes it difficult for women to work in a hostile environment. In a 1991 civil rights law, Congress gave women who have been harassed on the job the right to sue in federal court for damages. In 1998 the Court held employers liable for a supervisor's behavior even if it did not know of the misconduct. In another case the same year, the Court declared that the law included sexual harassment even if both parties were men or the same sex (*Oncale* v. *Sundowner*).

Despite these cross-currents, it is likely that more sex-based classifications will fall as a result of present standards applied by the courts.

ACTORS IN CIVIL LIBERTIES AND RIGHTS

Many players in the political game act on issues of civil liberties and rights. Within the government, the courts have been the most important, although Congress may pass laws and the president may issue executive orders. Outside the government a number of organizations champion the rights of particular groups, pressuring officials with street tactics like picketing and boycotts. The politics of civil liberties and rights involves struggles of group against group, as well as group against government, in ongoing attempts to strike a balance among competing claims.

Judges

Judges have been in the forefront of protecting and expanding civil rights and liberties. Activist judges (who along with other supporters of civil liberties are called *civil libertarians*) issue decisions in *class action suits* in which lawyers bring a case to court not only for their individual clients, but also on behalf of everyone in a similar situation—perhaps millions of people. Judges may rely on court-appointed experts to do the research needed to resolve complicated social issues. To decide a case, they may use not only previous cases and laws but also the equity powers of the judiciary.

Equity is used to prevent permanent damage in situations not covered by existing law. Suppose my neighbor, Jones, decides to cut down a tree in his yard. I see that the tree will crash into my house. My legal remedy is to sue Jones after my house is damaged. My equitable remedy is to obtain a court injunction that prevents Jones from cutting down the tree in the first place. Activist judges use equity powers to shape remedies that overcome the effects of discrimination. Take a school district that has been segregated by race because of state administrative action. Merely requiring that the system act without regard to race may not have any real effect if housing segregation exists so that schools will remain segregated in fact. Some federal judges have applied equitable remedies: They have required that the school districts take into account racial imbalances and come up with plans (some of which involve busing) to overcome these imbalances.

Other judges are more restrained in civil liberties and civil rights cases. They follow past decisions rather than expand the scope of constitutional protections. They place great weight on the policies of Congress, the president, and state legislatures, even when these are against civil rights and liberties. These judges will presume that elected officials are acting lawfully unless proven otherwise. Because elected officials are directly accountable to voters, these unelected judges hesitate to impose their own views. (See pp. 145–146 for more on activist and restrained judges.)

The Justice Department

Historically the Department of Justice has played a key role in protecting civil rights and liberties. Its lawyers in the U.S. Attorney's offices in each judicial district may prosecute persons, including state or federal officials, accused of violating people's civil rights. Under Republican presidents like Ronald Reagan, the Justice Department pulled back from support of civil rights groups. The department opposed busing plans to overcome segregation of schools, opposed some affirmative action hiring plans, and argued that job discrimination cases should be limited to the individuals involved and not cover patterns of employment.

President Clinton entered office aggressively backing civil rights enforcement. He appointed the first female attorney general, Janet Reno, as well as liberal judges and U.S. attorneys. Yet the Republican takeover of Congress in 1994 and the unpopularity of affirmative action programs put the administration between a rock and a hard place. Clinton worried about public opinion that was lukewarm toward civil rights. This attempt to steer a middle course led to joking in the Justice Department that they wanted to strongly enforce civil rights laws, as long as no one knew about it.

George W. Bush, elected with little black support, has steered a moderately conservative course toward civil rights. He has opposed affirmative action, which he equated with quotas and racial preferences. (After losing the University of Michigan case, Bush commended the Court "for recognizing the value of diversity on our nation's campuses.") Bush supported "affirmative access" such as the Texas 10 percent plan, where students graduating in the top 10 percent of their high school class are automatically admitted to a state university. In his first term, under his conservative attorney general, John Ashcroft, the Justice Department was considerably less active in civil rights enforcement.

"Private Attorneys General"

Various organizations have been created to support the rights of individuals and groups. These are called *private attorneys general* because they act, not on behalf of the government, but for groups bringing court cases against the government or against other groups. They are funded in part by foundations and wealthy donors, and in part by members who pay dues.

The largest such group is the *American Civil Liberties Union* (ACLU). The ACLU has a national staff and 50 state chapters handling more than 6,000 cases each year. The ACLU was organized in the 1920s to defend against the hysteria of "red scares" (a period when socialists were persecuted) and has fought against wire-tapping, surveillance, and "dirty tricks" by law enforcement agencies. It is especially active in First Amendment freedom of speech, press, and religion issues. Recently it has opposed speech codes on campuses and has defended the due process rights of citizens and others accused of terrorism.

The NAACP's Legal Defense and Educational Fund, Inc. (LDF) was created in 1939 and consisted at first of one lawyer, Thurgood Marshall, who later became the first black appointed to the Supreme Court. In the past, the LDF concentrated on school desegregation suits. Today its dozens of lawyers are focused on discrimination in employment and housing, and on abuses in the judicial system. The largest legal organization for women is the National Organization for Women (NOW) Legal Defense and Education Fund. It works to help women gain equal employment rights and to strike down legislation viewed as discriminating.

Legal Strategies

These organizations use a variety of legal tactics. They conduct research on the problems of their clients, hoping to find a pattern of discrimination for a large class of people. They offer their services to individuals whose rights may have been violated. Such people cannot afford the hundreds of thousands of dollars it takes to pursue a case all the way to the Supreme Court, so the assistance of the "private attorneys general," almost always provided free of charge, is crucial. Civil liberties lawyers can choose, from a large number of complaints, a *test case* for their arguments. Such a case offers the group its best shot because the violation is so obvious, the damage so great, and the person making the case so appealing.

The litigating organization hopes that its case eventually will wind up in the Supreme Court as a *landmark decision*—one that involves major changes in the definition of civil rights and liberties. Often similar cases will be filed in different courts, hoping for conflicting constitutional interpretations that will "force" the Supreme Court to rule on the issue. Such a decision creates a new precedent (such as the right to counsel in a state trial), which is then enforced by lower federal and state courts. After the landmark case is announced by the high court, the lawyers from these organizations then must bring dozens of cases in federal district courts to make sure that rights affirmed by the Supreme Court are followed by government officials. (For an example of a landmark decision, see *Brown* v. *Board of Education*, pp. 147–148.)

Obeying the Courts

These private organizations may ask judges to do several things. First, they may ask that a law, executive order, or private action be declared unconstitutional, or that actions of private individuals be found in violation of the law or the Constitution. Second, they may ask that a right be protected by judicial action. Of these, the most important are the *injunction*, which prevents someone from taking an action to violate someone else's rights, and the *order*, which requires someone to take a specified action to ensure someone else's rights.

In the event of noncompliance with a judicial injunction or order, the judges may issue a citation for contempt of court. Civil contempt involves the refusal to obey a court order granted to a party in a case and can lead to imprisonment. The court also may find someone in criminal contempt of court for disrupting the court or showing disrespect for the court's enforcement powers. This too may lead to imprisonment or a stiff fine.

The orders of a federal court are enforced by federal marshals, backed up by the state's National Guard (which may be brought into federal service by proclamation of the president) or by federal troops under the orders of the president. In 1957, for example, when Governor Orval Faubus of Arkansas refused to obey a federal court order to desegregate Little Rock Central High School, President Dwight Eisenhower took control of the Arkansas National Guard away from the governor and used federal troops to protect black students attending the school.

In writing their orders, federal courts can act as administrators over state agencies. At one time in the 1970s, federal judges in Alabama were running the state highway patrol, the prison system, and the mental hospitals, because the governor refused to obey federal court orders guaranteeing equal protection and due process of law in these agencies.

Sometimes state officials do not wish to comply with the spirit or letter of court orders. Consider the landmark decision of *Miranda* v. *Arizona* (1966), in which the Supreme Court held that once an investigation by police focused on an accused, that person had to receive the following warning:

> You have the right to remain silent.
> Anything you say may be used against you in a court of law.
> You have the right to be represented by an attorney of your choice.
> If you cannot afford an attorney, a public defender will be provided for you if you wish.

At first, there was only limited acceptance by many police departments of the new rules of the "cops and robbers" game. After all, unless there was a federal judge in every patrol car, voluntary compliance was the only practical way such a rule could be implemented. Some departments ignored the order; others gave only part of the warning. The courts gained compliance through the *exclusionary rule:* They threw out evidence obtained illegally, including confessions where *Miranda* warnings had not been given. The Supreme Court, while recently continuing *Miranda,* has narrowed the exclusionary rule, allowing evidence if police officers "acted in good faith," even if they did not follow all due process rules.

Public Opinion and Civil Liberties

Public agreement with decisions on civil rights and liberties cannot be taken for granted. A majority of the public, for example, does not believe that evidence should be thrown out in state criminal trials on "legal technicalities," which is what the *Miranda* rule requires. A year after 9/11, only 11 percent of Americans thought that the Bush administration had gone too far in limiting civil liberties in combating terrorism.

But it is because the rights of politically unpopular groups have been violated that judicial protection becomes necessary. (See "Uncle Sam: Enemy of Civil Liberties?" below.) Where support by local leaders does not exist and community sentiment runs against the decision, as with the ban on prayer in the public schools, compliance may be spotty. Often a Supreme Court ruling signals the start—not the end—of political debate. In the case of abortion rights, a Supreme Court decision (*Roe* v. *Wade*) affirming the right to abortion was followed by

Uncle Sam: Enemy of Civil Liberties?

Civil liberties in general have received broad support, but few people have come to their defense in unpopular cases. Throughout U.S. history, there are uncomfortable reminders of government actions that many now see as violating the Bill of Rights.

Not many years after the ink had dried on the Constitution, Congress passed the *Alien and Sedition Acts* of 1798. Aimed at the opposition party, these acts promised heavy fines and imprisonment for those guilty of writing or speaking anything false, scandalous, or malicious against any government official. Such a broad prohibition today would put an end to most political campaigns. The slavery issue in 1840 led Congress to pass the "Gag Rule" preventing antislavery petitions from being received by Congress (thus violating a specific First Amendment right).

Violations of civil liberties continued into the twentieth century. Within five months after the United States entered World War I, every leading socialist newspaper had been suspended from the mails at least once, some permanently. During World War II, Japanese Americans along the west coast were forced into internment camps. The Smith Act of 1940, which is still on the books, forbade teaching or advocating the violent overthrow of the government. In 1951, 11 Communist party leaders were convicted under it for activities labeled "preparation for revolution." This "preparation" involved advocating and teaching works like the *Communist Manifesto*, which today can be found in any college library. Ten defendants were sentenced to five years in prison.

In more recent times, the FBI infiltrated the anti–Vietnam War movement, spied on civil rights leaders like Martin Luther King Jr., and got into a shoot-out with a right-wing family at Ruby Ridge, Idaho. After 9/11, the government denied American citizens labeled terrorists a right to a lawyer and the chance to challenge their detention before a judge—fundamental due process rights. Down to the present, government respect for civil liberties remains a sometime thing.

congressional and state laws cutting off public funding for abortions and requiring parental consent for teenagers seeking an abortion.

The rightness of judicial action never rests on its popularity with the public. The federal judiciary is not elected and does not directly answer to the people. It is accountable to a Constitution that attempts to secure the rights of the people against governmental action. The judiciary protects the rights of people. Low levels of approval for some of its decisions are nothing to be alarmed about. If anything, it is a sign that the system is working.

Of course, for the courts to operate in the political game, and for their decisions to be enforced, they must function within the bounds of public opinion and the cooperation of other parts of the government. This is not automatically given, as the following case of due process in an age of terrorism illustrates.

CASE STUDY

FIGHTING TERROR, GUARDING LIBERTIES

The enemy has declared war on us. And we must not let foreign enemies use the forums of liberty to destroy liberty itself.
—George W. Bush

They that can give up essential liberty to obtain a little temporary safety deserve neither liberty nor safety.
—Benjamin Franklin

Two Indian men with box cutters were taken off an Amtrak train in Texas on September 12, 2001, and held in isolation for some three months without being brought before a court or being given a lawyer. Both were eventually cleared of any involvement with terrorism.

After 9/11, defending the country against terrorism and defending the Constitution's civil liberties seemed in conflict. President Bush, acting under his powers of commander-in-chief, took a number of aggressive actions. Without approval from Congress or the courts, the executive branch locked up over 1,200 people either for violating immigration laws or as material witnesses—though the real motive was to investigate their links to terrorism. (The attorney general refused to release their names, claiming, without a trace of humor, that he was protecting their privacy.) Secret deportation hearings were ordered for suspected terrorists. The administration held to a firm position in terrorist-related cases: no judicial review, no right to counsel, no public disclosure, no open hearings. A federal appeals court later ruled these secret hearings "undemocratic" and "in complete opposition to the society envisioned by the Framers of our Constitution."

Historically wartime presidents have found a way around civil liberties, and the Supreme Court usually goes along. George W. Bush's actions look mild compared to his predecessors: Abraham Lincoln detained thousands of rebel sympathizers, Woodrow Wilson banned antiwar publications during World War I, and Franklin D. Roosevelt interned tens of thousands of Japanese Americans in World War II. The courts avoided intervening in these presidential abridgements of civil liberties, and public opinion strongly supported them.

The men who wrote the Constitution wanted a strong president for protection against foreign attacks. But whether wartime needs could override fundamental rights like representation by a lawyer and a chance to contest detention before a civilian judge was questioned. The Bush administration argued that these were military decisions that the Constitution gave to the executive branch alone.

Yet the unusual nature of the terrorist threat complicated this argument. Terrorism, a criminal threat as much as a military one, was clearly not the equal of enemies like the Confederacy or Nazi Germany. And the ill-defined length of the terrorist war could mean that restrictions on liberty would continue indefinitely. One leading critic, Anthony Romero of the American Civil Liberties Union, said, "This is not the executive branch's war on terrorism. This is the American government's war on terrorism."

A Taliban and Due Process

In the year following the 9/11 terrorist attacks, the case *Hamdi* v. *Rumsfeld* brought up core civil liberties issues and the role of the courts in reviewing government actions.

Hamdi, a Saudi national, was captured in Afghanistan and along with other prisoners was taken to Guantanamo Bay in Cuba. When Hamdi said he was born in Louisiana and therefore an American citizen, he was declared an "enemy combatant," taken to Norfolk, and held incommunicado in a Navy jail. His father and a public defender tried to get access to him, but the government said for national security reasons he could not have visitors.

A federal district judge in Norfolk (an appointee of another Republican president, Ronald Reagan) ruled that Hamdi had a right to see a lawyer. The judge described the situation as "the first where an American citizen has been held incommunicado and subjected to an indefinite detention in the continental United States without charges, without any findings by a military tribunal, and without access to a lawyer." The Court of Appeals ruled against the judge, twice asking him to reconsider his decision, giving greater consideration to the executive branch's right to wage war. But the Court also questioned the administration's "sweeping proposition" that "any American citizen alleged to be an enemy combatant could be detained indefinitely without charges or counsel on the government's say-so."

The issue was not whether the government could detain an "enemy combatant." This had already been allowed under precedents from World War II. The issue was whether the executive could lock up U.S. citizens it *says* are enemy combatants and refuse them the opportunity to tell their side of the story to a court, to a lawyer, or to the public. Could they be held in solitary confinement for months or even years without a hearing? Does this accused citizen have the right to be heard?

The government responded to the appeals court by giving the district judge a two-page declaration of why Hamdi was an "unlawful enemy combatant" entitled to neither constitutional protections nor international prisoner-of-war status. The government declined to give the judge any further information. The district judge was not impressed: "I do think that due process requires something other than a basic assertion that they have looked at some papers and therefore they have determined he should be held incommunicado. Is that what we're fighting for?"

In the summer of 2004 the U.S. Supreme Court ruled in the Hamdi case against the government's claim of sweeping executive power. The Court declared that an American citizen detained as an enemy combatant had a due process right to a hearing to challenge his detention. Many observers thought that the abuses by the American military revealed at Abu Ghraib prison in Iraq had shown that the executive branch could not be trusted with its extensive claim to power. The reports of the torture of prisoners had also produced a climate of public opinion that made it politically easier for the Court to limit presidential powers, even in wartime.

By the end of September 2004, after nearly three years in solitary confinement, Yasser Hamdi was released from custody and flown home to Saudi Arabia. He was required to renounce his American citizenship. What the compelling national security concerns were that led the government to confine him and fight his release all the way to the Supreme Court were never revealed.

The Patriot Act

The Patriot Act, passed overwhelmingly by Congress on October 25, 2001, has been blamed by one side for things it doesn't do. It has been overhyped by others as a vital instrument in the antiterrorism war. (The attorney general declared that repealing any part of it would "disarm" the United States.)

The Act did strengthen law enforcement. It allowed the FBI and CIA to share evidence. It made it easier for the FBI to ask federal judges to force businesses (including libraries and bookstores) to turn over records in terrorism probes, and to delay telling people that their homes and offices were being searched. It also allowed "roving" wiretaps, under court orders, to listen to electronic devices.

For civil libertarians this may have been bad enough, but the Patriot Act did not include all that was alleged, often on TV cop shows:

- When the Justice Department detained hundreds of Middle Eastern men after 9/11, it was done under immigration laws.
- When the government locked up 650 suspected terrorists as "enemy combatants" at Guantanamo Bay, Cuba (as well as Yasser Hamdi and Jose Padilla, two U.S. citizens, in a Navy brig), it was done under the president's war powers.
- When the president authorized military tribunals to try noncitizens, this was done under Defense Department rules (although none has been held so far).

The main debate over extending the Patriot Act has focused on continuing the sunset provisions, which required that key parts of the Act expire at the end of 2005. But the question over what is included continued to be blurred in public. Senator Joseph Biden, Democrat of Delaware, blamed both sides for overselling their arguments. "It's always a disservice when you confuse the public."

Source: USA Today, February 26, 2004.

WRAP-UP

Civil rights and liberties are constitutional protections granted to all citizens. They protect people against violations of their rights by other people or by the government. Civil liberties refer to rights—such as freedom of speech and religion and guarantees of due process of law—which allow people full participation in a democratic political system. Civil rights guard groups against discrimination by other groups. Historically, both sets of rights have been deepened as to what they cover and widened as to whom they cover.

Using the Fourteenth Amendment concepts of "equal protection of the laws" and "due process of law," the courts have applied the Bill of Rights to the states as well as the national government. Freedom of speech has expanded to include freedom of expression, including symbolic speech. Privacy rights now include protection for consenting adult behavior. Due process rights cover bureaucracies as well as the state criminal justice system. Civil rights similarly have been widened with the use of suspect classifications to deal with racial prejudice. Although the strict scrutiny test does not apply to gender classifications, a large number of laws containing "protective" gender classifications have been removed from the books. Helping the process along have been activist judges and private attorneys general, whose test cases have changed the law, sometimes dramatically and sometimes slowly. The case study of terrorism and civil liberties illustrates how difficult it is to support constitutional protections for unpopular groups accused of planning vicious attacks.

Although the Bill of Rights is written in inspiring and absolute language—"Congress shall make no law"—these rights are seldom applied that way. Judges weighing civil liberties and rights (and students as well) are influenced by the political climate of the times. First Amendment freedoms are easier to support when we agree with the voices speaking. Liberals may not be quite as upset by violations of free speech when police rough up antiabortion demonstrators. Conservatives may not see an issue of freedom of the press involved when obscene words are used on a radio talk show. And no one wants to see terrorism flourish because of a blind dedication to due processs. But our individual support for these freedoms is their most important defense. As Judge Learned Hand wrote, "Liberty lies in the hearts and minds of men and women; when it dies there, no constitution, no law, no court can save it."

Civil rights and liberties not only protect individuals, but they also defend our system of government. These well-tested values balance and restrain the drives and ambitions of our leaders. They give us standards by which to judge the actions of these players. They underline the historical truth that majorities can be mistaken and that leaders can mislead. These rights admittedly grant, as Justice Oliver Wendell Holmes put it, "freedom for the thoughts that we hate." They also restrain the "tyranny of the majority," and may therefore be considered undemocratic. But by providing us with widely accepted freedoms and protecting our political communications, they become essential in making democracy work.

Thought Questions

1. How can individual citizens support civil liberties? Do they?
2. What accounts for the fact that not all of the Bill of Rights applies against state or other officials? Do you think it should?
3. Should affirmative action be used just to remedy the effects of discrimination? Or should it be used for broader goals of a more diverse society? Should affirmative action be limited to programs for minorities and women in poverty?
4. Why are civil liberties and rights more supported in some historic periods and not in others? Do you think that the threat of terrorism will mean a decline in popular support for these liberties in the United States?

Suggested Readings

Bovard, James. *Lost Rights.* New York: St. Martin's Griffin, 1995. Pb.
    An alarmist but readable critique of how "government officials are tearing the Bill of Rights to pieces."
Crier, Catherine. *The Case Against Lawyers.* New York: Broadway Books, 2002.
    A TV journalist tackles the American legal system—its complexity, unfairness, and expense.
Friendly, Fred W. *Minnesota Rag.* New York: Vintage Books, 1982.
    A delightful account of a famous case of freedom of the press.
Hentoff, Nat. *Living the Bill of Rights.* New York: HarperCollins, 1998.
    Entertaining flesh-and-blood examples of how Americans from Justice William O. Douglas to an Alabama homecoming queen have fought for their civil liberties.
Leone, Richard C., et al. *The War on Our Freedoms: Civil Liberties in an Age of Terrorism.* New York: Public Affairs, 2003. Pb.
    A collection of essays by experts worried about the impact of the war on terrorism on our freedoms at home.
Schlesinger, Arthur M., Jr. *The Disuniting of America.* New York: W.W. Norton, 1998.
    An eminent historian's brief, eloquent argument against the excesses of political correctness.
Sullivan, Andrew. *Virtually Normal: An Argument About Homosexuality.* New York: Alfred A. Knopf, 1995.
    An argument by the former editor of the *New Republic* that homosexuals be treated as equal public citizens in matters from marriage to the military.

CHAPTER 7

Voters and Political Parties

S o far we have only discussed half the story—the institutions and rules of government. Equally important are the "players" outside of government. We cannot assume that they have less influence in deciding issues than those within the government. The outcomes of the games they play will be determined by the skills and resources of the participants, as well as the nature of the issue. The next two chapters will discuss voters, political parties, interest groups, and media—their power and how they exercise it in American politics.

In this chapter, we will first look at voters—who they are and who they aren't. What leads some to vote and participate in politics, and others not to do either? Our political parties, whatever their shortcomings, are a critical link between voters and government. The history of the party system, its functions, and how well it performs its tasks today are the key topics. The case study at the end ("Blogs, Howard Dean, and the 2004 Campaign") shows how some voters were reached by their party, courtesy of the Internet.

VOTERS

Who Votes?

"Who votes in America?" may seem an easy question. Citizens who are 18 and older (because of the Twenty-sixth Amendment lowering the voting age) and who have satisfied their states' residency requirements can vote. But in most presidential elections about half don't; in elections between presidential years only about 40% show up. The good news is that voting turnout seems to be improving.

In the 2004 election almost 60% of those eligible voted. These estimated 120 million people represented 15 million more voters than in 2000. It was the highest turnout since Richard Nixon beat Hubert Humphrey in 1968 in the swirl of the controversies over the Vietnam War. Similarly this time experts saw the increase in voting coming from the strongly divided opinions of the Bush administration and the huge get-out-the-vote efforts by both political parties. Voting rates have been much lower in nonpresidential elections. In 2002, for example, only 39.3% turned up at election booths, a figure that remained 20 percent lower than midterm elections in the 1960s. As seen in the chart on the next page (Figure 7.1.) it is by no means certain that the longterm decline in voting has been reversed.

The questions grow. What leads some people to vote? What influences how they vote? And what has led to ever-greater numbers of people not voting?

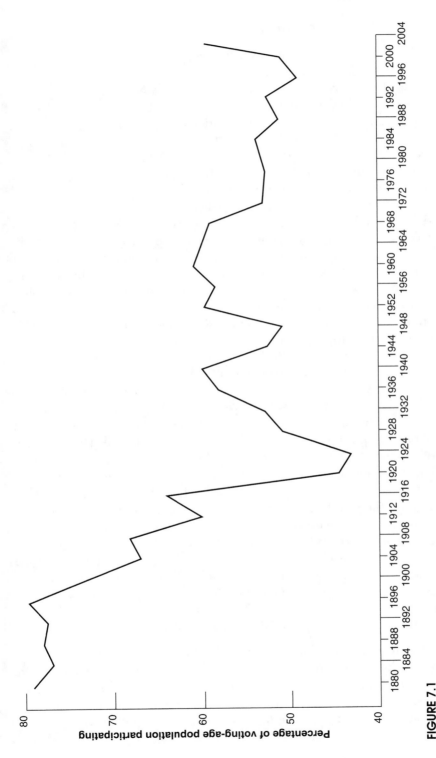

Political Socialization

Political socialization helps explain how, or if, people participate in politics. *Political socialization* is the *process of learning political attitudes and behavior.* The gradual process of socialization takes place as we grow up, in settings like the family and the schools. In the home, children learn about participating in family decisions—for example, the more noise they make, the better chance

they have of staying up late. Kids also learn which party their parents favor, how they generally view politics and politicians, and what are their basic values and outlook toward their country. Children, of course, don't always copy their parents' political leanings, but they are influenced by them. Most people stay with the party of their folks. Schools have a similar effect. Students salute the flag, take civics courses, participate in student politics, and learn that democracy (us) is good and dictatorship (them) is bad.

People's social characteristics also affect their participation in politics. Whether a person is young or old, black or white, rich or poor, and Northerner or Southerner will affect her or his political opinions and behavior. The views of a person's peer group (friends and neighbors), of political authorities ("The president knows what he's doing"), and of one's political party influence how people vote as well. The influence of religion and ethnic background can be seen in most large cities where parties in the past ran "balanced tickets" with Irish, Italian, and Jewish candidates—and, more recently, blacks, Latinos, and women as well. Besides the well-known tendency for people to vote for "one of their own," they also share certain political attitudes. Catholics tend to vote Democratic more often than do Protestants. Blacks and Jews generally support social programs. On specific issues, religion may also play a role: Many Catholics back aid to parochial schools, many Jews support aid for Israel, and many fundamentalist Protestants favor prayer in the schools.

Class and Voting

Class may be just as important in shaping people's political opinions and behavior. The term *social class* refers to a *group's occupation and income, and the awareness it produces of their relations to other groups or classes in the society.* In general we can speak of three broad overlapping categories: a working class, a middle class, and an upper class. The *working class,* which almost always includes the majority of people in a society, receives the lowest incomes and fills "blue-collar" jobs in factories and farms, as well as "white-collar" positions like clerical and secretarial jobs in offices. The *middle class* consists of most professionals (like teachers and engineers), small businesspeople, bureaucrats, and some skilled workers (say, those earning more than $50,000 a year). The *upper class* (often called the *elite* or *ruling class*) is composed of those who run our major economic and political institutions and receive the highest incomes for doing so.

At least as important as these "objective" categories that political scientists use is the "subjective" way in which people in these classes view their own position. Whether union members or teachers or housewives see themselves as members of the working class or the middle class also will influence their political attitudes. An important fact about class in the United States is that class identification is quite weak. People either don't know what class they are in or don't think it's important. Most Americans see themselves as members of the middle class no matter what "objective" class they may be put into.

Class as reflected in education, income, and occupation, however, does influence people's attitudes on a variety of issues. Studies have shown that people in the working class tend to be liberal in wanting greater economic equality and more social welfare programs. This liberalism on economic issues contrasts strongly with their ideas on civil liberties. Here, people of lower income and education tend to be intolerant of dissenters and not supportive of protection for minority views or different styles of behavior (such as homosexual rights). Members of the middle class are more conservative in their economic views and more liberal on issues such as free speech and respect for civil rights. Class attitudes on political questions, then, are both liberal and conservative depending on the type of issue.

Government policies and economic growth may also affect different classes differently. Even in the prosperous 1990s under a liberal Democratic administration, the income for 90 percent of families scarcely changed at all. Yet from 1986 to 1997 the *increase* in average income for the top 1 percent of Americans was $69,000. This increase was nearly triple the *total* average income of the bottom 90 percent, which was around $23,800.

The problem with figuring out how these various characteristics—race, class, and religion—influence a person's political behavior is that so many of them overlap. If we say that blacks are more likely to be nonvoters than whites, are we sure that race is the key category? We also know that poorer people, those with less education, and those who feel they have less effect on their government also are less likely to vote. All these categories include the majority of blacks. But we don't yet know which is more important in influencing behavior, and so even the "true" statement that blacks vote less may conceal as much as it reveals. We also have to examine whether blacks with more income or education also vote less—which they don't. We might then conclude that race is not as important in voter turnout as, say, class.

WHO DOESN'T VOTE?

Pollster: Do you think people don't vote because of ignorance or apathy?
Nonvoter: I don't know and I don't care.

The difficulty of answering the question of why people don't vote ought to be clear. As the charts indicate, turnout varies depending on education, race, gender, and age, and it changes over time.(See Figure 7.2.) Studies have shown that nonvoters most often are from the less educated, nonwhite, rural, southern, poor, blue-collar, and very young segments of the American population. Voters most often come from the white, middle-aged, college-educated, urban or suburban, affluent, white-collar groups. These are only broad tendencies, with a great many exceptions in each case. *Generally, people with the biggest stakes in society are the most likely to go to the polls:* older individuals and married couples, and people with more education, higher incomes, and good jobs.

There is other information, gathered from opinion polls, of which we are sure: First, Americans are poorly informed about politics. Surveys show that less than half the voters know the name of their representative in Congress, and only about one-fifth know how he or she has voted on any major bills. There is no doubt that the less income you have, the less likely you are to vote or participate in politics. One study found that in a recent presidential election, 68 percent of low-income people reported no activity (such as attending a meeting or wearing a campaign button). Only 36 percent of those identifying themselves as "upper middle class" said they had done nothing. Those earning over $75,000 a year accounted for nearly half of campaign contributions, while those earning less than $15,000 accounted for less than 3 percent.

Class differences in voting reflect differences in economic security. Low-income people who face immediate challenges like finding a job or paying bills may view politics as a luxury they can't afford. (This may help explain why voting by Latinos is so low, with roughly one-third turning out to vote.) Class differences in political socialization also have an effect. Children of working-class parents, whether because of their more rigidly structured families or because of poor

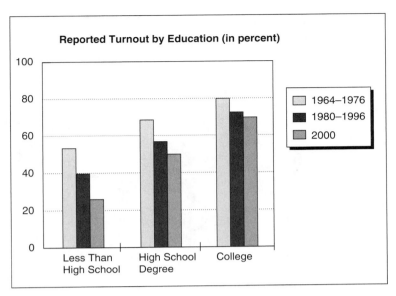

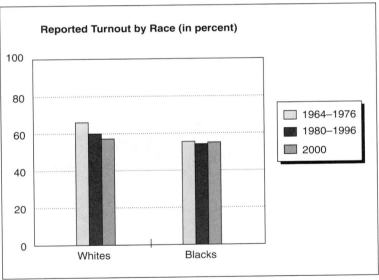

FIGURE 7.2
Presidential Voting Turnout of Eligible Voters by Education, Race, Gender, and Age, 1964–2000.
Source: Compiled by Mike Toppa, Gary Feld and Jennifer Ley.

education, are brought up to believe that they can have little influence on politics ("You can't fight City Hall"). At the same time, because of the disadvantaged reality they and their parents face, they tend to have a not-so-favorable image of political leaders. These children,

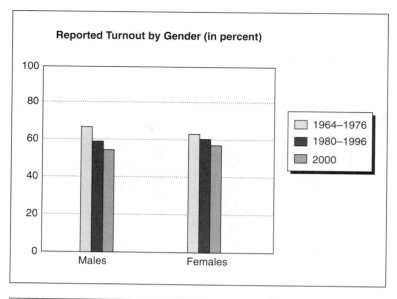

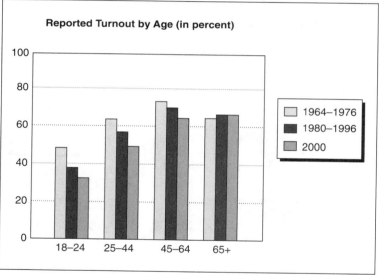

FIGURE 7.2 *(continued)*

then, end up being both more resentful and more passive toward politics. Middle- and upper-class children have a higher regard for political leaders and are taught in their schools to value participation in politics. They are encouraged to participate and are led to believe that the political system will respond favorably to their involvement. Of course, political leaders may be more likely to listen to people with a similar background and education as theirs—upper middle class.

Electoral barriers to voting, it is argued, also play a role in lower turnout. State registration laws—some requiring 50 days residency and periodic registration—make voting inconvenient. Making registration and voting two separate acts on different days clearly cuts out the "last-minute shoppers." As we learned in the 2000 election, older voting machines in poor neighborhoods may lead to more votes being disqualified and voters being discouraged.

Until recently, the U.S. government stood virtually alone in not helping citizens cope with voter registration. The so-called *motor voter* legislation made registration easier by allowing voters to register when they got drivers' licenses. The assumption behind the 1993 motor voter law was that the easier it was for people to register, the more likely they would be to vote. Yet fewer people registered to vote in 1996 and even fewer voted. Registration declined by 2 percent from 1992, and voting declined by 5 percent. By the time of the 2000 elections, registration numbers had increased, as had voting turnout, but only slightly.

While problems in registration cannot account for most of the decrease in voting, government can make voting easier. Making Election Day a national holiday, as it is in many European countries, or letting people vote on Saturday, or online, would help. Same-day registration—where any eligible citizen can roll out of bed on Election Day and register to vote at the polls—has seemed to work in Minnesota and Maine, which are two states among the top voting turnouts. This may also have to do with the higher turnout in rural areas, where personal communications reinforce a community feeling of a duty to vote.

Subjective Explanations

The objective categories describing nonvoters—younger, less educated, lower incomes—may conceal as much as they reveal. The term *nonvoters*, after all, covers half or more of the American population, and a great deal of variety. For example, surveys have shown that while nonvoters tend to be less well off financially, 43 percent have incomes of $30,000 or more. Nonvoters are significantly younger than voters, but one-quarter of nonvoters are 45 years old or older. When people who registered but did not vote were asked why, more than one in five said they couldn't take time off work or were too busy. Time constraints are now the biggest single reason given for not voting. Apathy was cited as a reason by 17 percent of registered nonvoters.

The ability to generalize about nonvoters gets cloudier when one examines negative feelings toward government. While it's true that nonvoters feel alienated from government, this is also true for voters. In one study of a recent election, about two-thirds of the population felt that to some extent "most elected officials don't care what people

The Vanishing Young Voter

Young voters have been disappearing on election day, with 2004 being a possible turnaround in the trend. In 1974 18 percent of voters were under 30; almost the same number (17 percent) were over 65. By 2000 those over 65 were turning out in greater numbers and represented over twice as many voters as those under 30. There are projections that in 20 years, seniors will outvote the young by 4 to 1. In 2004, however, the turnout of those under 30 went up along with everyone else's. Almost 21 million voters under 30 went to the polls up from 16 million votes in 2000. Because the overall turnout was higher the percent of the youth vote was almost the same as in 2000. Despite this significant gain, most of which went to the Democrats, scholars think the low youth vote will continue for a number of reasons.

Young people move more, marry and buy homes later in life, and have no strong identity to either political party—all factors that erode the voting habit. While young people are no more cynical than older ones about politics (equal percentages believe most politicians are crooks), young cynics vote almost 40 percent less than older ones. Polls have shown that most young voters don't consider it a constitutional duty to vote, while those over 30 overwhelmingly do.

No defining political crisis such as a depression or war has induced this generation of Xers to vote. Even the Get Out the Vote efforts that work are not terribly encouraging. At the University of Indiana, a "Vote Hard" registration drive got nearly 18,000 registration forms passed out when they expected only a few hundred. The difference was that a red Corvette was given away to those who signed up in a lottery after the election.

Source: The *Washington Post*, October 20, 2002 and November 9, 2004.

like me think." The percentage for nonvoters was exactly the same. Nonetheless, mistrust of government has grown in recent years parallel to the growth of nonvoting. This has likely had a cumulative effect, especially on the views of vulnerable young people as they formed their impressions of government and their role as citizens. (See "The Vanishing Young Voter.")

This lack of *political efficacy*—a sense that government will respond to peoples' needs—among both voters and nonvoters has several explanations. That people "don't think it makes any difference" in whether they participate may come in part from the way they were socialized or brought up. People may not consider politics relevant to their lives, identify with a political party, understand the political system, follow news about public affairs, or some combination of these. The less informed people are about politics, the less relevant it appears to their lives. And, in fact, government may not be responsive.

This lack of confidence in government has grown. In the early 1960s, three out of four Americans responded to survey questions by saying they trusted Washington all or most of the time. Today it is just the opposite: Three out of four no longer trust the government. There has been much debate over the causes of this lack of trust. In the 1960s, the government was remembered for having rescued people from the Great Depression and winning World War II. Since then the issues have gotten more complex and the victories fewer. Poverty, crime, discrimination, AIDS, and terrorism are just some of the problems that government is now expected to solve. At the same time, institutions like the family, religions, and political parties have all weakened in their ability to speak to many of society's ills. The media, with its negative advertising and skeptical reporting, has been blamed by many for encouraging nonparticipation. And, at least prior to 9/11, the argument was heard that big issues like the Great Depression or Vietnam were not around to shock the system and pull people into following political events.

The government is not exactly blameless in this cycle of distrust. At least beginning with memories of Vietnam and Watergate, leaders have misled. President Clinton, with half truths about his personal life from avoiding the Vietnam draft to not avoiding Monica Lewinsky, reinforced popular prejudices. The George W. Bush administration benefited from the public rallying around national leaders after 9/11, at least initially. Then came the invasion of Iraq. Justifying the war with undiscovered weapons of mass destruction and nonexistent ties to Al Qaeda undermined popular confidence in government. The TV images of American leaders squirming to avoid responsibility for intelligence lapses leading to 9/11 or for the widespread abuse of Iraqi prisoners only increased the public cynicism.

Election campaigns have traditionally been seen as a major vehicle of gaining public participation. Unfortunately, campaigns may actually be hurting turnout. The political scientist Thomas Patterson denounced the modern presidential campaign

> that starts far too early and lasts far too long, that runs on big money and responds to special interests, that has sapped the national party conventions of their energy and purpose, and that wears down the public as it grinds its way month after month toward November.

Partisan redistricting of congressional districts has made these elections noncompetitive and uninteresting. Even presidential campaigns usually focus on only a dozen or so states for intensive activities and advertising. The press has been blamed for coverage that is negative about candidates and absorbed with horse-race stories ("Who's ahead?") that minimize issues and maximize skepticism.

Of course, voting is not the only way of participating in politics. Politics saturates our lives. Participation in personal politics has likely increased in recent years. In the home, in dorms, and at work, political talk flourishes—between husband and wife, parents and children, and everyone on e-mail—often motivated by national news or outrageous television shows. Others join in the political game by wearing a "Thank You for Not Smoking" button, or by teaching younger kids to read nutrition labels at the supermarket. Young women and minorities who don't vote may do politics just by showing up in jobs where they were rarely seen before. Teens join class-action suits to remove asbestos in their schools, march for more funding for breast cancer research, or work to clean up a local park.

Isn't this politics—people influencing others on public issues? Professor Michael Schudson has made the argument well: "The changes that have made the personal political have been profound, arguably more so than the slackening of voter turnout."

Elections determine who leads the government and who shapes public policy. But they may not accurately demonstrate the overall vigor of America's civic health and political involvement. Detachment from government may not be merely a sign of apathy. It may reflect skeptical citizens willing to participate in politics, but on their own terms.

POLITICAL PARTIES

A *political party* is an organization that runs candidates for public office under the party's name. Although the framers seemed more concerned with factions and interests than with parties, they were well aware that parties could soon develop. George Washington, in his famed farewell address, warned against "the baneful effects of the spirit of party." Despite his advice, parties soon arose, and for good reasons.

The national government, as we have seen, is based on a system of dividing or *decentralizing* power. Political parties, on the other hand, are a method of organizing or *centralizing* power. The framers of the Constitution decentralized power in separate branches and separate states partly to avoid the development of powerful factions that could take over the government. This decentralization of power, however, created the need for parties that could pull together power to elect candidates who could then effectively govern.

For the rest of the chapter, we will ask and answer the following questions: What are the functions of parties? How have they historically developed? How are they organized? What are the consequences of our two-party system? How important are parties today? What about the future?

Party Functions

What is it that political parties do? Political parties throughout the world organize power in order to control the government. To do so, American political parties (1) contest elections, (2) organize public opinion, (3) put together coalitions of different interests, and (4) incorporate policy changes proposed by groups and individuals outside the party system and the government.

First, parties *contest elections.* They organize voters in order to compete with other parties for elected offices. To contest elections, parties—or, more commonly, their candidates—recruit people into the political system to work on campaigns. Parties provide people with a basis for making political choices. Most people in a party vote for the candidates of their party. (The other major motive behind a voter's choice is whether to favor or oppose the incumbent.) In addition, when parties contest elections, they express policy positions on important issues. This function of the parties serves to *educate* voters about the political process. Most people are not ordinarily involved in politics. They often rely on elections to keep them active and informed.

Second, parties *organize public opinion.* Despite the variety of views within them, parties give the public a limited channel of communication to express their desires about how government should operate. At the least, voters can approve the actions of the party that has been holding office by voting for it, or they can disapprove by voting for the opposition.

Third is building *coalitions.* Parties put together, or *aggregate, various interests.* The Democratic and Republican parties organize different regions, ethnic groups, and economic interests into large coalitions for the purpose of winning elections. Gathering special interests under the broad "umbrella" of a party label is an important function of American political parties. This can be seen clearly at the presidential level, where elected candidates often claim a *mandate,* or the widespread national support needed to govern.

Finally, the two major parties *incorporate changes* or reforms proposed by third parties or social protest movements. If third parties or political movements show that they have considerable support, their

Political Parties Around the World

One hundred years ago, political parties were confined mainly to Europe and North America. Elsewhere they were weak or nonexistent. At the beginning of this century, parties are found everywhere in the world. Generally they are larger, stronger, better organized, and with far more members than in 1900.

In their worldwide spread, parties have adapted to local forms. In Africa parties sometimes formed around a traditional ethnic base, with party leadership drawn from chiefs' families. In Asia membership in modern parties is often influenced by religious factors or by affiliation with ritual brotherhoods. Many parties in less developed countries are partly political, partly military.

The centralization and influence of parties mirror their political system. In Great Britain, where Parliament acts as both the legislative and executive branches of government, parties have a great deal of power. The members of Parliament choose the party leader, and even if he or she should attain government position, it is dependent on party support. So in 1990 the British Conservative Party overthrew Margaret Thatcher, despite her having been elected prime minister in three straight elections; the party's officials acted without any direct input from voters.

programs are often adopted, though usually in more moderate form, by one of the major parties. President Clinton's emphasis on deficit reduction reflected Ross Perot's positions in 1992 and was aimed to appeal to his supporters. (See "Political Parties Around the World.")

The Rise of Today's Parties

The *Federalists* and *Anti-Federalists,* the groups that supported and opposed the adoption of the Constitution, were not organized into actual political parties. They did not run candidates for office under party labels. There were, in fact, no political parties anywhere in the world at the time. Popularly based parties would evolve in the United States. At the time, what did exist were networks of communication and political activity struggling on opposite sides of a great dispute— ratification. The framers preached against political parties. Jefferson, who founded what would become the Democratic party, wrote a bit hypocritically that "if I could not go to heaven but with a party, I would not go there at all." Being called a "party man" was a stain against the political honor of this revolutionary generation. Yet these leaders found they needed parties as soon as the national government was operating.

After the Constitution was ratified, the Federalist faction grew stronger and more like a political party. Led by Alexander Hamilton, secretary of the treasury under President Washington, the Federalists championed a strong national government that would promote the financial interests of merchants and manufacturers. After Thomas Jefferson left Washington's cabinet in 1793, an opposition party formed under his leadership, due to the behind-the-scenes skill of James Madison. The new *Democratic-Republican party* drew the support of small farmers, debtors, and others who did not benefit from the financial programs of the Federalists. Under the Democratic-Republican label, Jefferson won the presidential election of 1800, which because it was the first peaceful transition from one party to another may have been the most important election in American history. Jefferson's party continued to control the presidency until 1828. The Federalists, without power or popular support, died out.

At the end of this 28-year period of Democratic-Republican control, the party splintered into many factions. Two of these factions grew into new parties, the *Democrats* and the *Whigs* (first called the *National Republicans*). Thus the Democratic party, founded in 1828, is the oldest political party in the world. The early Democratic party was led by Andrew Jackson, who was elected president in 1828. Jackson spread power down to the party ranks by creating national conventions to nominate presidential candidates. Under Jackson, the Democrats became known as the party of the common people. The Whigs, like the old Federalists, were supported by the wealthier conservative groups in society: bankers, merchants, and big farmers.

In 1854, a *coalition* (a collection of interests that join together for a specific purpose) of Whigs, antislavery Democrats, and minor parties formed the *Republican party.* One of the unifying goals of this new party was to fight the expansion of slavery. The Republicans nominated a *dark horse* (a political unknown), Abraham Lincoln, on the third ballot for president in 1860. The Democrats were so deeply divided over the slavery issue that the southern and northern wings of the party each nominated a candidate. Against this divided opposition, as well as a fourth candidate, Lincoln won the election in the electoral college with less than a majority of the popular vote, but more than any other candidate (known as a *plurality* of the vote).

Maintaining, Deviating, and Realigning Elections

For the past 145 years, the Democratic and Republican parties have dominated American politics. Their relative strength and the nature of their support have shifted back and forth. We can put this history into categories by looking at three types of presidential elections: maintaining, deviating, and realigning elections. *Maintaining elections* keep party strength and support as they are. *Deviating elections* show a temporary shift in popular support for the parties, usually caused by the exceptional popular appeal of a candidate of the minority party. *Realigning elections* show a permanent shift in the popular base of support of the parties, and usually a shift in the relative strength of the parties so that the minority party emerges as the majority party. The president who emerges from a realigning election, whether a Lincoln or a Franklin Roosevelt, has a fresh national coalition behind him able to change the course of the nation's history.

Most presidential elections between 1860 and 1932 were maintaining elections. The Republicans (or GOP for *Grand Old Party*) kept the support of a majority of voters, and controlled the executive branch, in all but 16 of those 72 years. When the Democrats did gain control of the presidency, they held office for only short periods. The two elections of Democrat Woodrow Wilson in 1912 and 1916, for example, were caused by temporary voter shifts in party support and by splits within the Republican party.

The great social and economic impact of the Great Depression of the 1930s destroyed the Republicans' majority support, and contributed to a realignment in the two-party system. Under Franklin Delano Roosevelt, the Democrats became the majority party and were known as the party of labor, the poor, minorities, the cities, immigrants, eastern liberals, and the white South. This "New Deal Coalition" has weakened down to the present and has only partly withstood growing Republican voting strength in the South and West and among the suburban middle class. Recent elections have posed the question of whether a Republican realignment similar to the Democratic one of 1932 is now taking place.

Beginning in 1968 and continuing through the two elections of Ronald Reagan in 1980 and 1984, and beyond, a rolling Republican realignment seemed to be occurring. The social earthquake called The 1960s led to divisions within the Democrats that the Republicans took advantage of. The independent presidential candidacy of segregationist Alabama Governor George Wallace exposed a traditionally Democratic white working class alienated from a party they felt to be too pro–civil rights and too anti–Vietnam War. Wallace's conservative populism claimed that pointy-headed bureaucrats and ivory-tower liberals were pushing government programs that helped minorities by taxing the white majority. Republicans saw the chance to steer blue-collar voters away from their New Deal enemy of Wall Street's Big Business to the new enemy in Washington and Harvard.

Riding this wave of conservative populism, with a smattering of racism, Republicans were elected president in five of the six elections before 1992, usually with an overwhelming electoral college vote. The southern and western states were consistently voting for Republican presidential nominees, the youth vote shifted to the GOP, and polls of party identification showed almost as many Republicans as Democrats.

The 1992 election of Bill Clinton complicated matters. Not only did Democrats capture the presidency, but they also added to their majorities in the House and Senate and picked up a majority of state legislatures and governorships. Analysts had to account for a changing electorate that refused to identify with either party. *Dealignment* came to be the buzzword of the moment, reflecting a decaying voter loyalty to either party. The emergence of Ross Perot as a nonparty presidential alternative in 1992 exposed the weakness of the two major parties. The Texas billionaire, for a short time that summer, outpolled both Democratic and Republican candidates.

2004: A Republican Realignment?

The 2004 elections seemed a convincing demonstration of a Republican realignment. Republicans were in firm control of all three branches of the federal government. George W. Bush expanded the Republican base in 2004 and won a higher vote total than any candidate in history. (Senator Kerry's total was second.) The Democrats, who had dominated the Congress for almost all of the 62 years up to 1994, had failed to control the House of Representatives for six straight elections. They had been a minority in the Senate for most of the last 10 years. The year 2002 saw the end of a half century in which Democrats held more state legislative seats; and now the GOP controlled more governorships. While equal numbers of voters declared themselves Democrats and Republicans (37%), and independents seemed to favor the Democrats, it didn't seem to matter. The country might be divided, the government was not.

Part of the explanation lay in a region: The South had changed parties. Since 1980 the South had consistently voted for Republican presidential nominees. Indeed the only Democrats to win the presidency since 1960 were from the South—Johnson, Carter and Clinton. The 1994 elections marked the first time that a majority of Southerners voted Republican for Congress. It was this realignment in the South that made the GOP the majority party in both houses of congress. The 2004 elections reaffirmed the trend; five conservative Republicans replaced retiring southern Democrats making the South's senators almost solidly Republican. And in Texas a Republican-engineered

redistricting switched 4 Democratic seats to the GOP. Reapportionment made it unlikely that the Democrats could win back a House
majority before the next census in 2010.

In the 2004 presidential contest the Democrats couldn't blame
voting machines, the electoral college, the Supreme Court or Ralph
Nader for their defeat. The Republican party was the stronger organization with the White House generating money, modern technology,
and successful campaign strategies. The GOP strength reflected the
broader development of a national conservative movement of foundations, think tanks, media outlets and religious groups. This ideological
network had grown in 40 years to dominate the nation's politics.
Bringing together working class evangelicals with Wall Street financial
clout, conservatives shifted the party to the Right. Republican leaders
delivered cultural populist speeches on the values of faith and family,
while more concretely delivering pro-business economic and tax policies. Presiding over his party was a president who stressed the dangers
of terrorism and the consequent need for strong federal government
leadership.

How long this coalition would rule remained uncertain. Second-
term presidents have tended to became more rigid in their beliefs and
more likely to see their administrations overtaken by scandal. Republicans might still turn off the still-moderate majority of Americans by
overplaying religious absolutes on issues like abortion and gay rights.
With Democrats promising to revive the economic populist roots of
their party, growing conservative dissent from an ever-rising deficit
and government expansion, and a domineering foreign policy alienat-
ing overseas allies, predicting the duration of this Republican realignment seemed hazardous at best.

Democrats Versus Republicans Versus Independents

The differences between the two major parties lie in both image
and reality. The image of the parties is usually based on a stereotype
of people who support the parties. Typical Republicans are white,
middle class, and Protestant; have a college education; and, with the
rise of the "gender gap" in the 1980s and 1990s, are less often
women. They support big business, law and order, limited government intervention in the economy and in peoples' private lives, and
a hard-line policy in foreign affairs, and they refer to themselves as
conservatives. (See Table 7.1.)

Typical Democrats are members of a minority, ethnic, or racial
group; belong to a labor union; and are working-class, non-Protestant,
and urban residents. They support social welfare measures to help

TABLE 7.1   HOW TO TELL A LIBERAL FROM A CONSERVATIVE

Here are some of the political beliefs likely to be preferred by liberals and conservatives.

	LIBERALS	CONSERVATIVES
On Social Policy:		
Abortion	Support "freedom of choice"	Support "right to life"
School prayer	Opposed	Supportive
Affirmative action	Favor	Oppose
On Economic Policy:		
Role of the government	View government as a regulator in the public interest	Favor free-market solutions
Taxes	Want to tax the rich more	Want to keep taxes low
Spending	Want to spend more on the poor, less on the military	Want to spend less on the poor, more on the military
On Crime:		
How to cut crime	Believe we should solve the problems that cause crime	Believe we should stop coddling criminals
Defendants' rights	Believe we should respect them	Believe we should stop letting criminals hide behind the law

the poor at home, government regulation of big business, more equal distribution of wealth, and more liberal, less forceful foreign policies, except perhaps in favoring trade restrictions to protect jobs.

Of course, the reality is more complex than the image. Leaders of the Democratic and Republican parties do disagree on major issues, more often than party members. Party *followers*, not actively involved with the party, tend to be more moderate (or indifferent) than *leaders* on issues. A number of voters straddle the positions of their parties, for example Democratic union members who favor expanded liberal social programs at home but stronger military actions abroad. Democratic and Republican party members, in fact, often agree more with each other than with their party leaders.

Another complicating factor in party differences is that each party is a coalition of often differing groups. The Democratic party includes, for example, liberal, black, urban, working-class supporters from the northern industrial cities, and moderate, white, wealthy suburbanites from the West. The GOP includes moderate business or professional people from the East, and small-town religious fundamentalists or conservative farmers from the South and Midwest.

Because of their conservative cultural and religious beliefs working class Southerners and Westerners have increasingly voted for Republicans. Despite what seems like their economic self-interest in

Democratic programs—job training, higher corporate taxes, and expanded healthcare—identification with conservative positions on abortion, school prayer and gay marriages, have so far out-weighed concerns for expanded public services. Cultural populism and anger at government elites has been more important than economic populism and resentment at corporate elites.

Voters identifying with neither political party are called independents. The 1996 election marked the first time since 1860 that votes for all third-party candidates topped 10 percent in two consecutive presidential elections. In 2001, according to opinion polls, 40 percent of adults were independents. In the 2004 election almost 30 percent still identified themselves as belonging to neither party. (However the number of people who strongly support one of the two parties—"strong partisans"—has increased in recent elections.)

Political scientists have developed two competing explanations for this change. The first is that voters have become less attached to any political party. This has occurred for several reasons: Voters now rely on the media rather than parties for political information, the rise of candidate-centered campaigns has decreased the role of parties in elections, and divisive events like the Vietnam War and the Clinton impeachment turned people off to politics, including parties. (A reversal of this trend after the terrorist attacks of 9/11 proved temporary.) This decline in partisanship has led to the rise of "issue voting," with voters becoming more "volatile." They are more prone to swing from one party's candidate to the other, more responsive to personality and issue appeals, and less predictable.

The second explanation says that there is a "myth of the independent voter." Since the mid-1960s, the increase in independents has been from upper-income and younger voters, who are as informed and active as other voters. Further, this rise may be neither real nor significant. Part of the increase in independents may come from the attractiveness of labeling oneself an "independent" when pollsters ask for a party identity. Most significant to this argument is that the majority of today's independents "lean" toward one of the parties. When it comes time to vote, they act just like people who identify with a party. An independent who "leans" Democratic votes Democratic about as much as someone who claims to be a Democrat. Despite many changes in voting behavior, party identification is still the single best predictor of how a person votes in a general election.

Although the debate between these two views has not ended, both the continuing distrust of government and the willingness of the electorate to consider candidates outside the major parties indicate that party loyalties are in a state of flux. While the two parties have polarized, the voters remain moderate in their views, certainly more moderate than either political party. Because the party elites are so angry with each other, they have helped alienate voters from party politics, and this may lead the "moderate middle" to consider new alternatives. The two major parties, drawn apart by their ideological divisions and their own special interest groups, may either pull centrist mainstream voters to the extremes or just alienate them from voting at all.

VIEW FROM THE INSIDE: PARTY ORGANIZATIONS

Historically American parties have been weak organizations. Traditionally there have been few ties knitting various local parties together, and fewer still binding them into a coherent national organization. The rise of candidate-centered campaigns, the breakdown in strong party loyalties, and the importance of money raised from interest groups and spent on media advertising have further threatened the role of parties today.

Currently the national parties, led by the Republicans, have centralized their organizations by controlling campaign technology, strategy and fundraising. Powerless parties have not always been the rule in the United States, and it's a rule that may be changing now.

Machines—Old and New

Particularly in the last half of the nineteenth century, many American parties at the local level were so tightly organized that they were called *political machines*. Party machines have a party *boss* (leader) who directly controls the political party workers at lower levels (usually city, district, or ward). Local leaders obey the boss because he controls party nominations, patronage positions (jobs that can be given to loyal supporters), political favors, and party finances. While an effective instrument for managing a city government and assuring immigrants a political network to respond to their needs, machines had a well-deserved reputation for corruption. Until his death in 1976, Richard Daley Sr., mayor of Chicago for more than 20 years, kept firm control of a strong Democratic party machine. Daley's machine acted as an informal government and social service agency, meeting the immediate needs of urban citizens. Chicago's political machine has declined (despite Mayor Daley's son, also Richard Daley, now serving as mayor) and this type of party organization, in general, seems to be a leftover from the past. (See "Machine Politics.")

Political machines lost much of their leverage early in the twentieth century when three things happened: (1) local, state, and federal agencies took over distributing benefits (like welfare) to the poor; (2) civil service reforms made most city jobs dependent on competitive

Machine Politics

During Richard Daley Sr.'s long reign as mayor of Chicago and boss of the "machine," he was seldom seriously challenged in an election. One who did run against him was a lawyer named Benjamin Adamowski. Mike Royko, a Chicago columnist, illustrates why he and other Daley opponents didn't get very far.

The owner of a small restaurant at Division and Ashland, the heart of the city's Polish neighborhood, put up a big Adamowski sign. The day it went up the precinct captain came around and said, "How come the sign, Harry?"

"Ben's a friend of mine," the restaurant owner said.

"Ben's a nice guy, Harry, but that's a pretty big sign. I'd appreciate it if you'd take it down."

"No, it's staying up."

The next day the captain came back. "Look, I'm the precinct captain. Is there anything wrong, any problem, anything I can help you with?" Harry said no. "Then why don't you take it down. You know how this looks in my job." Harry wouldn't budge. The sign stayed up. On the third day, the city building inspectors came. The plumbing improvements alone cost Harry $2,100.

Source: From *Boss: Richard J. Daley of Chicago* by Mike Royko, Copyright © 1971 by Mike Royko. Used by permission of Sutton Signet, an imprint of New American Library, a division of Penguin Books USA Inc.

examinations; and (3) direct primaries made gaining the party's nomination a contest anyone could enter and win.

Modern machines have appeared that allow political leaders to use the new technologies of fundraising and direct-mail campaigns to raise and give away money to party colleagues. These *leadership PACs* can cement loyalty to their creators and promote their ambitions for higher office. While they've been around since the 1970s, former Speaker Newt Gingrich is credited for starting the model for this fundraising machine. GOPAC was Gingrich's political action committee that raised millions for Republicans and aided his rise to House speaker. Congressional leaders in both parties are now expected to have a leadership PAC to raise money. Typically, committee chairmen raise funds from private interests with issues before their committees. They then distribute the booty to their more junior colleagues.

Recent White Houses have been accused of using their young campaign staff to form modern political machines. Labeled a "permanent campaign," many of the media advisers and organizers who shaped Bush's march to the presidency found jobs in the Republican

National Committee. But now they pushed for Bush's education and tax cut reform packages and, ultimately, his reelection. Direct-mail appeals, phone banks (using dozens of volunteers to phone supporters), and presidential visits were some of the techniques transferred from election campaigning to gathering national support for administration proposals.

American Party Structure

Picture the American party structure as a pyramid. Local political organizations or clubs are at the bottom, county committees are above them, and state committees are above the county. (See Figure 7.3.) The national committee of each party is over them all with the national conventions the ultimate elected authority. The strength of the party, which had traditionally been at the bottom, has now gravitated toward the top.

As a result of the welfare, civil service, and primary election reforms, most local parties have few resources with which to maintain a strong organization. Local parties range from virtual disorganization to still-powerful machines, with most parties falling closer to the pole of disorganization. In much of the United States, a handful of officials

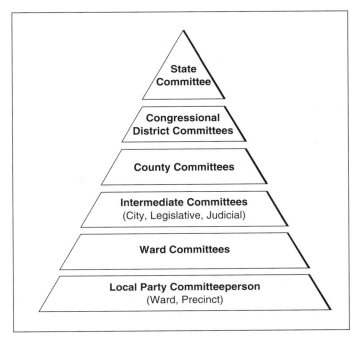

FIGURE 7.3
Typical State Party Organization.

meet occasionally to carry out the essential affairs needed to keep the party going. The party revives only around elections to support candidates who were generally selected by their own efforts.

What do the party's officers do in nonelection years? Their duties primarily depend upon whether they are the *in-party* or the *out-party*. The basic job of out-party officials is to show that the party is still alive. They may have booths at fairs, issue press releases criticizing public officials of the other party, and conduct voter registration drives. But all political activity takes money, which out-parties have difficulty raising. Systems for collecting regular contributions have been only modestly successful. State parties typically sponsor "Jefferson-Jackson Day" dinners (Democrats) or "Lincoln Day" dinners (Republicans). The success of these dinners is limited without the "clout" of a party member in a powerful public office.

One would guess that the in-party—the party with more of its own members in important government positions—has more power than the out-party. This isn't necessarily so. It's the public official, rather than the party, who actually exercises the power of the office. The government official uses the party organization, rather than vice versa. For example, a governor usually names the state party chairperson, who serves as a voice of the governor. The national Republican party clearly became an instrument for promoting President Bush's policies after he entered the White House.

State parties are generally stronger than local parties because of their connection to the national party. They have a professional staff of several people hired from funds supplied by the national party. Like the national structure, there is a state committee and a chairperson, all chosen by election or state convention. The committee's ability to select party nominees for state or national offices is severely limited by primaries. The state party frequently channels funds from the wealthy campaigns of incumbents to those of new, promising candidates, thus building party loyalty. Patronage, ranging from placing a traffic light to awarding a building contract, helps grease the wheels of state party activities.

National Party Organization

Historically the local party was the most effective link to the voter. Volunteers in the community would turn out the vote and deliver needed services (like that traffic light) to the party supporters. But in recent years the increased reliance on modern campaign technology (such as direct mail, the Internet, and media ads) has overshadowed the use of local volunteers to reach voters. It also has centralized party functions in professionals in the national organization and in outside consultants, known as "hired guns." Self-financing by wealthy candidates of their own campaigns, including the hiring of their staff, has further weakened the role of parties.

Each party is officially governed by its *national committee.* The national committee consists of representatives chosen from each state party organization and various other party groups. The committee is led by the *chairperson,* who is often chosen by the party's presidential nominee every four years. Under these authorities are the party's *professional staff.* These professionals have gained power through their understanding of the modern technology of campaigning and the complicated laws overseeing how money is raised and spent. The Republican staff is much larger than the Democratic staff because the Democrats contract out much of their work, such as direct-mail fundraising, to campaign consultants. The Republicans have also taken the lead in strengthening their national party.

In both fundraising and organization, the Republicans have done a better job than the Democrats. Though the gap between the parties narrowed when the Democrats controlled the White House, by 2002 the Republicans were clearly raising more money. Going into the 2002 elections, the GOP's election committees had raised $527 million to the Democrats' $344 million, a difference of $183 million.

In the 2004 elections Republican party committees, including those of the House and Senate, raised over $1.3 billion dollars—a record amount. Democratic committees raised almost $1.1 billion. These amounts were even more impressive because the parties could not raise 'soft money' in unlimited amounts in this election. The Republican total reflected their large pool of small donors and their lead in technology. The Democrats who almost doubled their fundraising totals from 2000 showed that they could match the GOP in the money race. Both parties defied predictions that the McCain-Feingold campaign finance reform would severely weaken their fundraising. The Republican party remained the single most important source of money in American politics. (See Table 7.2).

These funds were used to support the party's candidates and buy expensive campaign technology. The large amounts of money the Republicans have given to their candidates concentrated power in the national organization and encouraged loyalty in party members' votes in Congress. Besides increasing party discipline, the funds were spent on sophisticated media and computerized mail campaigns to reach and register Republican voters. Until recently, the Democrats have been the majority party, but the Republicans have the advantage in money and technology. The power of both national committees is

TABLE 7.2   A CONTINUING CLIMB

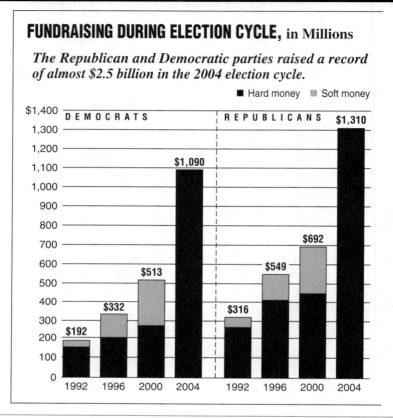

FUNDRAISING DURING ELECTION CYCLE, in Millions

The Republican and Democratic parties raised a record of almost $2.5 billion in the 2004 election cycle.

■ Hard money   ■ Soft money

DEMOCRATS — $192, $332, $513, $1,090
REPUBLICANS — $316, $549, $692, $1,310

Years: 1992, 1996, 2000, 2004

Source: Center for Responsive Politics, FEC, 12/2/04; *The Washington Post,* March 5, 2001.

likely to increase as the formerly weak parties strengthen their central organizations.

Soft Money

Before being restricted by recent reforms soft money provided important and controversial campaign funds for political parties. *Soft money* were large unrestricted donations that did not come under federal regulation because they were supposed to be for state and local parties, not candidates. (*Hard money* referred to funds for candidates in federal elections that since the Watergate scandal have been restricted to limited amounts.) After the 2002 election the national parties were prevented from using soft money in presidential campaigns. To avoid these limits allies of the two nominees formed independent 527 groups that were used in 2004 to raise funds to support their candidate. To many this looked like unrestricted soft money, just not raised by the political parties this time.

In the past soft money became an issue in campaigns because they became a loophole for channeling big bucks into elections. The Democrats in 1996, responding to their loss of control in Congress in 1994, developed an aggressive system of fundraising to pay for television advertisements for reelecting President Clinton. Some donors illegally represented foreign corporations, and some of the fundraising practices involved overnight stays in the Lincoln Bedroom. By the 2000 elections, record amounts of soft money were being raised by both political parties. The $245 million raised by Republicans and the $243 million collected by Democrats represented a record $488 million in soft money, a huge increase over the $263 million raised in the 1996 presidential campaign. By 2002, even these records were surpassed. (See "Money Talks, Nobody Walks.")

Both press coverage and public outrage grew at this avalanche of money into elections. The McCain-Feingold Campaign Finance Bill, which passed in early 2002, banned soft money going to national parties and restricted contributions to state and local parties. State parties were forbidden from transferring their soft money contributions to support or oppose federal candidates. At first the Democrats took

Money Talks, Nobody Walks

By providing a back door for wealthy interests, soft money has been involved in most of the scandals surrounding campaign contributions. One that emerged a few years ago involved an aggressive businessman, Charles H. Keating Jr., and five senators of both parties.

These "Keating Five" had attempted to intervene with the Federal Home Loan Bank Board to protect Lincoln Savings and Loan from regulatory penalties. Mr. Keating was the bank's owner and, not accidentally, had contributed over $1.3 million to the five senators' campaigns. Each of the senators claimed the intervention amounted to constituent service because Lincoln S&L had assets in their states. The S&L failed anyway, costing taxpayers some $2 billion in deposit insurance costs. Mr. Keating ended up in jail.

Afterward Keating himself raised and answered the question "whether my financial support in any way influenced several political figures to take up my cause. I want to say in the most forceful way I can, I certainly hope so."

Source: Time, September 11, 1995.

the lead in creating 527 groups and undermining the goals of campaign reform, but the Republicans soon caught up. By the end of the campaign, and with many reports still to be filed, both sides' 527 groups supporting presidential candidates had raised over $277 million in soft money contributions. Clearly the issue of big money in elections had not yet ended. (See Case Study, "Campaign Finance Reform," pp. 115–118.)

The National Convention

Much of the public attention the party receives comes at its *national convention*. Held during the summer before the presidential campaign, the national convention is attended by delegates chosen by the state parties in various ways. In late summer of 2004, the Republican convention in New York had 4,853 delegates, while the earlier Democratic convention in Boston had 4,319. The delegates to the convention adopt a platform, elect the party's presidential nominee, and act as the party's highest governing body assembled every four years.

The *party platform* actually is written by a platform committee and then approved by the convention. In the document, the party states its—and its presidential candidate's—views and promises on many issues. If the party is in power, the platform will boast of the party's achievements. If the party is out of power, the platform will criticize the policies of the incumbent party. The platform will emphasize the party's differences with the other major party and minimize the divisions within the party. Since the goal of the platform is to win elections, it may fudge on controversial issues.

Frequently, groups of convention delegates will organize into factions in order to press for statements to be included in the platform representing their minority political views. In 2000 a minority group of women at the Republican national convention pressed unsuccessfully for *planks* (parts of the platform) supporting abortion rights. Platforms are important in reconciling groups within the party before the election. Party platforms are surprisingly accurate in predicting what a president will actually try to do when in office.

Early in the 1970s—beginning with Democrats trying to recover popularity from their disastrous 1968 convention in Chicago—party reforms led to greater popular participation in the nominating process. Until these reforms, about 40 percent of convention delegates were chosen in states with *presidential primaries*—elections usually limited to registered voters from that one party. The rest were chosen by *caucuses*—party meetings dominated by party leaders. Since then, 70 percent of delegates have been chosen by voters supporting candidates in primary elections.

But something happened to the parties. Critics charged that these reforms made the news media central to presidential campaigns. The candidates for the party nomination now played to the press, not the party. The media coverage emphasized elections as horse races (who's ahead, who's behind) and stressed embarrassments that made attractive headlines (for example, Bush's long-ago arrest for drunken driving). The media focused on conflicts and negatives about politics, while neglecting issues. It did not promote coherent choices on how the nation will be governed or help build coalitions of groups that the candidates would need once in office. In short, primaries have undermined the party's central role of choosing their candidates. The press now fills that role—and, some would say, badly.

The names of the candidates for president are placed in nomination toward the end of the convention. A roll-call vote of the delegates is then taken. The final party nominee for the office of president is elected by a simple majority vote. In 1924, the Democratic convention took 103 ballots before it was able to reach a majority decision. In recent decades the presidential nominee has been named on the first ballot, reflecting the votes in the state primaries and caucuses. Conventions today can be described as *approving* or *ratifying* the candidate selected by the party voters. The delegates, who are mostly pledged to a candidate, don't make the choice themselves.

The presidential nominee chooses a vice presidential running mate who is then formally approved by the convention. A main goal has been to *balance the ticket*. Michael Dukakis, a liberal New England governor, in 1988 chose Lloyd Bentsen, a Texas conservative with Washington experience, to be the Democratic vice presidential nominee. The vice presidential choice may be a popular competitor of the nominee from the primaries, as was John Edwards when John Kerry chose him in 2004. Arkansan Bill Clinton's 1992 choice of Senator Al Gore from the neighboring state of Tennessee, while unusual in putting two Southerners on the ticket, reinforced the campaign's image of youth and change. The 2000 vice presidential choices of both parties were attempts to bolster weaknesses of the nominees. Richard Cheney's long public service compensated for George W. Bush's lack of government experience. Joe Lieberman's reputation for integrity was thought to be helpful in distancing Al Gore from President Clinton's moral lapses.

The national convention is the starting point of the fall presidential campaign. Party workers and supporters, boosted by free prime-time television coverage of at least some of the convention speeches, set out to make their party's nominee the winner of the presidential election in November. (See "Are Conventions Really TV Miniseries?")

Are Conventions Really TV Miniseries?

Don Hewitt, executive producer of CBS's 60 Minutes, *made the following remarks about political conventions:*

> There is no doubt whose convention this really is. The politicians meeting there are now extras in our television show. . . .
>
> In the old days, before the primaries took the steam out of political conventions, you could watch a good credentials fight or a good platform fight—even though a week later no one could remember what they were fighting about. Today, if you want to see a good fight at a political convention, let CBS News's sign be an inch bigger than NBC's. Now you'll see a fight at a convention. All hell breaks loose.
>
> It's time we gave the politicians back their convention. Tell them it's nothing but a big commercial and that it's not Rather's, Brokaw's, or Jennings's job to be the emcee of their commercial.

Source: Paul Allen Beck and Frank J. Sorauf, *Party Politics in America*, 7th ed. New York: HarperCollins, 1992, p. 301.

VIEW FROM THE OUTSIDE: THE TWO-PARTY SYSTEM

Despite the occasional calls for a third political party, the United States retains a *two-party system,* meaning that two parties dominate national politics. In a *one-party system,* a single party monopolizes the organization of power and the positions of authority. In a *multiparty system,* more than two political parties compete for power and electoral offices.

From the Civil War until at least the election of Dwight D. Eisenhower to the presidency in 1952, the 11 southern states of the Civil War Confederacy had virtually one-party systems. These states were so heavily Democratic that the Republicans were a permanent minority. The important electoral contests took place in the primaries, where blacks were excluded, and where factions within the party often competed like separate parties. Multiparty systems also have existed in the United States. With Jesse Ventura (loosely connected to the Reform party) elected as its governor in 1998, Minnesota could be said to have a three-party system, or did until he left his party, and then the office, in 2003.

Causes of the Two-Party System

There are four main reasons for the continued dominance of two parties in the United States. One is the *historic dualism* of American political conflict. The first major political division among Americans was dual, or two sided, between Federalists and Anti-Federalists. It is said that this original two-sided political battle established the tradition of two-party domination in this country.

The second reason is the *moderate views of the American voter.* Unlike European democracies, where radical political parties such as the Communists have legitimacy, American politics tends more toward the center. Americans may be moderate because their political party system forces them to choose between two moderate parties, or American parties may be moderate because Americans do not want to make more extreme political choices. As with the chicken and the egg, it's tough to know which came first.

Third, the *structure of our electoral system* encourages two-party dominance. We elect one representative at a time from each district to Congress, which is called election by *single-member districts.* The winning candidate is the one who gets the most votes, or a *plurality.* (A majority of votes means more than 50 percent of the votes cast; as mentioned earlier, a plurality simply means more votes than anyone else.) Similarly, in presidential elections, the party with a plurality in a state gets all the electoral votes of that state. This system makes it difficult for minor-party candidates to win elections, and without election victories parties fade fast.

Many countries with multiparty systems elect representatives by *proportional representation.* Each district has more than one representative, and each party that receives a certain number of votes gets to send a proportionate number of representatives to the legislature. For example, in a single-member district a minor party that received 10 percent of the vote would not be able to send its candidate to Congress. In a multimember district the size of ten congressional districts, however, that 10 percent of the vote would mean that one out of ten representatives sent from the district would be a minor-party member.

Finally, the Democratic and Republican parties continue to dominate national politics because they are flexible enough to *adopt some of the programs proposed by third parties,* and thus win over third-party supporters. The Socialist party in America, even during its strongest period, always had difficulty achieving national support partly because the Democratic party was able to *co-opt,* or win over, the support of most of organized labor with pro-labor economic programs. The Republican party lured voters away from Alabama Governor George Wallace's American Independent Party (AIP) by stressing law and order and ignoring civil rights in its 1968 presidential campaign. After seeing the disastrous results for Democrats of Ralph Nader running in 2000, in 2004 Democratic presidential candidate John Kerry made clear his support for some of the populist themes and anti-Bush tone of Nader's positions.

The End of the Two-Party System?

For all these historical and structural reasons, the odds are against either the emergence of a stable third party or an independent candidate being elected president. Operating as an "umbrella" over the broad moderate center, the two-party system has kept radical factions from winning power, thus preventing the country from being severely divided. This has meant that dissenting opinions traditionally got little consideration from voters. It kept the parties from taking extreme positions and led them to avoid controversial issues. It also meant that there was little room for third parties, except at the fringe.

And yet . . . the last decade has reinforced the weakness of the two political parties. Democrats saw large numbers of their elected representatives retire as the GOP tightened its grip on Congress and Democratic officials in the South switched parties. President Clinton moved his party toward the middle on domestic issues but helped drag his chosen successor, Al Gore, to defeat, dogged by his scandals. No Democratic presidential candidate has won a majority of the votes since 1976.

Further harming traditional Democrats was the apparent popular rejection of the party's core ideology—that government could be an effective instrument to improve the lives of working people. Voters now seem more worried about big government's flawed and expensive efforts to eradicate crime, poverty, and injustice. Adding to their party's problems, in a period of terrorist threats, polls showed people worried about the Democrats' alleged softness toward national security issues.

Republicans faced similar dilemmas. The drift toward the religious right by GOP leaders and the visible dominance by lobbyists for big corporations led to the question of whether the party could represent a new Republican majority that was neither very religious nor very wealthy. A rocketing deficit, a jobless economic recovery, and corrupt corporate executives on trial hardly enhanced the conservative party's popularity. Slogans about "compassionate conservatism" didn't conceal that the executive branch was undermining popular health and environmental programs, not to mention civil liberties. A bullying foreign policy relying on arrogance and military force isolated the United States from traditional allies and seemed stuck in Iraq, adding to an insecure and polarized politics at home.

Despite Republican control of the federal government, the two parties were equal in popular support. The election of 2004 reflected a moderate majority forced to choose between polarized parties. Most voters remained neither extreme nor particularly partisan in their political beliefs. The Republican victory reflected superior organizational skills in turning out their vote in key states, as well as the shrewd political use of national security fears. The Republican party was nationally dominant, but this did not reflect a broad shift in public opinion for the party. Whether either party would risk the loyalty of their own intense supporters to reach this moderate middle of voters may yet determine the direction party politics takes in the next few years.

CASE STUDY

BLOGS, HOWARD DEAN, AND THE 2004 CAMPAIGN

It's virtually impossible to talk about the Internet in the 2004 presidential election without talking about Howard Dean. His come-from-nowhere campaign used the Web in new and creative ways to raise money and recruit volunteers. Although he lost the Democratic nomination, Dean may have established a model that will become the norm for future presidential efforts.

Pre-2004

Prior to the 2004 presidential elections, the Internet was mainly used for two purposes: one was research, and the other was fundraising. The most frequent use of the Internet was easy to overlook—research. For research there was no faster or more economical way for a campaign to pull together information than to go online. And numerous Websites have sprung

up to meet these needs, from Opensecrets.org (for information on money in politics) to FirstGov.gov (for federal government data).

Internet fundraising had increased with each election. An estimated 2 percent of donations for elections came from online appeals in 1998, while some 10 percent was raised in 2000. The most notable example in the 2000 presidential campaign was John McCain raising $6 million after his surprise win over George W. Bush in the Republican New Hampshire primary. The ability to raise a large amount of money in a short period of time made the Internet a new weapon in campaign arsenals.

A Desperate Dean Meets the Blog

Howard Dean, the former governor of Vermont, improved on the existing fundraising and organizing techniques of using the Internet. Beginning as a virtual unknown, and without a national fundraising network, Dean was able to raise $41 million in 2003, breaking former President Bill Clinton's party record for money raised in one quarter of a year. His opposition to the war in Iraq gave him a clear, anti-establishment message that attracted supporters to his campaign. His exciting high-tech call to arms mobilized small donors to contribute using e-mail.

Like many innovations in politics, Dean's use of the Internet was born of desperation. It was January 2003 and, while talking with campaign manager Joe Trippi, Dean was bemoaning the fact that despite the crowds that flocked to their events, they had only $157,000 in the bank.

"We will never have any money," the governor complained.

"We have to use the Internet" to build the base, Trippi responded.

While Governor Dean understood the concept, the details escaped him. "What's a blog?" he asked.

Trippi knew the answer because he had spent the year before in California as a marketing consultant for dot-coms. While there, he had become a fan of political "blogs." These were Web pages where thousands of people could post thoughts and commentaries. These Web soapboxes allowed rapid responses in a never-ending virtual town hall meeting. Trippi wondered whether these Internet communities could be used for an Internet-based presidential campaign.

E-Campaigning

The Dean campaign enlisted the help of two Internet companies. One, Meetup Inc., set up gatherings for people with common interests who would pay to have business steered their way. The company focused on nonpolitical groups of, say, breast cancer survivors, sorting names by zip code and setting up local "meetups" for them. A nonprofit liberal Web group, MoveOn.org, was also enlisted. Begun to organize people against Clinton's impeachment ("Censure President Clinton and move on"), MoveOn had a large user-friendly e-mail list that they had successfully used for fundraising for liberal causes. They offered their expertise to all the Democratic candidates. Only the Dean campaign responded.

These two companies helped the campaign put together user-friendly blogs as electronic hangouts to chat with like-minded Dean supporters. People could communicate directly with the campaign, and with each other. In addition, these sites offered a range of online tools—a directory of supporters, a site that enabled them to find and schedule their own events, and an entry to Meetup.com. This last helped Dean people in scattered places find one another. The *blog* created a sense of community among dispersed supporters. More than 185,000 people signed up in support of Dean. It was a political organizing tool that allowed like-minded partisans to talk with each other, put on events, and raise money. It brought a national campaign to an effective community level.

It also raised a lot of money. In a few days in June, the campaign got tens of thousands of donors to give nearly $3 million, doubling the campaign's take for that quarter. The donations kept increasing from there, with nearly half of the money raised coming from contributions of less than $200. Internet fundraising was also efficient, netting more than 95 cents for every dollar given.

The Internet's Future

Howard Dean ended up losing his race for the Democratic nomination, rather badly. He lost early primaries and caucuses in Iowa and New Hampshire, and soon dropped out. But before that, Dean had led in opinion polls and raised more money than any other Democrat. Had he really changed presidential politics?

The failure of Dean's campaign led some to question the value of the Internet strategy. Arguably, that strategy reinforced his image as a fringe antiwar candidate. But his collapse can also be linked to a brash personality and lack of local organizing in key primary and caucus states. Whatever the causes, his online legacy may last longer than his campaign. His fundraising opened the possibility that the Democrats who have depended on wealthy Washington-based donors—mostly unions, trial lawyers, and some ethnic groups—can reorient their party toward small donors. In fact, by the end of the 2004 presidential campaign, the Democrats had almost matched President Bush's record fundraising, mostly in small donations and with help from the Internet. Basing campaigns on a large number of small donors offers the Democratic party the potential to move in more grassroots directions in the future—perhaps even bringing alienated young people back to the party.

The Dean campaign showed the potential for channeling blog links into electoral politics. Intensely committed people reaching out through the Internet to formerly isolated allies could organize a national movement. But successfully combining the energy and outrage of social networks with the broad coalitions needed to influence national politics remained for a future campaign.

Even the present situation is an improvement. Sociologist Robert Putnam, a noted critic of America's lagging participation, reflected on the impact of the Internet, "If people are getting together to talk about politics, that's better than people sitting watching a 30-second sound bite."

Sources: Jeanne Cummings, "Behind Dean Surge: A Gang of Bloggers," *The Wall Street Journal*, October 14, 2003; *National Journal*, October 14, 2000, pp. 3248–49; "Bandwagon," *Campaigns & Elections* (August 2000): 40–69; Brian Falter, "Dean Leaves Legacy of Online Campaign," The *Washington Post*, February 20, 2004; and The *New York Times*, January 25, 2004. Joe Trippi, *The Revolution Will Not Be Televised*. Reagan Books, 2004.

WRAP-UP

Voters are the broadest, most representative players in the political game. Elections legitimate how the government is run, and voters choose who is to run it. Many factors, like political socialization, party membership, religion, race, and class, influence how people vote or even *if* they vote. While participation in politics takes place outside of voting, substantial nonvoting and mistrust of Washington, especially among the young, pose serious questions about the representative nature of government.

The political parties provide a major link between voters and their elected officials. Historically the parties have evolved into a two-party system, with the Democrats and Republicans dominating elections for 145 years. Though the parties have been weakly organized, recent reforms including increased fundraising capabilities have strengthened the national organizations, resulting in high-tech operations, including the increasing use of the Internet pioneered in 2004 by Howard Dean's campaign. Through a process of primaries, nominating conventions, and election campaigns, parties put their labels on candidates who, through their own efforts in media-driven primaries, gain national leadership.

The traditional two-party system is now threatened by polarizing forces within the parties and by independent voters who feel little loyalty to either party. However, both parties still have a few cards left to play. They have shown great flexibility in adapting to the demands of newly mobilized groups, whether blacks and feminists, or Christian fundamentalists and angry white males. Demonstrating a willingness to grapple with the pressing national issues of the day will allow them to continue as vital links between people and their government. Not to do so will lead to the questioning of their own role as major players, and to the continued indifference of voters tuned out to the political game.

Thought Questions

1. If you voted in the last election, what influenced the way you voted? Can you relate your political views to your family, religion, or class background?
2. If you didn't vote, what led you not to vote? What would motivate you to vote in the future? How do you participate in politics even if you don't vote?
3. Are political parties obsolete? Can technology and modern media fill the role of connecting people to the campaigns of elected officials without parties acting as a bridge?
4. In the recent presidential campaign, how did both candidates try to move toward the moderate middle on major issues? Did that influence your vote?

Suggested Readings

Frank, Thomas. *Whats The Matter With Kansas?* Metropolitan Books, 2004.
  Subtitled,"How Conservatives Won the Heart of America," this book by a liberal Kansan, describes in personal terms how his state journeyed from economic populism to social conservatism.

Jamieson, Kathleen Hall. *Everything You Think You Know About Politics . . . and Why You're Wrong.* New York: Basic Books, 2000.
  Chatty insights of campaigns, news coverage, and voter turnout.

Lewis, Michael. *Trail Fever.* New York: Vintage, 1997. Pb.
  A funny, thoughtful account of life on the fringes of the 1996 presidential primaries.

Patterson, Thomas E. *The Vanishing Voter.* New York: Vintage Books, 2003.
  A political scientist expertly dissects why despite greater education and easier registration, fewer Americans turn out to vote.

Pomper, Gerald M. ed. *The Election of 2000.* New York: Chatham House Publishers, 2001. Pb.
> A collection of articles by academics and journalists on this unique election.

Riordan, William L. *Plunkitt of Tammany Hall.* New York: Dutton, 1963. Pb.
> The witty confessions of a New York City political boss covering the politics of his machine around the end of the nineteenth century.

Schudson, Michael. *The Good Citizen.* Cambridge, Mass.: Harvard University Press, 1998. Pb.
> A well-written history of Americans' participation in public affairs with some surprisingly positive conclusions about the state of modern citizenship.

CHAPTER 8

Interest Groups and the Media

SPECIAL INTERESTS

When one looks for who to blame for what is wrong with the modern political game, the finger is usually pointed at interest groups and media. "Special interests" are seen as the rich and powerful pulling strings behind the scenes. Media are more visibly seen distorting politics with simplistic sound bites of issues and negative images of leaders. Whatever our conclusions about them, both players are key to understanding today's politics.

The Constitution does not say much about either. Except for the First Amendment's guarantee of freedom of the press, neither is mentioned in the document. The framers of the Constitution recognized differing interests but not their role in government. Although they made wide use of the press in their efforts to get the Constitution adopted—*The Federalist Papers* began life as newspaper articles— the framers could not predict the influence of today's mass media. Indeed, what could the framers have said about them? Their unexpected growth has filled gaps in the political process left by the Constitution.

Both interest groups and media provide access to the government. Interest groups offer tools for people with common concerns to bring their views to public officials. The media are a communications link (and participants in their own right) by which people keep informed of politics. As instruments of power, the two change the political game they play. Who they are, what they do, and how interest groups and media shape and are shaped by politics are central to what follows.

INTEREST GROUPS

In his famous study *Democracy in America* in 1835, Alexis de Tocqueville, was impressed that Americans constantly joined groups of all kinds. The Frenchman thought these "associations" were essential to why democracy worked in the United States. The groups kept a balance between the state and the individual, and preserved individual liberties. As he put it,

> An association for political, commercial or manufacturing purposes, or even for those of science and literature, is a powerful and enlightened member of the community . . . which, by defending its own rights against the encroachments of government, saves the common liberties of the country.

Tocqueville's endorsement of the political importance of diverse group interests made him the father of what would later be called pluralism (see Chapter 9).

Though Tocqueville included local government when he wrote about associations, today we speak of *interest groups* as people organized to pursue a common interest by applying pressure on the political process. In the last chapter, we saw that American parties are not structured very well for representing specific interests. Interest groups help fill this gap.

Our parties and the electoral system are organized by geography. Senators and representatives represent us on the basis of the state or the district in which we live. But within one district there may be important group interests. Members of different religions, races, incomes, or economic associations may have different political concerns. Interest groups give Americans with common causes a way to express their views to decisionmakers. While interest groups may try to influence the outcome of elections, unlike parties they do not compete for public office. Candidates may be sympathetic to a certain interest, or even be a member of that group, but they will not run for election as representatives of that group.

Interest groups usually are more tightly organized than political parties. They are financed through contributions or dues-paying members. Organizers communicate with members through newsletters, mailings, and conferences. Union members, for example, will receive regular correspondence from their leadership informing them about political activities, positions they are expected to support, and which candidate to volunteer and vote for.

Types of Interest Groups

The largest and most important groupings are economic interests, including business, professional, labor, and farming groups. James Madison, in *The Federalist Papers* No. 10, expressed the fear that if people united on the basis of economic interests, all the have-nots in society would take control of the government. This clearly has not happened. The most influential groups are generally those who spend the most money. *Business groups* have a common interest in making profits, which also involves supporting the economic system that makes profits possible. The Chamber of Commerce, the National Association of Manufacturers, and the National Small Business Association are well-known business groups. Large, powerful companies, like Microsoft and General Motors, often act as interest groups by themselves.

Of course all business groups are seldom united on one side of an issue. Competitors within an industry extend their rivalries to the political arena. Long-distance phone companies bitterly fought local phone companies over recent telecommunications reforms. Railroads and truckers regularly battle over transportation policy. Even when a political conflict is characterized as business opposing, say, environmentalists, a closer look will reveal business groups on both sides of the issue. The Superfund cleanup of toxic waste sites saw environmentalists aligned with insurance and chemical companies opposing oil corporations and other insurance companies. Most contested political issues show splits in the business community.

Professional groups include the American Medical Association, the National Association of Realtors, and the American Bar Association, all of which have powerful lobbies in Washington. *Labor unions*, like the International Brotherhood of Teamsters and the unions that make up the American Federation of Labor and the Congress of Industrial Organizations (the AFL-CIO), are the most important financial supporters of the Democratic party. In many strongly Democratic districts, Election Day will find the local labor unions and the local party practically merging to turn out voters. Labor leaders, who tend to stay in power longer than most politicians, are powerful political figures in their own right. Although there have been recent signs of revival, the influence of organized labor has declined, along with its membership, in the last 50 years.

Agricultural business interests have a long history of influential lobbying activity. The American Farm Bureau Federation, the National Farmers Union, and the National Grange are powerful groups in Washington. Specialized groups, like the Associated Milk Producers, Inc. (AMP), will strongly lobby farm legislation.

Some interest groups are organized around religious, social, or political concerns. Groups like the NAACP, the Urban League, and the Southern Christian Leadership Conference (SCLC) focus on economic and religious constituencies within the black community that they represent in national forums. The Sierra Club lobbies in Washington to protect the environment but is considered more moderate than Greenpeace, a group of environmental activists who take direct action on issues like clear-cutting old-growth forests. Interest groups may represent people sharing similar political ideas. These include the liberal Washington-based People for the American Way, which has campaigned against censorship; Common Cause, which promotes bipartisan government reforms; and the conservative Christian Coalition. (See "The Christian Coalition.")

Lobbying

Lobbying is when individuals or interest groups pressure the government to act in their favor. Interest groups today maintain professional staffs of lobbyists or hire consulting firms in Washington to promote their concerns. These lobbyists include former members of

The Christian Coalition

One notable example of a successful religious interest group is the Christian Coalition. Organized in 1989 by religious broadcaster Pat Robertson, its 1.7 million members have been active within the Republican party on issues like abortion, funding for the arts, and school prayer. The conservative Christians they represent are given major credit for Republicans winning control of both Congress and the presidency for the first time in 50 years.

While not formally endorsing candidates, the Coalition has had a great influence on Republicans seeking the party's presidential nomination. Its grassroots organizations distribute voter guides in churches, track local school board activities, recruit volunteer organizers, and contact members of Congress and state legislatures. As part of the Evangelical movement, it was an important part of some state Republican parties. A spokesman summed up the Coalition's goals: "We think the Lord is going to give us this nation back one precinct at a time, one neighborhood at a time, and one state at a time."

Congress or the executive branch who are knowledgeable in a particular area, and may be personally connected to decisionmakers. When Senator Phil Gramm of Texas retired from the Senate in 2003, he joined the Wall Street firm of UBS Warburg for an annual salary of over $1 million. The former chairman of the Senate Banking committee had coauthored a bill in 1999 that permitted banks to merge with securities firms, a law that allowed UBS in 2000 to purchase a brokerage for $12 billion. Gramm's transition to Wall Street barely caused a ripple in Washington, where getting a job from firms that once lobbied you was a common practice.

More than 25,500 lobbyists spent at least $1.6 billion lobbying Congress in 2002. This comes to 48 lobbyists and more than $3 million per legislator. While lobbyists are required to register and are limited to $100 cap in gifts to public officials, the disclosure rules governing lobbying are not considered strict. The Center for Public Integrity took a survey of state lobbying laws and found that only three states had lobby disclosure rules that were as weak or weaker than those applying to the hired guns lobbying Congress. Occasional scandals historically have produced only modest gestures toward reform.

Direct lobbying usually takes place in congressional committees and executive bureaucracies. Although lobbying the legislature gets most of the publicity, lobbyists devote more attention to executive agencies in attempting to influence their regulations. It is said that the real decisions of government are made among lobbyists, bureaucrats, and congressional committees—the so-called *iron triangle.* Lobbyists provide information about their industry or association to committees and bureaucracies. They argue their position with congressional staffers, and they may have their powerful clients speak directly with decisionmakers. Knowledge, personal contacts, and frequent attendance at campaign fundraisers place lobbyists in a position to at least be heard on measures affecting their clients. (See "The Five Commandments of Lobbying.")

Indirect lobbying may involve massive letter-writing campaigns using phone banks to get voters' signatures and computers to make the letters look as if they had been individually written. Modern phone technologies allow lobbying firms to contact sympathetic voters and connect them directly to their member's office. The National Rifle Association has had notable success using mass mailings to fight gun control legislation. More subtle lobbying efforts involve "nonpolitical" public relations campaigns. Oil companies responded to criticism about oil spills with advertising showing their concern for the environment. Lumber companies don't discuss the clear-cutting of

The Five Commandments of Lobbying

In meeting with elected officials, lobbyists follow a set of "informal rules" that could be helpful to anyone lobbying Congress:

1. *Demonstrate a constituent interest.*
   One of the best ways to ensure attention is to show the impact on the representative's voters.

2. *Be well informed.*
   Officials want information in return for the time and attention they give.

3. *Be well balanced.*
   Compromise is inevitable in legislation. Lobbyists who present both sides leave the official with the impression that they have looked at all sides of the question and then arrived at a conclusion.

4. *Keep it short and sweet.*
   The challenge is to present the relevant information in the shortest time and in the most memorable way.

5. *Leave a written summary of the case.*
   It relieves officials of the necessity of taking notes and ensures that the correct information stays behind.

forests but instead show commercials of their employees planting trees. Op-eds, letters to the editor, and even editorials are often the results of lobbying campaigns funded by private interests.

Another form of indirect lobbying is for interest groups to persuade other groups to join them in a *grassroots campaign*. They will form a *coalition* of different groups often using a letterhead name, such as Americans for Free Trade, which is invented for the campaign. Using money from private interests, such as Japanese corporations opposing trade restrictions, the lobbyists managing the campaign try to give Congress the impression that much of the voting public supports their position. Sometimes these campaigns work to influence local opinion leaders, mobilize employees to write their member of Congress, and get allied businesses to join the coalition. At other times, these efforts merely produce Washington's famed "smoke and mirrors"—the illusion of broad popular support for what is in fact a narrow interest group spending lots of money. Congress and the press seem to be gaining experience in telling the difference. (See "Advocacy Ads: The John McCain Case.")

Advocacy Ads: The John McCain Case

Included in the Campaign Finance Reform of 2002 was a restriction on advocacy ads that mention a federal candidate and are run within 60 days of a general election or 30 days from a primary. Before this limit, these ads did not fall under campaign financing rules because they were not coordinated by campaign officials. A cosponsor of this law, Arizona Senator John McCain, found out how this loophole worked in his campaign for the Republican nomination for president in the spring of 2000.

Shortly before crucial primaries in California, New York, and Ohio, television stations began broadcasting ads that criticized McCain's record on the environment. They were sponsored by "Republicans for Clean Air." These turned out to be two Texas billionaires, Sam and Charles Wyly, who had spent $2.5 million on the ads. Both were long-time supporters of Governor Bush. McCain argued that the Wylys, as members of Bush fundraising committees, were not eligible to finance these issue ads. "Are we going to allow two Texas cronies of George W. Bush to hijack an election?" McCain asked. Bush replied that there was no coordination with his campaign and refused to ask the brothers to stop running them.

As John McCain learned, most voters can't tell the difference between a candidate's ads and an issue ad. One consultant concluded, "What separates issue advocacy and political advocacy is a line in the sand drawn on a windy day."

The essence of grassroots lobbying is getting constituents to contact their own elected representative. This demonstrates intensity and broad support, reflects the issue's local impact in the member's home district or state, and reminds elected officials of the political pain that awaits a wrong decision. Personal lobbying of this kind often is applied to members of Congress while they are visiting their districts. Organizations with a widespread geographic distribution of members, such as the American Association of Retired Persons (AARP), can make effective use of grassroots pressure just by contacting their members. Single-issue groups like the American Israel Public Affairs Committee (AIPAC) and the pro- and anti-abortion groups can use their members' intense feelings on an issue to influence legislators. These "passionate minorities" often are the only voices members hear on a policy. Elected officials know that their position on one of these "hot-button issues" will directly affect the vote, and the money, of these few but important activists.

Campaign Contributions and PACs

Money has been called the mother's milk of politics. Unlike milk, however, money in elections is combustible and controversial. By contributing money to a political campaign, interest groups can reward a politician who has supported them in the past and encourage support in the future. In the 2000 presidential election, corporation support went overwhelmingly to the Republican candidate; this included energy, tobacco and high-tech companies with specific  issues before the new administration. (See Table 8.1, "Bush's Top Corporate Donors.") The Democrats, while frequently pleading poverty, received millions in funding from labor unions and special interest groups like trial lawyers.

What does this money buy? At the least—*access*, the right to talk to the elected official. A campaign contributor may say: "I don't want any special promise from you; all I want is the right to come and talk to you when I need to." This seemingly modest request is critical. Access is power. Former Representative Michael Barnes of Maryland offered a congressman's perspective:

> You have to make a choice. Who are you going to let in the door first? You get back from lunch. You've got fourteen phone messages on your desk. Thirteen of them are from constituents you've never heard of, and one of them is from a guy who just came to your fundraiser two weeks earlier

and gave you $2,000. Which phone call are you going to return first?

As we saw in the last chapter, the money raised and spent in political campaigning has increased. Clearly this increase in funds has affected Congress. One representative remarked, "It is a simple fact of life that when big money enters the political arena, big obligations are entertained." There also may be relatively little that can be done to block the impact of money and the creative ways that campaigning politicians use to get it. As one lobbyist skeptically concluded, "Trying to cleanse the political system from the evils of money is like writing a law ordering teenagers not to think about sex. . . . You don't need a law, you need a lobotomy."

There is another side to the

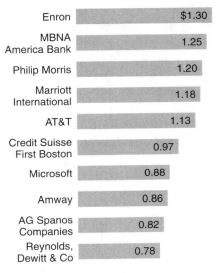

TABLE 8.1

Bush's Top Corporate Donors

Donors to Bush, the RNC, and the Inaugural Fund during the 2000 election cycle, in millions.

Enron	$1.30
MBNA America Bank	1.25
Philip Morris	1.20
Marriott International	1.18
AT&T	1.13
Credit Suisse First Boston	0.97
Microsoft	0.88
Amway	0.86
AG Spanos Companies	0.82
Reynolds, Dewitt & Co	0.78

Sources: Center for Responsive Politics; Federal Election Commission

From *The Wall Street Journal* March 6, 2001.

Washington money game. Most money is donated at the request of an elected official. Few contributions to politicians' campaigns start as the idea of the contributor. With this comes the implicit, and sometimes explicit, threat that without the contribution, the donor will not get much help from the member of Congress or from the White House. Shortly before a recent election, a Republican leader met with PAC directors and told them to give to GOP candidates or they could expect their "two coldest years in Washington." One senator bluntly put it: "I've had people who contribute to my campaign, and they get access; the others get good government." Of course, giving money doesn't guarantee that the representative will vote the right way. A lobbyist who had just seen his bill voted down and was shortly thereafter approached for another contribution said, "It's almost like blackmail. They ask for money from you as they're screwing you to the wall."

One of the most important changes in the role of interest groups in elections has been the rise of *PACs (political action committees).*

PACs are organizations set up by private groups such as businesses or labor unions to influence the political process by raising funds from their members. These organizations are not new in American politics. Their model was created in 1955 when the newly formed AFL-CIO (American Federation of Labor and Congress of Industrial Organizations) started the Committee on Political Education (COPE). Through its national and local units, COPE not only contributed money to pro-union candidates, but also organized Get Out the Vote drives and sought to politically educate its members.

The big expansion in business PACs occurred in the late 1970s as an unexpected result of campaign finance reforms. These laws, backed by labor, put strict limits on individual donations and provided for public disclosure. Before this legislation, money could legally go into campaigns in large amounts as individual donations from wealthy corporate leaders. There was thus little need for business PACs.

The reforms backfired. Instead of reducing the influence of large contributors, the reforms increased them. Corporations and trade associations organized PACs that more effectively channeled their money and influence into campaigns than individuals had been able to do. The number of PACs mushroomed from 608 in 1975 to 4,023 by 2003. Although there are many more corporate and trade association PACs, and they give more money, labor unions have been closing the spending gap. (See Table 8.2.)

The amounts of money skyrocketed. In 1974 interest group donations to congressional candidates totaled $12.5 million. By the 2002 elections, PAC contributions reached $280 million for the two-year election cycle. Incumbents collect most of the PAC money. In the same 2002 election cycle, incumbents received over $197 million in contributions out of the PAC funds contributed to federal candidates. In 1994 when Republicans won majorities in Congress, money from PACs started to flow toward them and away from the Democrats. For example, prior to the 1994 elections AT&T gave only 39 percent of its $1.3 million in PAC money to Republican candidates. After the Republican victory, 80 percent of its contributions went to Republicans. By 1995 Republicans received 58 percent of PAC contributions compared with 30 percent in 1993. The Democrats' revival and a large inflow of union money evened things out in the next elections. By 2002 GOP candidates got $144 million from PACs, while Democrats were close with $135 million.

The record spending in congressional elections continued and increased in 2004. For the first time it took an average of more than $1 million to win a seat in the House of Representatives. Senate fundraising increased even more. The $6.5 million raised by the average winning

TABLE 8.2   TOP PAC CONTRIBUTORS TO REPUBLICANS AND DEMOCRATS, 2004 ELECTION CYCLE

	COMMITTEE	REP TOTAL	DEM TOTAL	TOTAL AMOUNT
1	National Association of Realtors	1,956,803	1,806,280	3,763,083
2	Laborers Union	361,305	2,289,500	2,633,500
3	National Auto Dealers Association	1,796,749	664,551	2,461,300
4	National Beer Wholesalers Association	1,663,200	496,800	2,160,000
5	Association of Trial Lawyers of America	143,080	1,900,919	2,043,999
6	United Parcel Service	1,451,940	537,019	1,988,959
7	Intl Brotherhood of Electrical Workers	97,974	1,861,506	1,959,480
8	American Medical Association	1,505,513	376,378	1,881,891
9	United Auto Workers	18,582	1,839,618	1,858,200
10	National Assn of Home Builders	1,194,505	643,195	1,837,700
11	Credit Union National Association	1,057,933	766,090	1,824,023
12	Carpenters & Joiners Union	468,146	1,332,414	1,800,560

Source: www.opensecrets.org Center for Responsive Politics.

Senator was 47% more than it cost in 2002. These figures included safe seats where little money had to be spent by incumbents. (In fact only five incumbents in the House lost to challengers in 2004.) Spending more money than an opponent didn't guarantee victory. The Senate's most expensive race in 2004 was in the small state of South Dakota where Senate Minority Leader Tom Daschle lost to Republican challenger John Thune. Daschle spent over $17 million to winner Thune's $10 million. (See, "Can Millionaires Buy Their Own Elections?")

Attempts have been made to restrain and reform campaign spending. The attempts to limit overall campaign spending in early versions of the McCain-Feingold Campaign Reform bill proved unsuccessful. Members simply refused to have these constraints placed on their campaigns to keep their jobs. The obstacles that reforms have placed to limit contributions have also been overcome. The nonprofit 527 groups have accepted large unregulated amounts intended to help presidential campaigns. PACs, restricted in what they can give to a candidate, have *bundled* contributions from their members. This means that 50 corporate executives from the same industry can give $3,000 each, which the PAC then puts together and gives to the candidate. Presto, there appears to be a $150,000 contribution from a single industry.

Can Millionaires Buy Their Own Elections?

Candidates who bought their way into Congress got a lot of attention in the 2000 elections. Jon Corzine spent over $60 million of his own money to gain a New Jersey senate seat, while Mark Dayton got a bargain in spending $6 million in defeating an incumbent senator in Minnesota. The trend of self-financing elections seems to be growing since the Supreme Court allowed candidates unlimited spending on their own campaigns in *Buckley* v. *Valeo* (1976). This loophole on the limits to campaign spending was allowed because the Court saw spending one's own money as an exercise of constitutionally protected free speech.

But the hue and cry about buying your own election obscures the fact that most big spenders don't win. In the 1990s, 38 nonincumbent senate candidates financed $1 million or more of their own campaigns. Only six (16 percent) of them won. Those senate candidates who raised $1 million or more *from others* were twice as likely to win office. Because of recent candidates like Corzine who spent so much and won so big, it's easy to forget those who fell on their wallets. Michael Huffington blew $28 million on his unsuccessful California senate race, while Al Checchi in 1996 invested $40 million in not winning the governorship in the same state.

Source: Jennifer Steen, "Maybe You Can Buy an Election, But Not with Your Own Money," *Washington Post*, June 25, 2000.

Do Group Interests Overwhelm the Public Interest?

The idea that interest groups and their lobbyists dominate politics is widely accepted today. What the framers of the Constitution saw as multiple voices harmonized by the institutions of government has become for the liberal critic William Greider a "Grand Bazaar" of deal making. In Greider's view, modern lobbying has changed the art of governing into a haggling marketplace where special interests negotiate laws, regulations, and the use of public money. Political power, especially that of corporations, has become a tool for avoiding laws you don't like and passing laws you do like. Whatever the public purposes proclaimed in the laws, just below the surface lies the real spirit of lobbying—"universalized ticket fixing."

Despite newspaper headlines to the contrary, political scientists have traditionally downplayed the influence of lobbyists. Many studies have found that lobbyists have little success in persuading members of Congress to change their minds. Even campaign contributions can seldom be tracked down as the motive behind congressional votes. Part of the problem in studying these questions is that lobbyists' influence is often unclear and difficult to measure. Of course, lobbyists and journalists have every incentive to overstate this influence—one to boast, the other to make headlines.

Lobbyists' influence is more subtle than what surfaces in the occasional scandal of vote buying. Most of their impact takes place on hidden issues with low public visibility. In 2004, when the House passed a multi-billion-dollar transportation bill, the Republican leadership added corporate tax breaks at the last minute having nothing to do with transportation. Many Congress members of both parties didn't even know these tax loopholes were in the bill when they voted.

Where lobbying influence is felt on major policies, it needs to have public opinion favoring the position of the interest group. Lobbyists gain support by presenting their narrow cause as consistent with a national concern. This interpretation is very influential when it is done over a long period of time in hearings and through news reports, advertising, and personal conversations. Its impact can be seen when gun owners make gun control a violation of civil liberties, or environmentalists make forest clear-cutting an issue of global warming. Most importantly, members of Congress must see the lobbyists' cause as helping their own chances for reelection.

There is little argument that the volume of lobbying has increased vastly. Just between 1961 and 1982, corporations with Washington offices rose tenfold; the number of lobbyists doubled. With over 25,000 lobbyists now working Congress, it would seem foolish to argue that they don't have an impact on American politics. They are hired by wealthy interests to influence how the public officials treat those interests. The leaders of these interest groups are not people who are throwing away their money on activities that produce no benefits for their corporations, unions, or organizations. When compared to the relative decline in political parties, it seems fair to conclude that those seeking to influence American politics increasingly look to lobbyists to speak for them.

This rise in lobbying has produced increasing demands on government. Corporations, veterans, farmers, realtors, doctors, retirees, and universities push their claims for the resources of government. As the benefits provided by government increase, more groups organize to protect what they have or to get more. This results in what Jonathan Rauch calls *hyperpluralism,* too many groups making too many demands on government. Groups demand benefits, but these subsidies encourage new groups, until at last government begins to choke. Government loses its flexibility to change. There are too many intense narrow interests—and their lobbyists/lawyers/consultants—to overcome. Programs serving a general interest get less support, while those helping special interests keep their hold on public resources—almost forever.

Reforms to reduce the influence of wealthy interest groups have failed. Their lobbying, through modern technologies and campaign contributions, has increased. Government often appears to be held hostage by narrow groups resisting all changes not benefiting them. Average Washington deal making is not available to average American citizens. Nonetheless, "special" interests don't control everything.

Politicians still get elected on platforms calling for broad changes in government, and these officials have to explain to voters what they've accomplished when they run for reelection. The press investigates cozy deals by lobbyists, the civil service is competent and committed to their agencies' programs, and grassroots public interest groups often can elbow their issues onto the country's agenda. As we have seen, and will see, new forms of communications from radio talk shows to Internet blogs are constantly upsetting policy-making expectations.

The outcomes of the political game remain unpredictable. Lobbyists' success in defanging reforms aimed at their interests depend on the ability to convince the public, press, and politicians who focus on their issues. Their influence ultimately depends on the resistance, acceptance, or indifference by other players. As seen in the current debate over corporate corruption, public and political opinions may switch their loyalties back and forth depending on the skills and resources brought to bear. Any explanation of the political game based on the dominance of a few wealthy interests is unlikely to understand the surprising directions that American politics has taken, and will take in the future. Some of these unexpected turns will undoubtedly involve our last player—the media.

MEDIA

Both the highs and lows of America's war in Iraq seemed to be caught by competing media images of two figures on pedestals. Early spring 2003 may have seen the best image when American soldiers entered Baghdad, bringing an end to the regime of Saddam Hussein. The fall of that dictatorship was framed in televised pictures of GIs pulling down a large statue of Saddam from its pillar in the middle of his capital. Crowds of Iraqis cheered the American troops and kicked the metal statue as it was dragged through the streets.

A year later, in the spring of 2004, another figure on a pedestal symbolized a far different American involvement in the war. The news program Sixty Minutes II *broadcast photographs of Iraqi prisoners being abused at Abu Ghraib prison. One in particular became the icon or representative symbol of the humiliation—a hooded prisoner standing on a box with electrodes attached to his outstretched arms. The military prosecuted some of the guards involved, and apologies were made. But they were secondary to the visual impact on public opinion of Iraqi prisoners being tortured. These contrasting media images were broadcast repeatedly around the world and were key to how millions "saw" the conflict.* (See "A Marine's View of Embedded Reporters".)

Called "the fourth branch of government," the media have often rivaled the three official branches in political power. No one doubts the media's ability to shape the political agenda and public attitudes. But as those images from the war in Iraq illustrate, who shapes the media remains a debatable question. In this half of the chapter, we will come to grips with the following questions: What are the media? What do the media do? Who controls the media? How do the media influence politics, and how do the other players influence media content?

A Marine's View of Embedded Reporters

One of the most praised changes in coverage of the Iraq war was *embeds*—journalists traveling with and reporting on frontline troops. The following is from a Marine who served in the first Gulf War and tells how Marines treated reporters then.

> Our sergeant had suggested that we let the reporters into our circle, that we let them join us as though they were our fellows. He also said, "Don't tell them a thing." And we didn't because the reporters laid down for us. The mystique of the military and the military man overpowered their natural cynicism and skepticism. The reporter doesn't put pressure on the soldier because he doesn't want to be the bad guy. The young kid might die tomorrow, so why make him buckle today with intrusive questions? . . .
>
> The defining moments of this war are not occurring on screen. You can watch days of tanks traveling across the desert, but that's not war. Embeds serve up burly-chested kids full of charisma and grit; television reports soften war and allow it to penetrate even deeper into the living rooms and minds of America. War can't be that bad if they let us watch it. This is the danger of the embed.

Source: Anthony Swofford, "The Unknown Soldier," *The New York Times Magazine,* March 30, 2003, pp. 18–19.

WHAT ARE THE MEDIA?

Media are those means of communication that permit messages to be made public. Media such as television, radio, newspapers, and, recently, the Internet provide important links connecting people to one another. But these are links with an important quality: They have the ability to communicate messages to a great many people at roughly the same time. The major forms of media we will concentrate on are television and newspapers. (See Figure 8.1.)

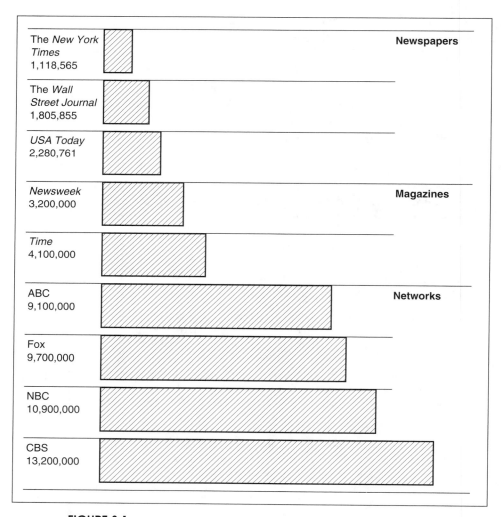

FIGURE 8.1

Audiences Reached by Leading Media, 2003–2004.

Source: Newspapers and Magazines: *Audit Bureau of Circulations.* Networks: John Consolin, *Adweek Magazines:* Special Report, April 26, 2004.

Over 98 percent of American households own at least one TV. These 125 million television sets dominate the mass media—as well as dominating American kids, who watch 22 hours of TV a week. Its political influence varies greatly. There is the exceptional event, like the first Bush-Kerry presidential debate in October 2004, watched by some 62 million Americans (still way down from the over 80 million who saw the Carter-Reagan debate in 1980). How closely people follow the presidential elections, even nail biters like the ones in 2000 and 2004, is not encouraging. One poll during the 2000 campaign found that only half of voting-age Americans thought about the election or could recall even one news story about it.

Although weakening, television continues to be led by the traditional major *television networks*—CBS, NBC, and ABC—and a fourth one, Fox Broadcasting. Under the sweeping telecommunications bill of 1996, the networks are allowed to reach up to 35 percent of the television audience with their local stations and to own cable systems. The networks sell programs with advertising to local broadcast stations called *affiliates.* Both NBC and ABC have over 225 affiliates, CBS has over 200, and Fox has almost 200. The networks contract with their affiliates to allow the networks to produce programs and sell time to advertisers for nationally broadcast programs. The affiliates get the shows, and the networks get the national coverage that allows them to sell time at $1 million for six minutes of advertising during prime evening viewing hours.

In recent years, the major television networks have been challenged by technologies that are widening the choices available to consumers. Now 65 million households get their signals not over the air but through cables. Over two-thirds of American homes have access to more than 30 cable channels. This has led to the rise of cable-only channels, such as CNN (Cable News Network), C-SPAN (Cable-Satellite Public Affairs Network), The Discovery Channel, and MTV (Music Television). As a result, the audience share of the broadcast networks has been declining, from 71 percent of viewers during the prime time evening hours in the 1991–1992 season to around 52 percent in the 2003–2004 season. In a 2004 survey, more people reported getting information about campaigns from cable network news than from nightly network news. The availability of news 24 hours a day seems to fit modern American lifestyles better than watching news at a fixed hour every evening.

New technologies are blurring the distinctions between television, computers, and telephones. The best known is the vast computer network known as the *Internet.* Started as an experiment by the U.S. military in 1969, it grew slowly into a grouping of 213 computers in 1981. Now it is a global network that by 2003 was used by over two-thirds of the adult population of the United States. The Internet provides countless sources of information and entertainment, as well as nearly instant communication by electronic mail— "e-mail"—to anyone who has an account. The graphic part of the Internet—the World Wide Web—has prompted many businesses, media, and political organizations to make themselves available online. People now are using the Internet to respond to opinion polls, write to newspapers, and find out about political candidates and government agencies.

Monica Lewinsky showed the Internet in the first full bloom of its political role. The news of President Clinton's sexual liaison first surfaced in January 1998 on a Website run by a freelance reporter named Matt Drudge. The scandal reached a crescendo of sorts in September when the House put Special Prosecutor Kenneth Starr's report on the Internet for public consumption. Throughout the controversy, tens of thousands of people were debating impeachment and more sordid aspects of the scandal in newsgroups and chat rooms. Reporters' news cycle for daily newspapers or evening news was accelerated with rumors surfacing 24/7 on the Internet. The mainstream press struggled to catch up. Whether the Internet allowed a positive expansion of public debate, or the cyberbabble of an electronic mob, was less certain. (See "Privacy on the Internet," p. 161.)

Despite the new technologies, the oldest of the mass media in the United States—newspapers—still prospers. More than 100 million Americans (80 percent of the adult population) read a daily newspaper regularly. There are a wide variety of papers, ranging in quality from the prestigious *New York Times,* carrying national and international news collected by its own reporters, to small-town dailies that relay crop reports and local fires, but provide sketchy coverage of national events reprinted from the wire services. (*Wire services* are specialized agencies like the Associated Press [AP] and United Press International [UPI] that gather, write, and sell news to the media that subscribe to them.)

However, newspapers are becoming less numerous and less competitive. In 1900, there were 2,226 daily papers in the United States. One hundred years later, though the population had more than tripled, there were only 1,647. The same period has seen a decline in the number of cities with competing newspapers. In 1920, there were 700 cities with competing daily papers. Currently, there are 13 cities with competing newspaper ownerships. Of major American cities, only New York has three separately owned daily papers—its fourth, *Newsday,* closed in 1995. We'll get to the reasons for this trend shortly.

What Do the Media Do?

The media provide three major types of messages. Through their *news reports, entertainment programs,* and *advertising,* the media help shape public opinion on many things—including politics. In news reports, the media supply up-to-date accounts of what journalists believe to be the most important, interesting, and newsworthy events, issues, and developments. But the influence of news reports goes well beyond relaying facts. The key to this power is *selectivity.* By reporting certain items (President Bush's jogging injuries) and ignoring others (President Roosevelt's crippled legs), the media suggest to us what's important. Media coverage gives status to people and events—a national television interview or a *Time* magazine cover creates a "national figure."

There are limits. Few people pay attention to political news. Most of us read the newspapers for the sports and comics and local events. Young people are notoriously indifferent to the news. Those under 30 are less likely than those over 30 to listen to or watch political news. This isn't because Generation Xers do not have enough time. Young people spend more time watching sports and entertainment on television than those over 30. One result of this is that the more they avoid coverage of politics, the less they know about American government.

The media perform two important political functions: agenda setting and framing. *Agenda setting is* putting together an agenda of national priorities—what should be taken seriously, what should be taken lightly, and what should be ignored altogether. "The media can't tell people what to think," as one expert put it, "but they can tell people what to think *about.*" The attention the media give to education in the inner cities, environmental pollution, the budget deficit, or the war in Iraq will affect how important most people think these issues are.

Framing defines problems, explaining *how* we see issues. Media coverage can present, or frame, an issue in many ways. Is crime linked to unemployment, to lax immigration laws, or to poor police training? How the problem is understood may influence whether the solution is a jobs program or barriers on the border. During the 2004 presidential campaign, a major objective of the two sides was to present a convincing negative frame for their opponent—Kerry as a waffler, Bush as arrogant. The effort was then made in the press to explain what the candidates did or said within these negative frames. Media scholar Kathleen Hall Jamieson has written, "Frames tell us what is important, what the range of acceptable debate on a topic is, and when an issue has been resolved."

Entertainment programs offer amusement while giving people images of "normal" behavior. Whether this television behavior offers socially acceptable models is another question. Soap characters (such as Tony Soprano of *The Sopranos*) engage in immoral business practices that bring wealth and power. These media programs may substitute for learning from life's more complex experiences, and become as important as real life. As one analyst of television observed: "If you can write a nation's stories, you needn't worry about who makes its laws. Today, television tells most of the stories to most of the people most of the time."

Finally, the programs and news that media present are built around a constant flow of *advertisements*. Television programs are constructed to reach emotional high points just before the commercials so that the audience will stay put during the advertisement. Newspapers devote almost two-thirds of their space to ads rather than to news, leading one English author to define a journalist as "someone who writes on the back of advertisements." Ads, especially television commercials, present images of what the audience finds pleasing about themselves. Presented in 30-second compelling symbols— "Reach Out and Touch Someone"—commercials offer viewers comfort, good looks, and amusement. They may change what we expect in other arenas, including politics. Media critic Neil Postman has charged that television's emphasis on entertaining visuals has altered how we look at our political leaders and how they present themselves: Instead of a public discussion of issues, we find a competition between reassuring visual images. In this case, the medium has changed the message of politics.

MEDIA AND THE MARKETPLACE OF IDEAS

The framers of the Constitution believed that a free flow of information from many voices was basic to their system of government. Ideas would compete with one another without restraint in a "marketplace of ideas." Fearing that the greatest enemy of free speech was the government, the framers added the First Amendment forbidding government officials from "abridging the freedom of speech, or of the press." The phrase since has been expanded to include radio and television. The principle remains the same, as Judge Learned Hand wrote:

> Right conclusions are more likely to be gathered out of a multitude of tongues than through any kind of authoritative selection. To many this is, and always will be folly; but we have staked upon it our all.

The ability of media to fulfill this goal of presenting a variety of opinion representing the widest range of political ideas has, to no one's surprise, been limited in practice. It is limited by (1) *the media*, (2) *the government*, and (3) *the public.*

Media, such as television stations and newspapers, are privately owned economic assets bought and sold to make money for their owners. Profitability, not public service, has led to the increasing concentration of media ownership. The decrease in competition among newspapers mentioned earlier has been a reflection of the increase in *chains*, which are companies that combine different media in different cities under one owner. More than 80 percent of the nation's newspapers are owned by chains, and only three corporations own most of the nation's 11,000 magazines.

In the last ten years, market calculations left all major media outlets concentrated in a few corporate hands. In 1995, Disney purchased ABC for $19 billion, Westinghouse paid $5.4 billion for CBS, and Time Warner bought Turner Broadcasting for $7.5 billion. Earlier, NBC had been bought by General Electric. In May 2000, the combination of Viacom (which owns Paramount Pictures, Blockbuster, MTV, Nickelodeon, and Simon & Schuster, among others) with CBS created the second-largest media company in the world. But this was soon surpassed. America Online, in 2001, acquired Time Warner, the largest media corporation. The *Christian Science Monitor* concluded: "The bulk of what we see, hear, learn, sing, play, rent and consume will shortly be controlled by a dozen corporate entities."

In the past, federal regulators prevented such mergers, arguing that monopolies over information didn't serve the public interest. Organizations like the Consumers Union have opposed these mergers, believing that the results will be soaring cable rates, shrinking entertainment options, and news coverage declining into sensationalism. Critics pointed to the incident where CBS lawyers prevented *60 Minutes* from airing an interview with a former tobacco executive on health issues in the industry (later made into a movie, *The Insider*, starring Al Pacino). They feared a lawsuit. This cautious attitude toward the news may have been connected to CBS's pending merger with Westinghouse, and concerns that a lawsuit would mess up the multi-billion-dollar deal.

Beyond the arguments concerning the *quality* or variety of views that are broadcast, there is no question that the *quantity* of information has increased. One of the new sources of information was CNN, providing news coverage 24 hours a day. Started in 1980 by Ted Turner, few people believed there would be enough demand for such a station, and it was jokingly called "Chicken Noodle News." CNN went on to become a success, and in times of crisis it has become the channel of choice for the general public, political leaders, and news junkies. Less popular C-SPAN provides continuous coverage of both houses of Congress, and many community cable stations provide similar coverage of state and local governments. The popularity of radio talk and call-in shows has made that medium into an important, often dissenting, political force. Jovial conservative talk-show host Rush Limbaugh was one of the few public figures to defend the Iraqi prisoner abuse, arguing that the guards "need to blow some steam off."

Most of the profits in the media industry come from advertising. Advertisers approach media with certain expectations. They want their ads to be seen by as many people as possible, they want the people seeing the ads to be potential customers, and they don't want the surrounding programs or articles to detract from the ads. As a result, advertising encourages media content—whether news or entertainment—to be conventional and inoffensive in order to keep the customer satisfied. Tobacco companies have contracts that keep their ads away from articles linking cigarette smoking to cancer. Ownership may bring "advertising" privileges. *NBC Nightly News* ran three segments, totaling 14 minutes, about a new device to detect breast cancer without mentioning that its parent corporation, General Electric, manufactured the machine.

Newscasts also affect the political information available. To get the largest possible audience, television news packages itself as entertainment. This means bite-sized, action-packed news with emphasis on stimulating visuals. The credibility of the news is largely dependent on the attractiveness of likable anchors—or "talking hairdos." Television news also is divided up by commercials that may make the news seem less serious, less complex, and perhaps less worth being concerned about. One critic noted how strange it was to see a newscaster who, having just presented a report on the likelihood of nuclear war, went on to say he will be right back after this word from

Burger King. *(What if I were to pause here, tell you that I will return to this discussion in a moment, and then write a few words about, say, Ben & Jerry's ice cream? If this were to happen several more times, you might think the text was not worth further attention.)*

Media and Government

Government and media in the United States have long engaged in an unsteady waltz. In the early years of the Republic, the press was consciously partisan, sponsored by one party or faction to appeal to their voters. By the mid-nineteenth century, this changed. Penny papers could depend on advertising for most of their revenues and wanted to reach customers, no matter what their political views. The Civil War increased the demand for human interest stories and up-to-date news not distorted by party loyalties. By the end of the century, advertisers and publishers, not politicians, bankrolled newspapers.

The media continued to depend on the government, but now it was through subsidies to the industry. Government support from cheap postal rates or profitable printing contracts helped keep afloat an often impoverished press. In the twentieth century, federal regulation in the form of the Federal Communications Commission (FCC), begun in 1934, generally took a pro-industry stance in restricting entry to competitors in radio and television, and in developing technology. Even today radio and television stations must renew their broadcast licenses every six years, though it is usually a formality. The media were exempted from a host of government laws and antitrust regulations, including making sure that minimum wage and child labor laws did not apply to newspaper boys. Perhaps the most important current subsidy is the one that every government agency provides—free information for the press through their public affairs office.

For campaigning politicians, the media are both opportunity and adversary. Sixty percent of the money in presidential races goes to advertising. Politicians—as noted in the case study at the end of this chapter—live and die by media coverage. Some of these activities have been called *pseudoevents*—not real news at all, but staged in order to be reported. One example, seen in 2004, was when President Bush took campaigning Republicans for rides on Air Force One with television cameras aboard. While coverage has been increased by the rise in media outlets such as cable, the quality of political news has not necessarily improved. For example, one study showed that the average *sound bite*—a video clip of a candidate speaking—had declined from 42 seconds in 1968 to just over 7 seconds currently. Newscasts emphasized

Leno, Letterman, and the Presidential Race

We make jokes about it but the truth is this presidential election really offers us a choice of two well-informed opposing positions on every issue. OK, they both belong to John Kerry, but they're still there.

—Jay Leno

John Kerry says that foreign leaders want him to be president, but that he can't name the foreign leaders. That's all right, President Bush can't name them either.

—David Letterman

The presidential election was on, and the late-night talk shows hosts—David Letterman, Jay Leno, Jon Stewart, and others—were drawing blood. These comics were legitimate political commentators with an impact. During the 2000 election, one survey showed that 47 percent of young adults got information about the presidential campaigns from late-night comedy shows. And why not? The comics presented politics in bite-size portions, though brutally simplifying the 2004 election by labeling Kerry as a waffler and Bush as dumb.

They also presented the candidates themselves. The Late-Night Visit was considered by the candidates as a way of humanizing themselves—John Kerry, for example, drove a motorcycle on stage. They showed the nation's leader, and potential leader, as funny and modest, joking about themselves in a relaxed setting. And the hosts responded with unusual kindness. One critic said that when the candidates appeared on their shows, the hosts gave them the equivalent of "a big wet kiss."

the quick and the dramatic in covering politics. People were not just getting their information on elections from television news. Now in our presidential elections, late-night talk shows play a surprisingly large role. (See "Leno, Letterman, and the Presidential Race.")

The examples of government leaders informally pressuring media are numerous. Presidents try to get on the good side of the media by giving favored reporters exclusive "leaks" of information and by controlling information going to the public. Often the president delivers the good news in person to the television cameras, like the release of 24 American fliers by China in 2001, while leaving it to others to communicate bad news, like their capture. The "spin" on an issue means presenting it in a way that makes the elected official look the best. When the Bush administration publicly presented its first tax cut in 2001, the president introduced smiling working-class families who would save on their taxes. The wealthy taxpayers who received most of the benefits were not shown. This is called *news management.*

Press conferences have been used by presidents since Theodore Roosevelt to give the media direct contact with the chief executive. Although disliked by both Clinton and George W. Bush, such conferences, when broadcast, can allow presidents to present their views directly to the public. Franklin Roosevelt's radio "fireside chats" were a brilliant way of personally reassuring people during the Great Depression. Television and politicians can also make uneasy partners. In 1960, presidential candidate Richard Nixon's streaky makeup, dull suit, and heavy beard made a poor impression—and may have cost him the election—in the first-ever televised debate with his opponent, John F. Kennedy. George W. Bush was widely criticized for being overly aggressive and 'unpresidential' in his debates with John Kerry.

Presidents now have a large stable of media experts and speechwriters to perfect their images. As a former movie actor and television personality, the late Ronald Reagan was known as "the Great Communicator" due to his unrivaled skill of looking and sounding absolutely forthright. (See "Mixed Media Messages.") President Clinton was an intelligent, articulate media celebrity. But Clinton's press relations came to a screeching halt at the feet of Monica Lewinsky where the president's negatives—questionable honesty, womanizing—were on display. The sex scandal also demonstrated the media's changing views of what was out of bounds in presidential privacy. (See "President Kennedy, Sex, and Newsworthiness.")

George W. Bush was not as good as Clinton in public performances, but then he didn't have to defend his private life. Near the end of his first term, President Bush had held 16 solo news conferences, compared to 43 for Bill Clinton, and 84 for George Bush, Sr., at the same point in their presidencies. He avoided unscripted press conferences and frequently garbled his few question-and-answer media sessions. Bush favored reporters from outside Washington (perhaps because they were less critical), usually in states important to his reelection. Vice President Cheney often acted as the administration's spokesman in complex areas such as foreign affairs. Bush showed discipline in "staying on message," which meant focusing only on a priority issue to communicate, and for tightly controlling leaks of information from the White House. The president could be charming and informal with the press and, on occasions such as his speech to Congress after 9/11, he rose to eloquence. But his weakness as a public communicator called into question his command of policies and issues he as president was expected to know.

Mixed Media Messages

During the 1984 presidential campaign, Lesley Stahl, a CBS reporter, prepared a critical commentary on how President Reagan used television. Her blunt report charged the president with manipulation, if not hypocrisy. She reported that he will appear at the Special Olympics or the opening of a senior housing facility, but no hint is given that he cut the budgets for subsidized housing for the elderly. He also distanced himself from bad news, Stahl reported. After he pulled Marines out of Lebanon, he flew off to his California ranch, allowing others to make the announcement.

To illustrate her piece, Stahl put together Reagan's video clips: Reagan greeting handicapped athletes, cutting the ribbon at a home for the elderly, and relaxing on his ranch in jeans.

"I thought it was the single toughest piece I had ever done on Reagan," Stahl said. She worried about the White House reaction.

After the piece aired, the phone rang. It was a senior White House official.

"And the voice said, 'Great piece.'"

"I said, 'What?'"

"And he said, 'Great piece!'"

"I said, 'Did you listen to what I said?'"

He said, "Lesley, when you're showing four and a half minutes of great pictures of Ronald Reagan, no one listens to what you say. Don't you know that the pictures are overriding your message because they conflict with your message? The public sees those pictures and they block your message . . . it was a four-and-a-half-minute free ad for the Ronald Reagan campaign for reelection."

I sat here numb. . . . None of us had figured that out.

She broke into laughter. "They loved it. They really did love it."

Source: Hedrick Smith, *The Power Game* (New York: Random House, 1988), pp. 413–14.

Media and the Public

The "definition of alternatives is the supreme instrument of power," wrote political scientist E. E. Schattschneider. By "definition of alternatives," he meant the ability to set limits on political debates, to define what is politically important and what is not, and to make certain solutions reasonable and acceptable, and others not. Media, to a great extent, have this power. Who influences the exercise of this power is another question.

President Kennedy, Sex, and Newsworthiness

During the Monica Lewinsky scandal, President Clinton argued, rather futilely, that a president's sex life was private and not newsworthy. Years before, an incident concerning President Kennedy underlined how the media's definition of newsworthy had changed.

Florence Kater was a middle-aged housewife who in 1958 rented an upstairs apartment in her Georgetown home to Pamela Turnure, an attractive aide to then-Senator John Kennedy. Mrs. Kater became incensed that Kennedy was conducting an indiscreet affair with Ms. Turnure. Kater ambushed the senator and took a photograph of him leaving the apartment at 3:00 a.m.

Despite attempts by Kennedy and his staff to stop Kater, she mailed the photo and a letter describing her encounter to a number of prominent Washington editors and columnists. (The FBI ended up with a copy and began keeping a file—on Kater.) Mrs. Kater explained in her letter that as an Irish Catholic, she took the photo hoping that Kennedy, as a presidential candidate, would change his behavior.

Although Kennedy's relationship with Turnure was known to reporters, no questions were ever asked the candidate. After Kennedy's inauguration, Mrs. Kater picketed in front of the White House, where passersby urged her to go back "to the nuthouse." Pamela Turnure became press secretary to Mrs. Kennedy.

Source: Seymour M. Hersh, *The Dark Side of Camelot* (Boston: Little, Brown, 1997), pp. 106–10.

Certainly media managers (editors, newscasters, producers, reporters) have a vital role in shaping political views. Advertisers, by buying space in some programs or papers and not in others, affect the messages sent out to the public. The owners of media, whether television networks, cable operators, or newspaper chains, play a part in selecting who will handle the day-to-day running of the press and what the general "slant" of the media they own will be. Owners may take a more direct involvement, as illustrated in late 2003 when Viacom's corporate leaders took a CBS drama on Ronald Reagan off the network because it had aroused criticism from conservative groups.

Government leaders have a range of tactics to pressure media into conforming to their political priorities. By dramatizing certain policies, by withholding information on other issues, and by favoring some reporters, experienced politicians can shape their coverage. For example, during the 2000 race for the presidency the Federal Trade

Commission issued a report attacking the entertainment industry for marketing violence to children. This supported the position of vice presidential candidate Joseph Lieberman, who denounced some moviemakers as "shameless salesmen" of "garbage." Of course, none of the candidates stopped attending Hollywood fundraisers.

People have a right to expect that the press will fulfill its two major political functions of (1) informing the public of what its leaders are doing and (2) acting as a watchdog monitoring government actions. The demands of the marketplace, by turning newscasts into entertainment, have limited the media's ability to fulfill either political function. As a result, the public is bombarded by more news from more outlets. But does the news provide any more understanding or any different points of view?

The public does not have to be passive. By watching or not watching certain programs, by buying or not buying publications, and by demanding or not demanding that dissenting voices be heard, the public can help "manage" the output of the media. The rise of talk radio, the Internet, and community-based programs on public access channels shows that flexibility and diversity are possible in today's media.

Yet, in the main, the messages that the media provide reflect the power of those in the political game. The official players, through press interviews, paid public relations advisors, and news management, can be fairly sure of reaching the public through the media. Using paid advertising, corporations can claim media time to persuade the public to act in certain ways—usually by buying the goods they produce, but sometimes (like oil or tobacco companies) simply by thinking well of them. The ability of members of the general public to address each other, as well as their political representatives, is more limited. Free speech without access to the modern medium of free speech remains a limited right for most people.

CASE STUDY

THE CANDIDATE: A DAY IN THE LIFE . . .

Elections allow interest groups and media to influence who will gain power in the political game. In this fictional account of a day in the life of a candidate, we see, through her eyes, the importance of these players.

Morning

The phone jars her awake. It is still dark outside. But months ago, she started leaving the light on in the bathroom of each motel she stayed in so that she could quickly get her bearings when, like this morning, she woke up disoriented.

"Yes?" she asks rasping into the mouthpiece, her voice slightly hoarse from too many speeches.

"Time to get moving, boss," an aide's voice says. There is an important breakfast meeting this morning with the state teachers' union. They have already given her the maximum allowable contribution, but she hopes they will get their national PAC to contribute and that they will encourage their members to volunteer for her campaign.

She has learned to travel light and dress quickly. Her short functional haircut is ready as soon as it dries. As she settles into the backseat of her midsize American-made car, she tries to recall what brought her to the southeast part of the state for two days of campaigning.

Her schedule is done by regions. To save travel time and money, she does events in neighboring communities. The two good-sized towns she will be in today offer her enough voters to make her stay worthwhile. More importantly, they offer opportunities for money and media. Every day must include a money event in the community being visited. And, of course, if you don't get media on a trip, you weren't there.

She works the crowd, prodded by an aide's earlier reminders of the key names, spouses, and previous times she has met them. As she eases into her seat at the head table, she turns to the aide for her purse, which reminds her of an argument at the beginning of the campaign.

Should she carry a purse? Her campaign manager said no. Why should a candidate for the U.S. Senate carry a purse? That wasn't even the worst of the special problems facing a woman running for office. How feminine should she look? Does she wear dresses or suits? Jewelry? Lipstick? Do heels make her look too tall, or do people want to look up at their next senator?

At the breakfast, she tries to eat the by-now-cold eggs because she has been losing weight and her face is looking haggard on television. Her major campaign promise is a cut in income taxes for the middle class, but she assures the teachers that savings in management will still allow for a cost-of-living increase in educational salaries. She thanks them for their contributions and makes a pitch that teachers are the best volunteers—bright but used to drudge work.

There is a ten o'clock news conference at the local press club. A reporter rides with her. He is doing a story about her family life. "But don't you feel bad about having to be away from your children so much?" he asks. It is a question she has fielded a hundred times before. "My husband is very good with them," she says, "and then Betsy, who's eleven, and Henry, who's fourteen, are very much involved in the campaign themselves, and they feel that what we are all doing together is very important."

The press conference goes smoothly. She reads the prepared statement, which explains how much her proposed income tax cut will mean for an average family. During the last two weeks of the campaign, she will issue two such statements each day, one for the morning newspapers and one for the afternoon papers. But the main hope is that she will get a segment on the nightly news. Television news is the key to a successful statewide campaign, and she has planned her campaign accordingly. In this case, she is well under the 2:00 p.m. deadline for the 6:00 p.m. local news.

Afternoon

At noon, she visits a senior citizen's center where hot lunches are served to about 60 retirees each day. Unfortunately, the local college student serving as her driver gets lost. She is late. This happens at least once a week.

After lunch, she goes back to her motel room for some urgent fundraising. She learns that she could lose some vital last-week television advertising spots unless she can come up with $30,000 before the day ends. At the motel, two wealthy supporters are waiting. She has another cup of coffee, pours them a beer, and makes the pitch. "I know you've given more than you should be asked to give, but we've got to raise the money for these spots." She always finds this a little demeaning. One of the men heads the state Bankers' Association. The other is a home-builder. She wonders, what will they want when she becomes senator?

Since they've already contributed the maximum $3,000 from each member of their family, the two commit to raising from friends another $20,000 and leave. She talks to more prospective contributors on the telephone, as each is dialed in turn by an aide. A number of these are directors of PACs in Washington, D.C. "Did you see the *Tribune* poll?" she asks. "We're really coming up, but these spots are crucial." With all but $4,000 of the needed money raised (which will probably be picked up through an aide's follow-up calls), she changes clothes and heads for a working-class cafe to film a television spot.

The cafe is crammed with television lights, reflectors, cameras, technicians, and spectators anxious to get into the picture. The candidate briefly studies a script, which will take 45 seconds to recite. With the cafe and its customers as backdrops, she looks into the camera on cue and begins. "In the closing days of this campaign, ordinary people have increasingly been joining with me in demanding a cut in income taxes. . . ."

"Hold it!" the producer says. "We're getting a buzzing on the sound track from the ice machine."

She starts again. "In the closing days of this campaign. . . ."

"Wait a minute," the producer interrupts. "There's some kind of funny shadow on her face."

The lights are adjusted, and she begins again—and again, and again. A minute spot takes two hours to film.

After filming the television spot she hurries to two "coffees," one at the home of a wealthy friend active in environmental groups, the other sponsored by the sisterhood of a local synagogue. She makes a brief opening statement at each coffee, and then answers questions. At the end of each session, she asks those who are willing to help with telephoning, canvassing, stuffing envelopes, or other campaign chores to sign a pledge sheet. After she leaves, her hosts make a pitch for money. Almost $15,000 is promised at the two coffees.

Evening

Back at the motel, she takes the phone from an aide and responds to a prearranged, live radio interview for 15 minutes. She spends 20 minutes with her campaign manager going over the latest poll results. "We're cutting down the general," her chief opponent in the race, "but I'm worried about the increase in your 'negatives'; maybe we should soften our attack a little," the manager says. She knows that her attacks on an opponent will also increase voters' negative feelings toward her. She agrees.

"Then there's the soft money contribution by Sleaze. We've really got the state party steamed at us for telling them to wait on this one." She nods. She knows that "soft money" is given to the state party to fund their Get Out the Vote efforts to help candidates like her, without having to worry about campaign laws or disclosure. Now, Ben A. Sleaze, the owner of Jefferson S&L, wants to give $100,000 to the state party for Get Out the Vote activities aimed indirectly at supporting her campaign. She knows that the S&L has some regulatory problems, and clearly Sleaze is going to expect help from her if she wins.

Besides the fact that her campaign desperately needs the money, the party also wants the funds to build up their voter contact program. The party chairman, who says he's amazed Sleaze would even offer help to a nonincumbent, is leaning on her to OK the money. It's all perfectly legal, he tells her. Yet she worries about the bad press when it leaks out, and she doesn't trust or like Sleaze. But, as her manager said, "It's only a press problem. You need the money now; you can deal with the media later, when you're senator." She decides to talk with her husband about it and tells her manager she'll let him know her decision in the morning.

Her stomach tightens as she begins to think ahead to the last of the day's activities, a televised "debate" with the other senatorial candidates before a League of Women Voters' audience. Too tense to eat, she turns down a sandwich and goes over her notes. "Should I be rough with the general or not?" she asks nobody in particular.

Riding back to the motel after the debate, she feels good. She is sure that the local news tomorrow evening will make a "sound bite" out of her statement, "The general may want to be a senator as an honor to cap off his career, but I want to be a senator because I feel deeply about what we ought to be doing for our people."

She talks to her husband and one of the children by telephone; the younger child is already asleep. Her husband is enthusiastic about the debate, and that is a good note to end the day on. Maybe that's why she doesn't raise the issue of Sleaze's soft-money contribution, or maybe she's too tired to remember. Just before she gets into bed, she calls the motel desk. "Would you ring me in the morning at five o'clock?"

WRAP-UP

Both interest groups and media are bridges over which people and players can reach the political game. Interest groups provide the means for business, labor, professional, or citizens' organizations to make their views known to government officials. They unify people with common concerns to bring pressure on decisionmakers through grassroots campaigns, fundraising, lobbying, or publicity. Those interest groups with the most resources tend to be the most effective. Reforms to limit the influence of wealthy interests have been notably unsuccessful.

Media seem to be everywhere. As both a communications tool and a profitable economic asset, media affect politics. Through news reports, entertainment, and advertisements, media shape the national agenda and frame the nation's issues and personalities. What is and is not broadcast and printed establishes political figures, sets priorities, focuses attention on issues, and largely makes politics understandable to most people. The media in turn are affected by the corporations that own them, the advertisers that pay for their messages, the managers who run them, and the public that looks, reads, and listens to what they offer. Technology has increased the variety of media outlets and led to the merger of many of them under giant corporate banners. Political leaders grant them licenses (if they're television or radio), stage pseudoevents, and spin information as it serves their interests. Campaigning candidates spend much of their days seeking free access to media or raising the money for ads. As a player and a communications link, the media are among the political game's most powerful, complex, and controversial forces.

Interest groups and media offer the potential for wide public participation. The rise in interest groups and the explosion of media outlets provide linkages that could be used by a broader public. But it is the public that is more likely to be used—by players enhancing their own political positions. Interest groups through lobbying campaigns mobilize parts of the public to support their own policies. Media offer the public news-as-entertainment for the commercial and political benefits that come from claiming a larger share of the audience. The public is the object of the efforts, not the creator. These instruments of power remain in the hands of the powerful.

Thought Questions

1. Which interests are represented best by American interest groups? How would you reform interest groups so that groups that are now poorly represented would have a greater voice?
2. By making news entertaining, are media putting their commercial needs ahead of the goal of an informed public? Are public education and media entertainment contradictory goals?
3. What are the arguments for and against changing the media to make them more available for differing political viewpoints? Must this change mean more government control and regulation?
4. Do you think our candidate for the Senate (see Case Study, "The Candidate: A Day in the Life . . . ," pp. 248–252) will accept the "soft money" contribution? If you were her aide, what would you recommend? How should she "spin" her responses to press questions about the contribution?

Suggested Readings

Interest Groups

Berry, Jeffrey M. *The Interest Group Society*, 3rd ed. New York: Longman, 1997.
  A concise overview of how, and how much, interest groups influence American politics.
Buckley, Christopher. *Thank You for Smoking*. New York: Random House, 1994. Pb.
  A funny, smart novel of a tobacco lobbyist and his uphill struggle to preserve truth, justice, and the American smoker.
Rauch, Jonathan. *Demosclerosis: The Silent Killer of American Government*. New York: Times Books, 1995. Pb.
  Argues that what ails the body politic is too many interest groups clogging the arteries of government.
Sherrill, Robert. *Why They Call It Politics*, 6th ed. Fort Worth, Tex.: Harcourt College Publishers, 2000. Pb
  A populist book on American government with the viewpoint that corporate money is undermining democracy.
West, Darrell M., and Burdett A. Loomis. *The Sound of Money*. New York: W.W. Norton, 1999. Pb.
  Two experts answer the subtitle—How Political Interests Get What They Want—by looking at four case studies and hearing the clanking of coins.

Media

Bennett, W. Lance. *News: The Politics of Illusion*, 5th ed. New York: Longman, 2003.

A critical discussion of the many ways that the media influence—and distort—contemporary politics.

Cook, Timothy E. *Governing with the News*. Chicago: University of Chicago Press, 1998.

Traces the history of the media as a political institution tied closely to the functions of government.

Gabler, Neal. *Life: The Movie*. New York: Vintage Books, 2000. Pb.

How the media have turned everything of importance, including the news, into entertainment.

Goldberg, Bernard. *Bias: A CBS Insider Exposes How the Media Distort the News*. New York: Harperperennial, 2003. Pb.

An entertaining argument attacking liberal bias in the news, which also describes how events become "news."

Jamieson, Kathleen Hall, and Paul Waldman. *The Press Effect*. New York: Oxford, 2003. Pb

Analyzes how the press fails to inform citizens of what their leaders are doing.

CHAPTER 9

Who Wins, Who Loses: Pluralism Versus Elitism

A re we starting to understand American politics? Or have we spent so much time describing the players and rules, the terms and institutions, that we've lost sight of the game? In this last chapter, we will step back from analyzing the trees to take a look at the woods. Put another way, we will ask our basic questions: Who (if anyone) is running the game? Who wins, who loses? Who plays and who watches?

It should be no surprise that there is no single accepted answer to these questions. Rather, there are two competing approaches to an answer. The traditional one, supported in some form by most political scientists and most of the players in the political game, is *pluralism*. Its competitor, the *elite* school of thought, has attracted supporters on both the Right and Left who are critical of the American political game. More recent views have modified and attempted to close the gap between the two sets of ideas.

PLURALISM

Pluralism is a group theory of democracy. Pluralism states that society contains a variety of competing groups with access to government officials, and that these organizations struggle and cooperate to influence policy decisions. Although people as individuals don't usually have much power in politics, they can gain influence through their membership in what de Tocqueville called "associations." These groups bargain among themselves and with government institutions. The compromises that result become public policy.

Several key concepts make up the pluralist argument: *fragmentation of power, bargaining, compromise,* and *consensus.*

Fragmentation of power is the pluralists' way of saying that no one group dominates the political game. Power is divided, though not equally, among a large number of groups—labor unions, corporations, nonprofits, religions, ethnics, and many others. To gain their goals, the groups must *bargain* with each other. Within this bargaining process, the government, though it may have its own interests, acts essentially as a referee. The government will make sure the rules of the game are followed and may intervene to help groups that consistently have less power than their opponents. It also is to the advantage of all the groups to follow the "rules of the game," for the bargaining-compromise method is the most effective way to win changes.

The result of this bargaining process is inevitably a series of *compromises.* Because no single group dominates, each must take a little less than it wants in order to gain the support of the others. This accommodation is made easier because both the interests and the membership of the groups overlap. Groups disagreeing on one issue know that they may need each other's support in the future on another issue on which they agree. Individuals may be a member of two groups with different views on an issue. Their membership in both will tend to reduce the conflict between them. A black doctor may be a member of the American Medical Association (AMA), which opposes many expanded programs of government-sponsored health care, but also be a member of the National Association for the Advancement of Colored People (NAACP), which supports these programs. As a member of both, this doctor may influence the groups to reach a compromise with each other.

Underlying this bargaining-compromise process is a *consensus*— an agreement on basic political questions that reasonably satisfies most of the groups. This agreement on the rules of the game, and also on most of its results, is the basic cooperative cement that holds society together. Aspects of this consensus in American society are the general agreement on the importance of civil liberties, on equal opportunity for all citizens, on the necessity for compromise, and on the duty of citizens to participate in politics. The pluralists maintain not only that there is widespread participation (open to all who wish to organize) in political decisions, but also that the decisions themselves, and the procedures by which they are reached, have a consensus in society behind them. Government decisions, in the pluralist universe, essentially reflect the compromises reached by the major groups in the political system.

The picture that pluralism presents is of a process of bargaining among organized groups, and also between these groups and various parts of the government. The bargaining results in a series of compromises that become public policy and determine who gets what, when, and how. A widespread consensus on the rules and results of this process keeps the political game from descending into unmanageable conflict.

Examples of Pluralism

Pluralists have no difficulty pointing to examples of the bargaining-compromise process. When major environmental groups decided that a new law regulating air pollution was needed, they formed a Clean Air Coalition to lead the fight. Helped by environmental lobbyists, the Coalition raised funds from members of wealthy groups like the Environmental Defense Fund and the Sierra Club. Chemical and oil companies, tired of fighting lawsuits brought under what they considered unrealistic regulations, reluctantly supported compromise proposals. They also worried about public opinion, which strongly supported the environmentalists' health arguments over business' cost objections. The press weighed in with editorials and generally favorable coverage. The Environmental Protection Agency (EPA), making sure its concerns were covered, supported the bill with studies and testimony. The appropriate committees of the House and Senate, reacting to competing substantive arguments, political pressures and, yes, fundraising, approved a bill that became the Clean Air Act. Pluralists would say the law reflected the relative power of the various groups as well as the compromises they reached.

One well-known study supporting the pluralist model is Robert Dahl's book on politics in New Haven, Connecticut, *Who Governs?* Dahl examined several important issues, such as urban development and public education, to see who made the key decisions. He concluded that the people influential in education policy were not the same as those involved in urban development or political nominations. Dahl concluded that there was not just one economic and social elite wielding political power in New Haven. In his 1998 book, *On Democracy*, Dahl updates and argues the virtues of democracy, and under what conditions it exists in modern societies. (See "The Pluralist View.")

Criticisms of Pluralist Theory

Pluralism has run into numerous criticisms. One argument condemns pluralism for emphasizing *how* the political game is played rather than *why* people play it. Critics say that the pluralists do not give enough importance to how benefits really are distributed. A consensus supporting equal opportunity is not the same as actually having equality. A system of democratic procedures may simply conceal the powerful getting their way. The argument often goes on to say that there can be no political equality without social and economic conditions being equal for all. Critics of pluralism ask: What good are the rules of the game to the majority of people who never get a chance to play?

Other critics point out that pluralists believe that groups will balance off each other, producing a self-regulating stable system. But what if everyone sees the value in forming a group to gain more benefits from the government? Political inflation leads to so many competing groups making so many demands that the government begins to choke on budget deficits caused by trying to please all the groups. This *hyperpluralism* is for some observers a more accurate, if more pessimistic, portrait of current American politics than is traditional pluralism.

The Pluralist View

The fact is that the Economic Notables operate within that vague political consensus, the prevailing system of beliefs, to which all the major groups in the community subscribe. . . . Within limits, they can influence the content of that belief system; but they cannot determine it wholly. (p. 84)

In the United States the political stratum does not constitute a homogeneous class with well-defined class interests. (p. 91)

Thus the distribution of resources and the ways in which they are or are not used in a pluralistic political system like New Haven's constitute an important source of both political change and political stability. If the distribution and use of resources gives aspiring leaders great opportunities for gaining influences, these very features also provide a built-in throttle that makes it difficult for any leader, no matter how skillful, to run away with the system. (p. 310)

Source: Robert A. Dahl, *Who Governs?* New Haven, Conn.: Yale University Press, 1961.

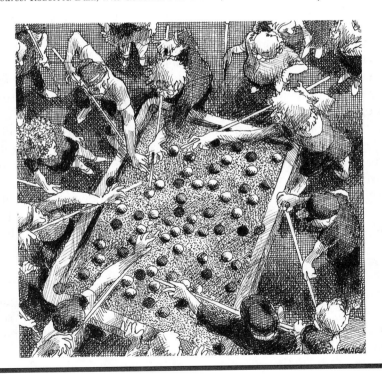

ELITE

Many of those disagreeing with pluralism believe instead that an *elite* approach more realistically describes American politics. Supporters of this approach see society as dominated by unified and nonrepresentative leaders often called the *power elite*. This elite secures the important decision-making positions while encouraging powerlessness below. Those in power do not represent the varied interests in society. Instead, they look after their own interests and prevent dissenting views from surfacing. American politics is not a collection of pluralist groups maintaining a balance of power among themselves, but an elite of economic, political, and military leaders in unresponsive control of the political game.

This elite rules the country through the positions that its members occupy. Power does not come from individuals but from *institutions*. Thus, to have power you need a role of leadership in a key institution of the society—you have to be the chief executive of a large corporation or a cabinet secretary, or a full admiral in the Navy. The argument extends to a criticism of the broader society's social classes, which limit who can climb up to these leadership positions. They are open only to the rich and the powerful, the *ruling class* of the country, whose names can be found in major newspapers' society columns and whose children go to the "right" schools. This influential class controls the country's economy and uses political power to preserve the status quo and their own privileges.

The results of this elite control, needless to say, are different from the pluralist outcome. Political decisions, rather than representing a consensus in society, merely represent the *conflict* within it. Society is held together not by widespread agreement but by force and control: the control the elite has over the majority. The only consensus that exists is that some have power and others do not. From this pessimistic viewpoint, politics is a constant conflict between those with power (who seek to keep it) and those without power (who seek to gain it). The policies that result from this political game reflect the conflict between elite and majority, and the domination of the elite.

Elite Examples

One of the best-known, and sometimes denounced, elite policy organizations is the *Council on Foreign Relations*. It was founded after World War I by what would loosely be called the eastern Establishment—socially connected, New York–based bankers, lawyers, and academics. One study found that 23 of the country's largest banks and corporations had four or more directors who were members of the Council. Its members played key roles after World War II in creating the International Monetary Fund, the World Bank, and the United Nations. Its journal, *Foreign Affairs,* is a must-read by foreign policy decisionmakers, most of whom are members of the Council. Its discussion groups bring together leaders from business, government, universities, and the military. To those in the Council, it is a policy-oriented group analyzing issues and producing broad leadership agreements on American foreign policies. To critics of the elite, it looks more like an old boy network dividing up jobs and deciding issues among themselves.

The classic study of elite control in the United States, *The Power Elite*, was written by sociologist C. Wright Mills, who maintained that American politics was dominated by a unified group of leaders from corporations, the military, and politics. More recently, William Greider's *Who Will Tell the People* continues the Mills tradition. In his study of Washington politics in the 1990s, Greider sees a policy-making elite working with wealthy economic interests to dominate the creation and implementation of laws and regulations. Even reforms of the system, such as campaign funding and protecting the environment, are "fixed" to protect the big corporations. Parties and media, rather than mobilizing citizens around authentic national needs, manipulate them to promote the interests of the elite. The answer to the question that begins Greider's book, "Who speaks for the people?" is "No one." (See "The Elite View.")

Criticisms of the Elite View

Critics have been quick to join the fight with the elite view. Although they may agree that only a few people participate in politics, they argue that this minority of activists is much less unified than elite theory assumes. They point to political conflicts over taxes or the environment, or any presidential election, as examples of how elites check each other. These elites compete, and democracy consists of people choosing between them through the vote. Besides, some critics argue, the political ideals of democracy are probably in better, if fewer, hands than they would be under the control of an uninformed majority. Public surveys have shown intolerance for dissent among the less educated and lower classes. Hence greater participation might, curiously enough, mean fewer liberties, not more.

Another criticism aimed at some careless power elite supporters is that they are *conspiracy theorists*. Ideologues of both the Right and Left may veer close to blaming certain racial, religious, or economic groups for betraying democracy. The reasoning often becomes circular: American politics is governed by a secret conspiracy "covered up" by certain groups or people. Such conspiracies are responsible for everything from President Kennedy's assassination to the World Trade Center bombings, the AIDS epidemic, and the Iraq war. Sadly, conspiracies remove

The Elite View

Instead of popular will, the government now responds more often to narrow webs of power—the interests of major economic organizations and concentrated wealth and the influential elites surrounding them. (p. 12)

Government responds to the public's desires with an artful dance of symbolic gestures—hollow laws that are emptied of serious content in the private bargaining of Washington. (p. 12)

The high art of governing—making laws for the nation and upholding them—has been reduced to a busy commerce in deal making. (p. 105)

Source: William Greider, *Who Will Tell the People.* New York: Simon & Schuster, 1992.

politics from analysis and allow demagogues to manipulate naïve followers, usually to raise money.

THE DEBATE

The debate between supporters of the pluralist and elite theories does not boil down to *whether* a small number of people dominate the political game. Even in the pluralist model, the bargaining among the groups is carried on by a relatively few leaders on behalf of their groups. Clearly only a minority of people directly participate in politics, and this small group has more influence than the majority of people. The central questions are how *competitive* and *representative* these elites are.

To what degree do elites compete rather than cooperate with one another over who gets what, when, and how? How much conflict is there between, say, heads of government agencies and corporations over regulation and taxes? Or how much do they share views on major questions of policy and cooperate among themselves regardless of the "public good"? Certainly anyone reading the newspaper can point to numerous examples of conflicts over policy among groups in the political arena. Are these conflicts to be dismissed as mere bickering among a small, tight group on the top? Or are vital issues being resolved in fairly open free-for-all contests?

Next is the question of how representative these elites are of the broader public. Do powerful groups reflect, however imperfectly, the wishes of the majority? In recent years, elite circles in America have opened their doors, not always voluntarily, to minorities and women. Has this made these institutions more representative or at least more aware of the wishes of formerly excluded groups? Is this just tokenism, or can the leaders of these associations, businesses, parties, or government agencies claim to represent a more diverse public opinion?

Is there, in fact, a "public opinion," or has that been manipulated beyond recognition? Take the question of what we watch from Hollywood entertainment. After the Columbine High School shootings in Colorado, it was charged that movies, television programs, and video games were undermining traditional family values. But do we know why? Some say it's because an elite seeking its own profits controls what we see. Others argue that abundant violence, casual sex, and silly commercials reflect what the majority wants, as shown by opinion polls. But do these polls reflect what people actually want or what they are conditioned to want? Do elites, including elected officials, follow public opinion? Or do they use polls to manipulate the public to follow their own preferences?

A glance back at the case studies at the end of most chapters in this book is a reminder of how difficult it is to put the political game under a single umbrella of ideas. The case study of Congress passing campaign finance reform shows political leaders using widespread public outrage to overcome legislative inertia and powerful elected officials. And yet the reform was instantly, if only partially, undermined. The case study of the decline and fall of racial segregation seems even more clear-cut—widespread pluralist participation resolving a difficult political conflict, but requiring enormous effort.

The other cases are not as clear. The president's response to 9/11 was both timely and appropriate, but it hardly reflected broad debate among a diversity of voices. Even in calmer times, the courts had difficulty getting the government to apply restrictive civil liberties to the war on terrorism. The use of the Internet in Howard Dean's 2004 campaign was an encouraging sign of grassroots participation but, then, he did lose. In the case study, "The Candidate: A Day in the Life" (in Chapter 8), a woman running for the Senate aims to win a popular vote, but her immediate targets are narrowed to special interest groups and media. Both in process and results, the pluralist and elite frameworks highlight certain parts of America's politics, but ignore others.

Newer Views

The pluralist and elite approaches are two ends of a range of ideas about American politics. Recent modifications have attempted to bridge the gap between the two. One has discussed a *plural elitism.* This stresses that politics is divided into separate policy arenas where narrow elites dominate, usually at the expense of the public interest. So, for example, when it comes to deciding on government spending levels for the Army, a trio of military leaders, defense contractors, and key congressional committees dominate the decisions, making sure they benefit, usually at the public expense. The general public is confused by ideology and patriotic symbols from clearly seeing the elite dominance that is occurring in these issue arenas.

Underlying this approach is the view that whether pluralists or the power elite school is right depends on which political conflict we are talking about. Sometimes, as in town meetings held in many New England towns, we can see a number of views being expressed and a democratic decision being reached by the community. In other areas, such as the making of antiterrorism policies, a small number of high officials meeting behind closed doors decide issues that will affect the lives of millions. The issue being decided is likely to affect how decisions will be made and who participates. Pluralism may be most appropriate in describing a small community's politics, but the elite approach may help us understand the making of national security policy.

Other students of American politics have emphasized how the *government* itself acts. In both pluralism and elitism, government actions are basically viewed as the result of outside forces: in one case, compromises between different groups; in the other, the wishes and interests of a unified elite. But clearly government—its major branches and agencies—is more than a passive mirror of dominant outside groups. Government has interests of its own and may even, at times, act to represent a broad national interest.

The concepts we adopt as most accurately reflecting political reality are bound also to reflect our own ideals. The pluralists and elitists (and those in between) are asking not only what *is* but what *should be.* The pluralists state that politics in America is democratic, with widespread participation in decisions to which most people agree. The elitists say that politics is dominated by an elite that controls and manipulates the rest of us in its own interest. The elitists contend that basic changes in the American system are needed to create a pluralist democracy, whereas the pluralists argue that we have one and that the means for change are available within it.

What do you think? The position you take will reflect not only your understanding and study of politics, but also your political ideals, interests, and experience. Further, the position you take will guide your future political choices.

WRAP-UP

The book has presented American politics as a game. We have discussed the nature of the game and how the competition takes place. We talked about the rules of the conflict, many of them in the Constitution, and how they have changed. Most of the book has introduced the major governmental and nongovernmental players, and their history, organization, and influence. This last chapter has looked at two schools of thought that try to analyze how the game is really played and sum up who wins and loses. But we're not quite finished.

What we have called this "game" of politics is more than that. It is a contest that defines who we are as a people: whether we are selfish or generous, arrogant or compassionate, brave or fearful. Like any country, America is a mix of conflicting values and interests, amplified by great wealth and power. Which America will win out? Will it reflect an America of pioneers who expanded on the democratic principles they inherited, offering them to those who had been excluded, while defending them at great cost in blood and treasure? Or will it be a self-righteous America so lulled by material comfort, which it assumes reflects the entitlement of winners, that it can refuse to listen to dissenting voices at home and abroad? The answers lie in the political game.

We did say that most of us are spectators of the game—nonparticipants. But just as politics is a special kind of game, so too are we a special kind of audience. We *can* participate in the game and, by participating, change the way the game is played and even its outcome. As a respected scholar of politics once wrote:

> Political conflict is not like a football game, played on a measured field by a fixed number of players in the presence of an audience scrupulously excluded from the playing field. Politics is much more like the original primitive game of football in which everybody was free to join, a game in which the whole population of one town might play the entire population of another town moving freely back and forth across the countryside.

Many conflicts are narrowly confined by a variety of devices, but the distinctive quality of political conflicts is that the relations between the players and the audience have not been well defined and there is usually nothing to keep the audience from getting into the game.

In whatever way you think best, join in. American politics today is too important to just watch others play.

Thought Questions

1. Give examples from throughout the book that support the pluralist approach. Give other examples that lean toward the power elite.
2. Pluralism has been described as essentially "liberal," whereas elitism can be either "radical" or "conservative." Do you agree?
3. Which approach, pluralism or elitism, do you feel best describes the political game in your own community? Give examples.
4. Do you think interest in politics is growing among students? Why? Is political participation by students encouraged or discouraged? How?

Suggested Readings

Dahl, Robert A. *Who Governs?* New Haven, Conn.: Yale University Press, 1961. Pb.
   A case study showing pluralism operating in New Haven's city government.
———*On Democracy.* New Haven, Conn.: Yale University Press, 1998.
   Intelligently reviews and argues the merits of democracy.
D'Souza, Dinesh. *What's So Great About America?* New York: Regnery Publishing, 2002.
   An articulate conservative immigrant fires away at critics of the United States of America, including Michael Moore.
Greider, William. *Who Will Tell the People.* New York: Simon & Schuster, 1992.
   This *Rolling Stone* editor gives a muckraking view at how issues are wheeled and dealed in Washington with little regard for the American people.
Mills, C. Wright. *The Power Elite.* New York: Oxford University Press, 1959. Pb.
   The well-known attempt to show that an elite governs America in its own interest.
Moore, Michael. *Stupid White Men.* New York: HarperCollins, 2002.
   The populist behind the movie *Fahrenheit 9/11*, writes a funny diatribe against the elites running our "nation of idiots."
Schattschneider, E. E. *The Semisovereign People.* New York: Holt, Rinehart & Winston, 1961. Pb.
   This landmark work presents a basic explanation of how and why some people get into politics and some stay out.

APPENDIX

The Declaration of Independence

In Congress, July 4, 1776

THE UNANIMOUS DECLARATION OF THE THIRTEEN UNITED STATES OF AMERICA

When in the Course of human events, it becomes necessary for one people to dissolve the political bands, which have connected them with another, and to assume among the powers of the earth, the separate and equal station to which the Laws of Nature and of Nature's God entitle them, a decent respect to the opinions of mankind requires that they should declare the causes which impel them to the separation.—We hold these truths to be self-evident, that all men are created equal, that they are endowed by their Creator with certain unalienable Rights, that among these are Life, Liberty and the pursuit of Happiness.—That to secure these rights, Governments are instituted among Men, deriving their just powers from the consent of the governed,—That whenever any Form of Government becomes destructive of these ends, it is the Right of the People to alter or to abolish it, and to institute new Government, laying its foundation on such principles and organizing its powers in such form, as to them shall seem most likely to effect their Safety and Happiness. Prudence, indeed, will dictate that Governments long established should not be changed for light and transient causes; and accordingly all experience hath shown, that mankind are more disposed to suffer, while evils are sufferable, than to right themselves by abolishing the forms to which they are accustomed. But when a long train of abuses and usurpations, pursuing invariably the same Object evinces a design to reduce them under absolute Despotism, it is their right, it is their duty, to throw off such Government, and to provide new Guards for their future security.—Such has been the patient sufferance of these Colonies; and such is now the necessity which constrains them to alter their former Systems of Government. The history of the present King of Great Britain is a history of repeated injuries and usurpations, all having in direct object the establishment of an absolute Tyranny over these States. To prove this, let Facts be submitted to a candid world.—He has refused his Assent to Laws, the most wholesome and necessary for the public good.—He has forbidden his Governors to pass Laws of immediate and pressing importance, unless suspended in their operation till his Assent should be obtained; and when so suspended, he has utterly neglected to attend to them.—He has refused to pass other Laws for the accommodation of large districts of people, unless those people would relinquish the right of Representation in the Legislature, a right inestimable to them and formidable to tyrants only.—He has called together legislative bodies at places unusual, uncomfortable, and distant from the depository of their public Records, for the sole purpose of fatiguing them into compliance with his measures.—He has dissolved Representative Houses repeatedly, for opposing with manly firmness his invasions on the rights of the people.—He has refused for a long time, after such dissolutions, to cause others to be elected; whereby the Legislative powers, incapable of Annihilation, have returned to the People at large for their exercise; the State remaining in the meantime exposed to all the dangers of invasion from without, and convulsions within.—He has endeavored to prevent the population of these States; for that purpose obstructing the Laws for Naturalization of Foreigners; refusing to pass others to encourage their migrations hither, and raising the conditions of new Appropriations of Lands.—He has obstructed the Administration of Justice, by refusing his Assent to Laws for establishing Judiciary powers.—He has made Judges dependent on his Will alone, for the tenure of their offices, and the amount and payment of their salaries.—He has erected a multitude of New Offices, and sent hither swarms of Officers to harass our people, and eat out their substance.—He has kept among us, in times of peace, Standing Armies without the Consent of our legislatures.—He has affected to render the Military independent of and superior to the Civil power.—He has combined with others to subject us to a jurisdiction foreign to our constitution, and unacknowledged by our laws; giving his Assent to their Acts of pretended Legislation.—For quartering large bodies of armed troops among us:—For protecting them, by a mock Trial, from punishment for any Murders which they should commit on the Inhabitants of these States:—For cutting off our Trade with all parts of the world:—For imposing Taxes on us without our Consent:—For depriving us in many cases, of the benefits of Trial by Jury:—For transporting us beyond Seas to be tried for pretended offenses:—For abolishing the free System of English Laws in a neighboring Province, establishing therein an Arbitrary government, and enlarging its Boundaries so as to render it at once an example and fit instrument for introducing the same absolute rule into these Colonies:—For taking away our Charters, abolishing our most valuable Laws, and altering fundamentally the Forms of our Governments:—For suspending our own Legislatures, and declaring themselves invested with power to legislate for us in all cases whatsoever.—He has abdicated Government here, by declaring us out of his Protection and waging War against us.—He has plundered our seas, ravaged our Coasts, burnt our towns, and destroyed the lives of our people.—He is at this time transporting large armies of foreign Mercenaries to complete the works of death, desolation and tyranny, already begun with circumstances of Cruelty & perfidy, scarcely paralleled in the most barbarous ages, and totally unworthy the Head of a civilized nation.—He has constrained our fellow Citizens taken Captive on the High Seas to bear Arms against their Country, to become the executioners of their friends and Brethren, or to fall themselves by their hands.—He has excited domestic insurrections amongst us, and has endeavored to bring on the inhabitants of our frontiers, the merciless Indian Savages, whose known rule of warfare, is an undistinguished destruction of all ages, sexes and conditions. In every stage of these Oppressions We have Petitioned for Redress in the most humble terms: Our repeated Petitions have been answered only by repeated injury. A Prince whose character is thus marked by every act which may define a Tyrant, is unfit to be the ruler of a free people. Nor have We been wanting in attentions to our British brethren. We have warned them from time to time of attempts by their legislature to extend an unwarrantable jurisdiction over us. We have reminded them of the circumstances of our emigration and settlement here. We have appealed to their native justice and magnanimity, and we have conjured them by the ties of our common kindred to disavow these usurpations, which would inevitably interrupt our connections and correspondence. They too have been deaf to the voice of justice and of consanguinity. We must, therefore, acquiesce in the necessity, which denounces our Separation, and hold them, as we hold the rest of mankind, Enemies in War, in Peace Friends.—

We, therefore, the Representatives of the United States of America, in General Congress, Assembled, appealing to the Supreme Judge of the world for the rectitude of our intentions do, in the Name, and by the Authority of the good People of these Colonies, solemnly publish and declare, That these United Colonies are, and of Right ought to be Free and Independent States, that they are Absolved from all Allegiance to the British Crown, and that all political connection between them and the State of Great Britain, is and ought to be totally dissolved; and that as Free and Independent States, they have full Power to levy War, conclude Peace, contract Alliances, establish Commerce, and to do all other Acts and Things which Independent States may of right do.—And for the support of this Declaration, with a firm reliance on the protection of divine Providence, we mutually pledge to each other our Lives, our Fortunes and our sacred Honor.

The Constitution of the United States

Submitted on September 17, 1787 by the Constitutional Convention, and became effective on March 4, 1789.

We the People of the United States, in Order to form a more perfect Union, establish Justice, insure domestic Tranquility, provide for the common defence, promote the general Welfare, and secure the Blessings of Liberty to ourselves and our Posterity, do ordain and establish this CONSTITUTION for the United States of America.

ARTICLE I

Section 1. All legislative Powers herein granted shall be vested in a Congress of the United States, which shall consist of a Senate and House of Representatives.

Section 2. (1) The House of Representatives shall be composed of Members chosen every second Year by the People of the several States, and the Electors in each State shall have the Qualifications requisite for Electors of the most numerous Branch of the State Legislature.

(2) No Person shall be a Representative who shall not have attained to the Age of twenty-five Years, and been seven Years a Citizen of the United States, and who shall not, when elected, be an Inhabitant of that State in which he shall be chosen.

(3) [Representatives and direct Taxes[1] shall be apportioned among the several States which may be included within this Union, according to their respective Numbers, which shall be determined by adding to the whole Number of free Persons, including those bound to Service for a Term of Years, and excluding Indians not taxed, three fifths of all other Persons.][2] The actual Enumeration shall be made within three Years after the first Meeting of the Congress of the United States, and within every subsequent Term of ten Years, in such Manner as they shall by Law direct. The Number of Representatives shall not exceed one for every thirty Thousand, but each State shall have at Least one Representative; and until such enumeration shall be made, the State of New Hampshire shall be entitled to choose three, Massachusetts eight, Rhode-Island and Providence Plantations one, Connecticut five, New York six, New Jersey four, Pennsylvania eight, Delaware one, Maryland six, Virginia ten, North Carolina five, South Carolina five, and Georgia three.

(4) When vacancies happen in the Representation from any State, the Executive Authority thereof shall issue Writs of Election to fill such Vacancies.

(5) The House of Representatives shall choose their Speaker and other Officers; and shall have the sole Power of Impeachment.

---

[1] The Sixteenth Amendment replaced this with respect to income taxes.

[2] Repealed by the Fourteenth Amendment.

Section 3. (1) The Senate of the United States shall be composed of two Senators from each State, [chosen by the Legislature][3] thereof, for six Years; and each Senator shall have one Vote.

(2) Immediately after they shall be assembled in Consequence of the first Election, they shall be divided as equally as may be into three Classes. The Seats of the Senators of the first Class shall be vacated at the Expiration of the second Year, of the second Class at the Expiration of the fourth Year, and of the third Class at the Expiration of the sixth Year, so that one-third may be chosen every second year; [and if Vacancies happen by Resignation, or otherwise, during the Recess of the Legislature of any State, the Executive thereof may make temporary Appointments until the next Meeting of the Legislature, which shall then fill such Vacancies].[4]

(3) No person shall be a Senator who shall not have attained to the Age of thirty Years, and been nine Years a Citizen of the United States, and who shall not, when elected, be an Inhabitant of that State for which he shall be chosen.

(4) The Vice President of the United States shall be President of the Senate, but shall have no Vote, unless they be equally divided.

(5) The Senate shall choose their other Officers, and also a President *pro tempore,* in the Absence of the Vice President, or when he shall exercise the Office of President of the United States.

(6) The Senate shall have the sole Power to try all Impeachments. When sitting for that Purpose, they shall be on Oath or Affirmation. When the President of the United States is tried, the Chief Justice shall preside: And no Person shall be convicted without the Concurrence of two thirds of the Members present.

(7) Judgment in Cases of Impeachment shall not extend further than to removal from Office, and disqualification to hold and enjoy any Office of honor, Trust or Profit under the United States: but the Party convicted shall nevertheless be liable and subject to Indictment, Trial, Judgment and Punishment according to Law.

Section 4. (1) The Times, Places and Manner of holding Elections for Senators and Representatives, shall be prescribed in each State by the Legislature thereof; but the Congress may at any time by Law make or alter such Regulations, except as to the Places of choosing Senators.

(2) The Congress shall assemble at least once in every Year, and such Meeting shall [be on the first Monday in December,][5] unless they shall by Law appoint a different Day.

Section 5. (1) Each House shall be the Judge of the Elections, Returns and Qualifications of its own Members, and a Majority of each shall constitute a Quorum to do Business; but a smaller Number may adjourn from day to day, and may be authorized to compel the Attendance of absent Members, in such Manner, and under such Penalties as each House may provide.

---

[3]Repealed by the Seventeenth Amendment.

[4]Changed by the Seventeenth Amendment.

[5]Changed by the Twentieth Amendment, Section 2.

(2) Each House may determine the Rules of its Proceedings, punish its Members for disorderly Behavior, and, with the Concurrence of two thirds, expel a Member.

(3) Each House shall keep a Journal of its Proceedings, and from time to time publish the same, excepting such Parts as may in their Judgment require Secrecy; and the Yeas and Nays of the Members of either House on any question shall, at the Desire of one fifth of those Present, be entered on the Journal.

(4) Neither House, during the Session of Congress, shall, without the Consent of the other, adjourn for more than three days, nor to any other Place than that in which the two Houses shall be sitting.

Section 6. (1) The Senators and Representatives shall receive a Compensation for their Services, to be ascertained by Law, and paid out of the Treasury of the United States. They shall in all Cases, except Treason, Felony and Breach of the Peace, be privileged from Arrest during their Attendance at the Session of their respective Houses, and in going to and returning from the same; and for any Speech or Debate in either House, they shall not be questioned in any other Place.

(2) No Senator or Representative shall, during the Time for which he was elected, be appointed to any civil Office under the Authority of the United States, which shall have been created, or the Emoluments whereof have been increased during such time; and no Person holding any Office under the United States, shall be a Member of either House during his Continuance in Office.

Section 7. (1) All Bills for raising Revenue shall originate in the House of Representatives; but the Senate may propose or concur with Amendments as on other Bills.

(2) Every Bill which shall have passed the House of Representatives and the Senate, shall, before it becomes a Law, be presented to the President of the United States; If he approve he shall sign it, but if not he shall return it, with his Objections to that House in which it shall have originated, who shall enter the Objections at large on their Journal, and proceed to reconsider it. If after such Reconsideration two-thirds of that House shall agree to pass the Bill, it shall be sent, together with the Objections, to the other House, by which it shall likewise be reconsidered, and if approved by two thirds of that House, it shall become a Law. But in all such Cases the Votes of both Houses shall be determined by Yeas and Nays, and the Names of the Persons voting for and against the Bill shall be entered on the Journal of each House respectively. If any Bill shall not be returned by the President within ten Days (Sundays excepted) after it shall have been presented to him, the Same shall be a Law, in like Manner as if he had signed it, unless the Congress by their Adjournment prevent its Return, in which Case it shall not be a Law.

(3) Every Order, Resolution, or Vote to which the Concurrence of the Senate and House of Representatives may be necessary (except on a question of Adjournment) shall be presented to the President of the United States; and before the Same shall take Effect, shall be approved by him, or being disapproved by him, shall be repassed by two-thirds of the Senate and House of Representatives, according to the Rules and Limitations prescribed in the Case of a Bill.

Section 8. (1) The Congress shall have Power To lay and collect Taxes, Duties, Imposts and Excises, to pay the Debts and provide for the common Defense and general Welfare of the United States; but all Duties, Imposts and Excises shall be uniform throughout the United States;

(2) To borrow money on the credit of the United States;

(3) To regulate Commerce with foreign Nations, and among the several States, and with the Indian Tribes;

(4) To establish a uniform Rule of Naturalization, and uniform Laws on the subject of Bankruptcies throughout the United States;

(5) To coin Money, regulate the Value thereof, and of foreign Coin, and fix the Standard of Weights and Measures;

(6) To provide for the Punishment of counterfeiting the Securities and current Coin of the United States;

(7) To establish Post Offices and post Roads;

(8) To promote the Progress of Science and useful Arts, by securing for limited Times to Authors and Inventors the exclusive Right to their respective Writings and Discoveries;

(9) To constitute Tribunals inferior to the supreme Court;

(10) To define and punish Piracies and Felonies committed on the high Seas, and Offenses against the Law of Nations;

(11) To declare War, grant Letters of Marque and Reprisal, and make Rules concerning Captures on Land and Water;

(12) To raise and support Armies, but no Appropriation of Money to that Use shall be for a longer Term than two Years;

(13) To provide and maintain a Navy;

(14) To make Rules for the Government and Regulation of the land and naval Forces;

(15) To provide for calling forth the Militia to execute the Laws of the Union, suppress Insurrections and repel Invasions;

(16) To provide for organizing, arming, and disciplining the Militia, and for governing such Part of them as may be employed in the Service of the United States, reserving to the States respectively, the Appointment of the Officers, and the Authority of training the Militia according to the discipline prescribed by Congress;

(17) To exercise exclusive Legislation in all Cases whatsoever, over such District (not exceeding ten Miles square) as may, by Cession of particular States, and the Acceptance of Congress, become the Seat of the Government of the United States, and to exercise like Authority over all Places purchased by the Consent of the Legislature of the State in which the Same shall be, for the Erection of Forts, Magazines, Arsenals, dock-Yards, and other needful Buildings;—And

(18) To make all Laws which shall be necessary and proper for carrying into Execution the foregoing Powers, and all other Powers vested by this Constitution in the Government of the United States, or in any Department or Officer thereof.

Section 9. (1) The Migration or Importation of such Persons as any of the States now existing shall think proper to admit, shall not be prohibited by the Congress prior to the Year one thousand eight hundred and eight, but a tax or duty may be imposed on such Importation, not exceeding ten dollars for each Person.

(2) The Privilege of the Writ of Habeas Corpus shall not be suspended, unless when in Cases of Rebellion or Invasion the public Safety may require it.

(3) No Bill of Attainder or ex post facto Law shall be passed.

(4) No Capitation, or other direct, Tax shall be laid, unless in Proportion to the Census or Enumeration herein before directed to be taken.[6]

(5) No Tax or Duty shall be laid on Articles exported from any State.

(6) No Preference shall be given by any Regulation of Commerce or Revenue to the Ports of one State over those of another; nor shall Vessels bound to, or from, one State, be obliged to enter, clear, or pay Duties in another.

(7) No Money shall be drawn from the Treasury, but in Consequence of Appropriations made by Law; and a regular Statement and Account of the Receipts and Expenditures of all public Money shall be published from time to time.

(8) No Title of Nobility shall be granted by the United States: And no Person holding any Office of Profit or Trust under them, shall, without the Consent of the Congress, accept of any present, Emolument, Office, or Title, of any kind whatever, from any King, Prince, or foreign State.

Section 10. (1) No State shall enter into any Treaty, Alliance, or Confederation; grant Letters of Marque and Reprisal; coin Money; emit Bills of Credit; make any Thing but gold and silver Coin a Tender in Payment of Debts; pass any Bill of Attainder, ex post facto Law, or Law impairing the Obligation of Contracts, or grant any Title of Nobility.

(2) No State shall, without the Consent of the Congress, lay any Imposts or Duties on Imports or Exports, except what may be absolutely necessary for executing its inspection Laws: and the net Produce of all Duties and Imposts, laid by any State on Imports or Exports, shall be for the Use of the Treasury of the United States; and all such laws shall be subject to the Revision and Control of the Congress.

(3) No State shall, without the Consent of Congress, lay any duty of Tonnage, keep Troops, or Ships of War in time of Peace, enter into any Agreement or Compact with another State, or with a foreign Power, or engage in War, unless actually invaded, or in such imminent Danger as will not admit of delay.

ARTICLE II

Section 1. (1) The executive Power shall be vested in a President of the United States of America. He shall hold his Office during the Term of four Years, and, together with the Vice-President, chosen for the same Term, be elected, as follows:

(2) Each State shall appoint, in such Manner as the Legislature thereof may direct, a Number of Electors, equal to the whole Number of Senators

---

[6]Changed by the Sixteenth Amendment.

and Representatives to which the State may be entitled in the Congress; but no Senator or Representative, or Person holding an Office of Trust or Profit under the United States, shall be appointed an Elector.

[The Electors shall meet in their respective States, and vote by Ballot for two persons, of whom one at least shall not be an Inhabitant of the same State with themselves. And they shall make a List of all the Persons voted for, and of the Number of Votes for each; which List they shall sign and certify, and transmit sealed to the Seat of the Government of the United States, directed to the President of the Senate. The President of the Senate shall, in the Presence of the Senate and House of Representatives, open all the Certificates, and the Votes shall then be counted. The Person having the greatest Number of Votes shall be the President, if such Number be a Majority of the whole Number of Electors appointed; and if there be more than one who have such Majority, and have an equal Number of Votes, then the House of Representatives shall immediately choose by Ballot one of them for President; and if no Person have a Majority, then from the five highest on the List the said House shall in like Manner choose the President. But in choosing the President, the Votes shall be taken by States, the Representation from each State having one Vote; A quorum for this purpose shall consist of a Member or Members from two-thirds of the States, and a Majority of all the States shall be necessary to a Choice. In every Case, after the Choice of the President, the Person having the greatest Number of Votes of the Electors shall be the Vice-President. But if there should remain two or more who have equal Votes, the Senate shall choose from them by Ballot the Vice-President.][7]

(3) The Congress may determine the Time of choosing the Electors, and the Day on which they shall give their Votes; which Day shall be the same throughout the United States.

(4) No person except a natural born Citizen, or a Citizen of the United States, at the time of the Adoption of this Constitution, shall be eligible to the Office of President; neither shall any Person be eligible to that Office who shall not have attained to the Age of thirty-five Years, and been fourteen Years a Resident within the United States.

(5) In case of the Removal of the President from Office, or of his Death, Resignation, or Inability to discharge the Powers and Duties of the said Office, the same shall devolve on the Vice-President, and the Congress may by Law provide for the Case of Removal, Death, Resignation or Inability, both of the President and Vice-President, declaring what Officer shall then act as President, and such Officer shall act accordingly, until the Disability be removed, or a President shall be elected.[8]

(6) The President shall, at stated Times, receive for his Services, a Compensation, which shall neither be increased nor diminished during the Period for which he shall have been elected, and he shall not receive within that Period any other Emolument from the United States, or any of them.

---

[7]This paragraph was superseded in 1804 by the Twelfth Amendment.

[8]Changed by the Twenty-fifth Amendment.

(7) Before he enter on the Execution of his Office, he shall take the following Oath or Affirmation:—"I do solemnly swear (or affirm) that I will faithfully execute the Office of President of the United States, and will to the best of my Ability, preserve, protect and defend the Constitution of the United States."

Section 2. (1) The President shall be Commander in Chief of the Army and Navy of the United States, and of the Militia of the several States, when called into the actual Service of the United States; he may require the Opinion in writing, of the principal Officer in each of the executive Departments, upon any subject relating to the Duties of their respective Offices, and he shall have Power to Grant Reprieves and Pardons for Offenses against the United States, except in Cases of Impeachment.

(2) He shall have Power, by and with the Advice and Consent of the Senate, to make Treaties, provided two-thirds of the Senators present concur; and he shall nominate, and by and with the Advice and Consent of the Senate, shall appoint Ambassadors, other public Ministers and Consuls, Judges of the supreme Court, and all other Officers of the United States, whose Appointments are not herein otherwise provided for, and which shall be established by Law: but the Congress may by Law vest the Appointment of such inferior Officers, as they think proper, in the President alone, in the Court of Law, or in the Heads of Departments.

(3) The President shall have Power to fill up all Vacancies that may happen during the Recess of the Senate, by granting Commissions which shall expire at the End of their next Session.

Section 3. He shall from time to time give to the Congress Information of the State of the Union, and recommend to their Consideration such Measures as he shall judge necessary and expedient; he may, on extraordinary Occasions, convene both Houses, or either of them, and in Case of Disagreement between them, with Respect to the Time of Adjournment, he may adjourn them to such Time as he shall think proper; he shall receive Ambassadors and other public Ministers; he shall take Care that the Laws be faithfully executed, and shall Commission all the Officers of the United States.

Section 4. The President, Vice President and all civil Officers of the United States, shall be removed from Office on Impeachment for, and Conviction of, Treason, Bribery, or other high Crimes and Misdemeanors.

ARTICLE III

Section 1. The judicial Power of the United States, shall be vested in one supreme Court, and in such inferior Courts as the Congress may from time to time ordain and establish. The Judges, both of the supreme and inferior Courts, shall hold their Offices during good Behavior, and shall, at stated Times, receive for their Services a Compensation which shall not be diminished during their Continuance in Office.

Section 2. (1) The judicial Power shall extend to all Cases, in Law and Equity, arising under this Constitution, the Laws of the United States, and Treaties made, or which shall be made, under their Authority;—to all Cases affecting Ambassadors, other public Ministers and Consuls;—to all Cases of admiralty and maritime Jurisdiction;—to Controversies to which the United States shall be a Party;—to Controversies between two or more states;—[between a State and Citizens of another State];[9]—between Citizens of different States;—between Citizens of the same State claiming Lands under Grants of different States, and [between a State, or the Citizens thereof, and foreign States, Citizens or Subjects].[10]

(2) In all Cases affecting Ambassadors, other public Ministers and Consuls, and those in which a State shall be Party, the supreme Court shall have original Jurisdiction. In all the other Cases before mentioned, the supreme Court shall have appellate Jurisdiction, both as to Law and Fact, with such Exceptions, and under such Regulations as the Congress shall make.

(3) The trial of all Crimes, except in Cases of Impeachment, shall be by Jury; and such Trial shall be held in the State where the said Crimes shall have been committed: but when not committed within any State, the Trial shall be at such Place or Places as the Congress may by Law have directed.

Section 3. (1) Treason against the United States, shall consist only in levying War against them, or in adhering to their Enemies, giving them Aid and Comfort. No Person shall be convicted of Treason unless on the Testimony of two Witnesses to the same overt Act, or on Confession in open Court.

(2) The Congress shall have Power to declare the Punishment of Treason, but no Attainder of Treason shall work Corruption of Blood, or Forfeiture except during the Life of the Person attained.

ARTICLE IV

Section 1. Full Faith and Credit shall be given in each State to the public Acts, Records, and judicial Proceedings of every other State. And the Congress may by general Laws prescribe the Manner in which such Acts, Records and Proceedings shall be proved, and the Effect thereof.

Section 2. (1) The Citizens of each State shall be entitled to all Privileges and Immunities of Citizens in the several States.

(2) A Person charged in any State with Treason, Felony, or other Crime, who shall flee from Justice, and be found in another State, shall on demand of the executive Authority of the State from which he fled, be delivered up, to be removed to the State having Jurisdiction of the Crime.

(3) [No Person held to Service or Labor in one State, under the Laws thereof, escaping into another, shall, in Consequence of any Law or Regulation therein, be discharged from such Service or Labor, but shall be delivered up on Claim of the Party to whom such Service or Labor may be due.][11]

Section 3. (1) New States may be admitted by the Congress into this Union; but no new State shall be formed or erected within the Jurisdiction of

---

[9]Restricted by the Eleventh Amendment.

[10]Restricted by the Eleventh Amendment.

[11]This paragraph was superseded by the Thirteenth Amendment.

any other State; nor any State be formed by the Junction of two or more States, or Parts of States, without the Consent of the Legislatures of the States concerned as well as of the Congress.

(2) The Congress shall have Power to dispose of and make all needful Rules and Regulations respecting the Territory or other Property belonging to the United States; and nothing in this Constitution shall be so construed as to Prejudice any Claims of the United States, or of any particular State.

Section 4. The United States shall guarantee to every State in this Union a Republican Form of Government, and shall protect each of them against Invasion; and on Application of the Legislature, or of the Executive (when the Legislature cannot be convened) against domestic Violence.

ARTICLE V

The Congress, whenever two-thirds of both Houses shall deem it necessary, shall propose Amendments to this Constitution, or, on the Application of the Legislatures of two-thirds of the several States, shall call a Convention for proposing Amendments, which, in either Case, shall be valid to all Intents and Purposes, as part of this Constitution, when ratified by the Legislature of three-fourths of the several States, or by Conventions in three-fourths thereof, as the one or the other Mode of Ratification may be proposed by the Congress; Provided that no Amendment which may be made prior to the Year One thousand eight hundred and eight shall in any Manner affect the first and fourth Clauses in the Ninth Section of the first Article; and that no State, without its Consent, shall be deprived of its equal Suffrage in the Senate.

ARTICLE VI

(1) All Debts contracted and Engagements entered into, before the Adoption of this Constitution, shall be as valid against the United States under this Constitution, as under the Confederation.

(2) This Constitution, and the Laws of the United States which shall be made in Pursuance thereof; and all Treaties made, or which shall be made, under the Authority of the United States, shall be the supreme Law of the Land; and the Judges in every State shall be bound thereby, any Thing in the Constitution or Laws of any State to the Contrary notwithstanding.

(3) The Senators and Representatives before mentioned, and the Members of the several State Legislatures, and all executive and judicial Officers, both of the United States and of the several States, shall be bound by Oath or Affirmation, to support this Constitution; but no religious Test shall ever be required as a Qualification to any Office or public Trust under the United States.

ARTICLE VII

The Ratification of the Conventions of nine States, shall be sufficient for the Establishment of this Constitution between the States so ratifying the Same.

DONE in Convention by the Unanimous Consent of the States present the Seventeenth Day of September in the Year of our Lord one thousand seven hundred and Eighty seven and the Independence of the United States of America the Twelfth. In Witness whereof We have hereunto subscribed our Names.

Go. Washington
President and deputy from Virginia

Articles in Addition to, and Amendment of, the Constitution of the United States of America, Proposed by Congress, and Ratified by the Legislatures of the Several States, Pursuant to the Fifth Article of the Original Constitution.

AMENDMENT I[12]

Congress shall make no law respecting an establishment of religion, or prohibiting the free exercise thereof; or abridging the freedom of speech, or of the press; or the right of the people peaceably to assemble, and to petition the Government for a redress of grievances.

AMENDMENT II

A well regulated Militia, being necessary to the security of a free State, the right of the people to keep and bear Arms, shall not be infringed.

AMENDMENT III

No Soldier shall, in time of peace be quartered in any house, without the consent of the Owner, nor in time of war, but in a manner to be prescribed by law.

AMENDMENT IV

The right of the people to be secure in their persons, houses, papers, and effects, against unreasonable searches and seizures, shall not be violated, and no Warrants shall issue, but upon probable cause, supported by Oath or affirmation, and particularly describing the place to be searched, and the persons or things to be seized.

AMENDMENT V

No person shall be held to answer for a capital, or otherwise infamous crime, unless on a presentment or indictment of a Grand Jury, except in cases arising in the land or naval forces, or in the Militia, when in actual service in time of War or public danger; nor shall any person be subject for the same offense to be twice put in jeopardy of life or limb; nor shall be compelled in any

---

[12]The first ten amendments were adopted in 1791.

criminal case to be witness against himself, nor be deprived of life, liberty, or property, without due process of law; nor shall private property be taken for public use without just compensation.

AMENDMENT VI

In all criminal prosecutions, the accused shall enjoy the right to a speedy and public trial, by an impartial jury of the State and district wherein the crime shall have been committed, which district shall have been previously ascertained by law, and to be informed of the nature and cause of the accusation, to be confronted with the witnesses against him; to have compulsory process for obtaining witnesses in his favor, and to have the Assistance of Counsel for his defense.

AMENDMENT VII

In Suits at common law, where the value in controversy shall exceed twenty dollars, the right of trial by jury shall be preserved, and no fact tried by a jury, shall be otherwise reexamined in any Court of the United States, than according to the rules of the common law.

AMENDMENT VIII

Excessive bail shall not be required, nor excessive fines imposed, nor cruel and unusual punishments inflicted.

AMENDMENT IX

The enumeration in the Constitution, of certain rights, shall not be construed to deny or disparage others retained by the people.

AMENDMENT X

The powers not delegated to the United States by the Constitution, nor prohibited by it to the States, are reserved to the States respectively, or to the people.

AMENDMENT XI[13]

The Judicial power of the United States shall not be construed to extend to any suit in law or equity, commenced or prosecuted against one of the United States by Citizens of another State, or by Citizens or Subjects of any Foreign State.

---

[13]Adopted in 1798.

AMENDMENT XII[14]

The Electors shall meet in their respective states and vote by ballot for President and Vice-President, one of whom, at least, shall not be an inhabitant of the same state with themselves; they shall name in their ballots the person voted for as President, and in distinct ballots the person voted for as Vice-President, and they shall make distinct lists of all persons voted for as President, and of all persons voted for as Vice-President, and of the number of votes for each, which lists they shall sign and certify, and transmit sealed to the seat of the government of the United States, directed to the President of the Senate;—The President of the Senate shall, in presence of the Senate and House of Representatives, open all the certificates and the votes shall then be counted;—The person having the greatest number of votes for President, shall be the President, if such number be a majority of the whole number of Electors appointed; and if no person have such majority, then from the persons having the highest numbers not exceeding three on the list of those voted for as President, the House of Representatives shall choose immediately, by ballot, the President. But in choosing the President, the votes shall be taken by states, the representation from each state having one vote; a quorum for this purpose shall consist of a member or members from two-thirds of the states, and a majority of all the states shall be necessary to a choice. [And if the House of Representatives shall not choose a President whenever the right of choice shall devolve upon them, before the fourth day of March next following, then the Vice-President shall act as President, as in the case of the death or other constitutional disability of the President.][15]—The person having the greatest number of votes as Vice-President, shall be the Vice-President, if such number be a majority of the whole number of Electors appointed, and if no person have a majority, then from the two highest numbers on the list, the Senate shall choose the Vice-President; a quorum for the purpose shall consist of two-thirds of the whole number of Senators, and a majority of the whole number shall be necessary to a choice. But no person constitutionally ineligible to the office of President shall be eligible to that of Vice-President of the United States.

AMENDMENT XIII[16]

Section 1. Neither slavery nor involuntary servitude, except as a punishment for crime whereof the party shall have been duly convicted, shall exist within the United States, or any place subject to their jurisdiction.

---

[14]Adopted in 1804.

[15]Superseded by the Twentieth Amendment, Section 3.

[16]Adopted in 1865.

Section 2. Congress shall have power to enforce this article by appropriate legislation.

AMENDMENT XIV[17]

Section 1. All persons born or naturalized in the United States, and subject to the jurisdiction thereof, are citizens of the United States and of the State wherein they reside. No state shall make or enforce any law which shall abridge the privileges or immunities of citizens of the United States; nor shall any State deprive any person of life, liberty, or property, without due process of law; nor deny to any person within its jurisdiction the equal protection of the laws.

Section 2. Representatives shall be apportioned among the several States according to their respective numbers, counting the whole number of persons in each State, excluding Indians not taxed. But when the right to vote at any election for the choice of electors for President and Vice-President of the United States, Representatives in Congress, the Executive and Judicial officers of a State, or the members of the Legislature thereof, is denied to any of the male inhabitants of such State, being twenty-one years of age, and citizens of the United States, or in any way abridged, except for participation in rebellion, or other crime, the basis of representation therein shall be reduced in the proportion which the number of such male citizens shall bear to the whole number of male citizens twenty-one years of age in such State.

Section 3. No person shall be a Senator or Representative in Congress, or elector of President and Vice-President, or hold any office, civil or military, under the United States, or under any State, who, having previously taken an oath, as a member of Congress, or as an officer of the United States, or as a member of any State legislature, or as an executive or judicial officer of any State, to support the Constitution of the United States, shall have engaged in insurrection or rebellion against the same, or given aid or comfort to the enemies thereof. But Congress may by a vote of two-thirds of each House, remove such disability.

Section 4. The validity of the public debt of the United States, authorized by law, including debts incurred for payment of pensions and bounties for services in suppressing insurrection or rebellion, shall not be questioned. But neither the United States nor any State shall assume or pay any debt or obligation incurred in aid of insurrection or rebellion against the United States, or any claim for the loss or emancipation of any slave; but all such debts, obligations and claims shall be held illegal and void.

Section 5. The Congress shall have power to enforce, by appropriate legislation, the provisions of this article.

------

[17]Adopted in 1868.

AMENDMENT XV[18]

Section 1. The right of citizens of the United States to vote shall not be denied or abridged by the United States or by any State on account of race, color, or previous condition of servitude.

Section 2. The Congress shall have power to enforce this article by appropriate legislation.

AMENDMENT XVI[19]

The Congress shall have power to lay and collect taxes on incomes, from whatever source derived, without apportionment among the several States, and without regard to any census or enumeration.

AMENDMENT XVII[20]

The Senate of the United States shall be composed of two Senators from each State, elected by the people thereof, for six years; and each Senator shall have one vote. The electors in each State shall have the qualifications requisite for electors of the most numerous branch of the State legislatures.

When vacancies happen in the representation of any State in the Senate, the executive authority of such State shall issue writs of election to fill such vacancies: *Provided,* That the legislature of any State may empower the executive thereof to make temporary appointments until the people fill the vacancies by election as the legislature may direct.

This amendment shall not be so construed as to affect the election or term of any Senator chosen before it becomes valid as part of the Constitution.

AMENDMENT XVIII[21]

Section 1. After one year from the ratification of this article the manufacture, sale, or transportation of intoxicating liquors within, the importation thereof into, or the exportation thereof from the United States and all territory subject to the jurisdiction thereof for beverage purposes is hereby prohibited.

Section 2. The Congress and the several States shall have concurrent power to enforce this article by appropriate legislation.

Section 3. This article shall be inoperative unless it shall have been ratified as an amendment to the Constitution by the legislatures of the several

---

[18]Adopted in 1870.

[19]Adopted in 1913.

[20]Adopted in 1913.

[21]Adopted in 1919. Repealed by Section 1 of the Twenty-first Amendment.

States, as provided in the Constitution, within seven years from the date of the submission hereof to the States by the Congress.

AMENDMENT XIX[22]

The right of citizens of the United States to vote shall not be denied or abridged by the United States or by any State on account of sex.

Congress shall have power to enforce this article by appropriate legislation.

AMENDMENT XX[23]

Section 1. The terms of the President and Vice-President shall end at noon on the 20th day of January, and the terms of Senators and Representatives at noon on the 3rd day of January, of the years in which such terms would have ended if this article had not been ratified; and the terms of their successors shall then begin.

Section 2. The Congress shall assemble at least once in every year, and such meeting shall begin at noon on the 3rd day of January, unless they shall by law appoint a different day.

Section 3. If, at the time fixed for the beginning of the term of the President, the President elect shall have died, the Vice-President elect shall become President. If a President shall not have been chosen before the time fixed for the beginning of his term, or if the President elect shall have failed to qualify, then the Vice-President elect shall act as President until a President shall have qualified; and the Congress may by law provide for the case wherein neither a President elect nor a Vice-President elect shall have qualified, declaring who shall then act as President, or the manner in which one who is to act shall be selected, and such person shall act accordingly until a President or Vice-President shall have qualified.

Section 4. The Congress may by law provide for the case of the death of any of the persons from whom the House of Representatives may choose a President whenever the right of choice shall have devolved upon them, and for the case of the death of any of the persons from whom the Senate may choose a Vice-President whenever the right of choice shall have devolved upon them.

Section 5. Sections 1 and 2 shall take effect on the 15th day of October following the ratification of this article.

Section 6. This article shall be inoperative unless it shall have been ratified as an amendment to the Constitution by the legislatures of three-fourths of the several States within seven years from the date of its submission.

---

[22]Adopted in 1920.

[23]Adopted in 1933.

Amendment XXI[24]

Section 1. The eighteenth article of amendment to the Constitution of the United States is hereby repealed.

Section 2. The transportation or importation into any State, Territory, or possession of the United States for delivery or use therein of intoxicating liquors, in violation of the laws thereof, is hereby prohibited.

Section 3. This article shall be inoperative unless it shall have been ratified as an amendment to the Constitution by conventions in the several States, as provided in the Constitution, within seven years from the date of the submission hereof to the States by the Congress.

Amendment XXII[25]

Section 1. No person shall be elected to the office of the President more than twice, and no person who has held the office of President, or acted as President, for more than two years of a term to which some other person was elected President shall be elected to the office of the President more than once. But this Article shall not apply to any person holding the office of President when this Article was proposed by the Congress, and shall not prevent any person who may be holding the office of President, or acting as President, during the term within which this Article becomes operative from holding the office of President or acting as President during the remainder of such term.

Section 2. This article shall be inoperative unless it shall have been ratified as an amendment to the Constitution by the legislatures of three-fourths of the several States within seven years from the date of its submission to the States by the Congress.

Amendment XXIII[26]

Section 1. The District constituting the seat of Government of the United States shall appoint in such manner as the Congress may direct:

A number of electors of President and Vice-President equal to the whole number of Senators and Representatives in Congress to which the District would be entitled if it were a State, but in no event more than the least populous State; they shall be in addition to those appointed by the States, but they shall be considered, for the purposes of the election of President and Vice-President, to be electors appointed by a State, and they shall meet in the District and perform such duties as provided by the twelfth article of amendment.

---

[24]Adopted in 1933.

[25]Adopted in 1951.

[26]Adopted in 1961.

Section 2. The Congress shall have power to enforce this article by appropriate legislation.

Amendment XXIV[27]

Section 1. The right of citizens of the United States to vote in any primary or other election for President or Vice-President, for electors for President or Vice-President, or for Senator or Representative in Congress, shall not be denied or abridged by the United States or any state by reasons of failure to pay any poll tax or other tax.

Section 2. The Congress shall have power to enforce this article by appropriate legislation.

Amendment XXV[28]

Section 1. In case of the removal of the President from office or of his death or resignation, the Vice-President shall become President.

Section 2. Whenever there is a vacancy in the office of the Vice-President, the President shall nominate a Vice-President who shall take office upon confirmation by a majority vote of both Houses of Congress.

Section 3. Whenever the President transmits to the President *pro tempore* of the Senate and the Speaker of the House of Representatives his written declaration that he is unable to discharge the powers and duties of his office, and until he transmits to them a written declaration to the contrary, such powers and duties shall be discharged by the Vice-President as Acting President.

Section 4. Whenever the Vice-President and a majority of either the principal officers of the Executive departments or of such other body as Congress may by law provide, transmit to the President *pro tempore* of the Senate and the Speaker of the House of Representatives their written declaration that the President is unable to discharge the powers and duties of his office, The Vice-President shall immediately assume the powers and duties of the office as Acting President.

Thereafter, when the President transmits to the President *pro tempore* of the Senate and the Speaker of the House of Representatives his written declaration that no inability exists, he shall resume the powers and duties of his office unless the Vice-President and a majority of either the principal officers of the executive departments or of such other body as Congress may by law provide, transmit within four days to the President *pro tempore* of the Senate and the Speaker of the House of Representatives their written declaration that the President is unable to discharge the powers and duties of his office. Thereupon Congress shall decide the issue, assembling

---

[27]Adopted in 1964.

[28]Adopted in 1967.

within forty-eight hours for that purpose if not in session. If the Congress, within twenty-one days after receipt of the latter written declaration, or, if Congress is not in session, within twenty-one days after Congress is required to assemble, determines by two-thirds vote of both houses that the President is unable to discharge the powers and duties of his office, the Vice-President shall continue to discharge the same as Acting President; otherwise, the President shall resume the powers and duties of his office.

Amendment XXVI[29]

Section 1. The right of citizens of the United States, who are 18 years of age or older, to vote shall not be denied or abridged by the United States or any state on account of age.

Section 2. The Congress shall have power to enforce this article by appropriate legislation.

Amendment XXVII[30]

Article the Second . . . No law, varying the compensation for the services of the Senators and Representatives, shall take effect, until an election of Representatives shall have intervened.

---

[29]Adopted in 1971.

[30]See "The Long and Winding Road of the Twenty-seventh Amendment," p. 31.

GLOSSARY

104th Congress—the Congress elected in 1994 with the first Republican majority in both houses since the 1950s.

108th Congress—current Congress elected in 2002.

527 Groups—private groups usually organized to support a presidential candidate by raising unregulated money; they are a way to get around the ban on parties raising unlimited soft money; named after the part of the tax code under which they are registered.

advocacy ads—used by interest groups to indirectly promote or defeat candidates for election; also called issue ads, they are a way of avoiding campaign spending limits.

affirmative action—an effort to remove effects of discrimination by requiring and expanding minority job, admission, and promotion opportunities.

agenda setting—a listing of national priorities; a major media function.

anarchy—a society without government.

Anti-Federalists—group opposing adoption of Constitution; they preferred stronger state governments and more popular participation.

appellate jurisdiction—the authority of some courts to hear appeals from lower courts.

Articles of Confederation—a document that from 1781 to 1789 loosely unified the newly independent American states; its shortcomings led to the U.S. Constitution.

authority—legitimate power.

"balance the ticket"—the effort by parties to represent different population groups and regions in their candidates for office.

bicameral—a legislature with two houses, such as the U.S. Congress with the House of Representatives and Senate.

Bill of Rights—the first ten amendments to the Constitution, including freedoms of speech, press, religion, due process, and jury trial.

blogs—internet websites used to form networks of people to support a political candidate or to share views on a common issue; represent an important fundraising innovation in the 2004 presidential campaign.

bureaucrat—an administrator in a large organization, often government; may refer to someone who slows things down by enforcing too many rules and red tape.

cabinet—the major departments of the federal government such as State and Defense, of which there are now 15.

calendars—the agendas or schedules for legislation in Congress.

casework—the efforts by members of Congress to solve voters' individual problems with the government; an important part of their constituency service.

caucus—a gathering of all the members of a political party serving in either house of Congress.

chain—companies that combine media in different cities under one ownership.

checks and balances—the constitutional principle that mixes together separate powers to give each branch some powers of the others; protects and balances the functions of government.

chief executive—the president's role as head of the executive branch and its federal bureaucracy.

chief of state—the role of the president as head of the nation as well as of the government.

civil liberties—legal protections against government restrictions on freedoms of speech, press, and religion.

civil rights—legal protections against discrimination because of race, religion, ethnicity, or gender.

class action suits—cases representing a whole class of people whose rights may have been violated.

coalition—a political grouping representing diverse interests organized to represent popular opinion on a particular issue.

commander-in-chief—the president's authority over the military; the principle behind civilian supremacy.

complete incorporationists—a judicial position that the entire Bill of Rights was incorporated into the Fourteenth Amendment.

concurrent powers—those powers shared by the states and federal government, such as the power to tax.

conference committee—a temporary body of members from the two houses of Congress set up to resolve different versions of legislation passed by both houses.

consensus—a general agreement among the population on basic political questions and "rules of the game."

conspiracy theory—an unprovable argument that the United States and specific activities are dominated by a unified, secret elite.

dealignment—a recent phase that refers to the growing lack of support for either major party.

democracy—a form of government in which the people effectively participate.

deviating elections—elections that show a temporary shift in popular support for the majority party.

due process—a phrase in the Fourteenth Amendment used to incorporate freedoms of the Bill of Rights to cover states' actions, including the rights to procedural fairness and impartiality by government officials.

electoral barriers—legal obstacles to voting, such as residency and registration requirements.

electoral college—an antiquated constitutional provision whereby voters on Election Day select electors to reflect their state's choice for president.

elites—those who get most of society's values, especially wealth and power.

embeds—reporters who travel with American frontline troops in the fighting in Iraq and the earlier Gulf War.

equal protection—a clause in the Fourteenth Amendment used to prevent state officials and others from engaging in racial or sex discrimination.

equity—a flexible judicial doctrine that allows judges to resolve a case based on a sense of fairness.

exclusionary rule—a judicial rule that excludes any evidence obtained by illegal means.

exclusive and concurrent jurisdiction—refers to whether federal courts have sole authority over a case (exclusive) or whether they share that authority with state courts (concurrent).

exclusive powers—those powers only exercised by the federal government, such as the right to coin money.

executive agencies—major departments of the government that are not in the Cabinet—for example, the National Aeronautics and Space Administration (NASA).

executive agreements—international agreements only needing approval by the president because they are usually less important than treaties.

federalism—the distribution of political authority between the federal government and the governments of the states.

Federalists—supporters of the Constitution in the struggle to adopt it; they wanted a strong conservative central government.

filibuster—the right under Senate rules to delay action by speaking for an unlimited amount of time, only stopped by a cloture vote.

First Amendment freedoms—freedoms of religion, speech, press, and assembly.

Fourteenth Amendment—the post–Civil War amendment that has been used to extend the protections in the Bill of Rights to actions by state and local governments and by private individuals and groups.

fragmentation of power—a key pluralist perspective that no one group dominates American politics.

gerrymandering—designing legislative districts to favor one party's candidates over another's.

GOP—Grand Old Party; the traditional nickname of the Republican Party.

government—a political association that makes rules determining the distribution of values of a society and is the ultimate regulator of legitimate force.

grassroots campaigns—the effort to bring pressure on elected officials by mobilizing voters in their own districts and states using mail, phones, the Internet, or visits.

hard money—funds for candidates in federal elections that since the mid-1970s have been strictly regulated.

hyperpluralism—the view that participation by too many groups demanding too many resources from the government leads to political paralysis.

impeachment—the power of Congress to remove high officials of the executive or judicial branches from office for misconduct.

incumbent—an elected official currently in office with all the advantages that confers.

independents—voters who publicly identify with neither major political party.

injunction—a court order preventing someone from violating someone else's rights.

interest group—an association organized to pursue a common interest by bringing pressure on the political process.

Internet—a global computer network allowing near-instant communication.

iron triangle—refers to public policy being shaped by a trio of lobbyists, bureaucrats, and congressional committees.

joint committees—permanent bodies including both senators and representatives, for example, the Joint Economic Committee.

judicial activism—the concept that the courts should be an active partner with the other branches of government in shaping policy.

judicial restraint—the opposing concept that the courts should not impose their views on other branches of the government except in extreme instances; a passive role for the courts.

judicial review—the courts' authority to decide on the constitutionality of the acts of state, local, and federal governments.

lame duck—the negative description of a president weakened because he is in the last months of his final term.

landmark decision—a judicial decision involving major changes in the law.

leadership PACs—modern political machines established by congressional leaders to further their ambitions by raising funds for party colleagues. See PACs.

legitimacy—a publicly recognized quality of an institution like a family or government that makes the actions of people connected to that institution both legal and correct.

limited government—the constitutional principle by which the powers of government are limited by the rights and liberties of the people.

lobbying—the process of influencing government officials by private interests.

maintaining elections—elections that continue the parties' popular support at the same level.

marblecake federalism—the modern mix of overlapping relations between the states and the federal government.

Mayflower compact—an early example (1620) of American settlers' (Pilgrims) desire to be governed by a publicly accepted rule of law.

media—those means of communications, such as television, radio, and newspapers, that permit messages to be made public.

memorandum orders—the method by which the Supreme Court decides most cases without the need for oral arguments.

national agenda—the important political issues that are the current focus of public attention; gaining control of this agenda is a major aspect of presidential power.

national convention—an assembly of party delegates usually selected by primaries who meet every four years to nominate their party's candidates for president and vice president.

news management—techniques used by public officials to control information going to the media.

order—when the court requires someone to take a specified action to ensure someone else's rights.

original jurisdiction—the authority of the court to initially try cases.

oversight—a nonlegislative power of Congress to investigate and examine the activities of executive branch agencies.

PACs (political action committees)—legally sanctioned organizations set up by private groups to raise campaign funds.

partial incorporationists—judicial position that believes only preferred rights, such as the First Amendment freedoms, should be included in the Fourteenth Amendment and applied to the states.

party platform—a document stating the party's positions on issues.

plural elitism—a view of American politics as being divided into different policy arenas where various special interest elites dominate.

pluralism—a group theory of democracy that positively views the competition between many different groups as resulting in compromises that produce public policies.

political conflict—a widespread dispute over society's values—for example, wealth.

political efficacy—the sense of political effectiveness, for example that efforts like voting will produce results like a change in government policies.

political machine—a traditional locally based political organization led by a boss who controlled government jobs and services through loyalty and corruption.

political party—an organization that runs candidates for public office under the party's name.

political questions—controversial issues that the courts refuse to deal with because they feel they lack the capacity and that other branches are most suited to resolve.

political science—the study of those social relations involving power and authority, especially those including government.

political socialization—the process of learning political attitudes and behavior.

politics—the process of who gets what, when, and how; actions among a number of people involving influence.

populism—American protest movements that periodically arise to protest dominance by an elite of the government or economy; present-day cultural populists represent religious conservatives opposing what they see as liberal control of the government and media.

pork barrel—laws designed to produce visible local benefits.

power elite—a theory that American politics is dominated by a unified nonrepresentative elite.

power—the ability to influence another's behavior.

precedent, or *stare decisis*—the judicial practice by which the courts generally follow previous court decisions involving the same issue.

presidential primaries—elections held by states to determine which nominee's delegates will be sent to the national convention.

realigning elections—elections that show a long-term shift in the popular base of support of the parties.

reciprocity—the congressional practice of members looking for guidance on legislation to members of their party on committees specializing in that area.

regulatory commissions—agencies semi-independent from the rest of government charged with regulating parts of the economy—for example, the Federal Communications Commission (FCC).

Rehnquist court—the current Supreme Court, since 1986, named after Chief Justice William Rehnquist.

representative democracy—government in which the people rule indirectly through elected representatives.

reserved powers—those powers not delegated to the federal government that are reserved to the states or people by the Tenth Amendment.

residual powers—those powers not spelled out in the Constitution but necessary for the president to carry out his other responsibilities; used to expand the duties of the president.

ruling class—the economically privileged group that controls the major institutions of society according to the power elite view.

select or special committees—temporary congressional panels established to do specific tasks, usually investigations; a recent example was the Senate Special Committee on Whitewater.

Senate majority leader—leader of the Senate majority party and the Senate equivalent to the House speaker, currently Republican Bill Frist of Tennessee.

senatorial courtesy—the practice of the Senate to only approve judicial nominees who are acceptable to the senator from that state.

seniority—an informal congressional rule by which the chairman of a committee is automatically the member from the majority party who has served the longest on the committee.

separation of powers—a constitutional principle that the powers of government should be separated into three branches of government—legislative, executive, and judicial.

single-member district—an electoral system of electing one member of Congress from each district; considered an obstacle to the rise of minor parties.

social class—a major social division based on occupation and income and the awareness this produces of relations toward other classes.

social sciences—the academic disciplines, such as history, economics, or political science, that study relationships among people.

soft money—unregulated funds that in the past were used for state and local parties because they could be contributed in large amounts and used as a loophole to raise money for federal candidates; under the McCain-Feingold campaign reform parties can no longer raise soft money.

sound bite—a brief video clip of a candidate or political official speaking.

speaker of the House—the head of the House of Representatives and the leader of the majority party, currently Republican J. Dennis Hastert of Illinois.

specialization—an expectation that members will remain on the same committee and become experts in its issues.

spin—slang for putting a favorable interpretation or slant on information given to the media and public.

spoils system—process of filling government positions with supporters of the winning politicians; largely replaced by the civil service.

standing committees—the permanent specialized units of both houses that draft legislation in subject areas like taxes and agriculture.

State of the Union address—a presidential speech before Congress at the beginning of the year outlining his legislative program.

Supreme Court of the United States—the head of the federal court system, composed of a chief justice and eight associate justices.

suspect classifications—a judicial doctrine that laws involving race, religion, or ethnicity will be subject to close scrutiny by the courts because they are presumed invalid.

term limits—popular effort to limit the number of times that state legislators or members of Congress can run for reelection.

test case—brought by lawyers to court as the best example of a major violation affecting a large group of people.

TV networks—corporations owning nationwide local television outlets to whom they produce and sell programs.

U.S. courts of appeals—thirteen federal courts above the district courts, which mainly hear appeals from those courts.

U.S. district courts—the federal courts where most cases involving federal law are first tried.

veto—a president's constitutional power to refuse to sign legislation, thus preventing it from becoming law unless overridden by a two-thirds vote of both houses of Congress.

whips—floor leaders who work to coordinate votes and assist the party leaders.

writ of certiorari—order of a higher court to a lower court to send the record of a case for review.

INDEX